ECONOMIC POLICY AND THE MARKET PROCESS

Austrian and Mainstream Economics

Edited by

K. GROENVELD
Prof. Mr. B.M. Telderstichting
's-Gravenhage, The Netherlands

J.A.H. MAKS
Department of Economics
University of Groningen
Groningen, The Netherlands

J. MUYSKEN
Department of Economics
University of Limburg
Maastricht, The Netherlands

1990

NORTH-HOLLAND
AMSTERDAM • NEW YORK • OXFORD • TOKYO

ELSEVIER SCIENCE PUBLISHERS B.V.
Sara Burgerhartstraat 25
P.O. Box 211, 1000 AE Amsterdam, The Netherlands

Distributors for the United States and Canada:
ELSEVIER SCIENCE PUBLISHING COMPANY, INC.
655 Avenue of the Americas
New York, N.Y. 10010, U.S.A.

Library of Congress Cataloging-in -Publication Data

Economic policy and the market process: Austrian and mainstream economics / edited by K. Groenveld, J.A.H. Maks, J. Muysken.
p. cm.
Proceedings of a 1986 symposium.
Includes bibliographical references.
ISBN 0-444-88106-9
1. Capitalism --Congresses. 2. Austrian school of economists--Congresses. 3. Economics--Congresses. I. Groenveld, K. II. Maks, J.A.H. III. Muysken, J.
HB501.E256 1990
330.15'7--dc20 89-48986
CIP

ISBN: 0 444 88106 9

Printed in The Netherlands

ECONOMIC POLI[illegible]ARKET PROCESS

Austrian and Mainstream Economics

Preface

The Departments of Economics of the Universities of Groningen and Maastricht and the Professor Mr. B.M. Telders Foundation, organized a symposium entitled: "Economic Policy of the Welfare State and the Market Process: Success or Failure".

The central theme of this gathering was the so-called neo-Austrian position on the adaptation processes in a market economy. Broadly speaking, the neo-Austrian position considers government intervention in these processes by and large unnecessary and frequently undesirable, since intervention tends to increase instability.

During the symposium a number of leading economists were given the opportunity to defend the classical-liberal ideas of the neo-Austrian school against a party of mainstream (Keynesian, neo-classical and institutional) economists. This book contains the proceedings of this conference.

We would like to thank our sponsors, the Stichting voor Oeconomische Politiek, Bonaventura, De Nederlandsche Bank, the Department of Economics of the University of Groningen, the Department of Economics of the University of Limburg and the Telders Foundation. Their financial support made this symposium possible.

K. Groenveld
J.A.H. Maks
J. Muysken

Contents

The Monetary System

K. GROENVELD, J.A.H. MAKS AND J. MUYSKEN

Diverging views

In this chapter we attempt to identify congruent and divergent views of the neo-Austrians on the one hand and mainstream economists on the other, as manifested in the contributions to the present volume. But first a summary of the views of the neo-Austrians is given.

1. Neo Austrian Economics

The neo-Austrian school of thought, which particularly manifests itself in the United States of America, derives its name from its representatives build upon the work of the Austrian school of thought. The Austrian school came into being in Vienna in the last quarter of the 19th century. Its principal representatives were Karl Menger, Eugen von Böhm-Bawerk, Friedrich von Wieser and Ludwig von Mises. The last two fled the nazi-regime in the 1930's and settled down in Anglo-Saxon countries. Under their wings the neo-Austrian school of thought was born. Leading neo-Austrians include Friedrich Hayek, Israel Kirzner, Ludwig Lachmann and Lawrence White, among others.

The neo-Austrians, joined by certain neo-classical economists (which include the new classical economists) and the monetarists, are of the opinion that the adaptation processes proceed successfully and smoothly. Through this process, with adequate institutionalized circumstances, there is continually a tendency towards economic equilibrium. Contrary to the monetarists and neo-classical economists, the neo-Austrians believe that although there is a tendency towards equilibrium, the economic process should not be analysed on the basis of a model of equilibrium based on perfect competition. (Because, with such an analysis the view on the nature of the adaptation processes, which are characteristic of the dynamics of disequilibrium in a market economy, disappears.) According to Hayek and Kirzner, the problem of economic choice and ultimately the analysis of economic behaviour in the neo-classical theory is in essence reduced to optimal behaviour under familiar limiting conditions. These limiting conditions then apply to (1) preferences, (2) technological data and (3) the availability of the means of production.

Characteristically the neo-Austrian view gives emphasis to the existence of fundamental uncertainty and ignorance regarding these limiting conditions. On the one hand this uncertainty leads to permanent disequilibrium, on the other hand the disequilibrium implies uncertainty with regard to the limiting conditions. Disequilibrium and uncertainty are thus two sides of one coin. Subsequently the price signals generated by the market processes at any given moment, produce incomplete information regarding the actual scarcity relations. Therefore the economic problem in such a setting is in essence a problem of identification.

Identification of the limiting conditions is followed by the query of optimization and it is notably the alert participants of the market process, whom the neo-Austrians define as "entrepreneurs", who try to get a picture of the nature of the disequilibria on the markets. In their dealings they are stimulated by a pursuit of greater profits in broad terms. If subsequently a successful identification leads to an extraordinary profit for these "entrepreneurs", then this profit becomes a signal. The adaptations which are brought about in this manner generate market signals through which a tendency is created towards a general economic equilibrium. However, due to continuous change in the limiting conditions, this equilibrium is never achieved.

Due to the disequilibrium and its inherent uncertainty, the model of perfect competition is inadequate. In this model the agents in the market are mere optimal quantity adapters in a general economic equilibrium. That is why it is better to speak of monopolistic or monopsonistic competition in which alert agents pursue an extraordinary surplus themselves by procuring a (temporary) monopoly position. Once they succeed in their efforts, this position is subsequently put under pressure which is caused by the behaviour of the "followers", but also by the actions of other alert producers who in turn are equally pursuing a monopoly- (monopsony) position.

The agents in the market who are continuously trying to gain profits by solving the identification problem, are viewed by the neo-Austrians as those who generate information through their conduct, in this way reducing the disequilibra. In this respect the neo-Austrian's view differs from that of the Keynesians and institutionalists. Particularly the Keynesians contend that disequilibria in the different markets fortify each other due to quantity restrictions on the behaviour of the market parties. In this view price adjustments are such that quantity adjustments lead to spill-overs. In other words: the disequilibrium on one market is transmitted to other markets and the resulting disequilibria fortify each other. There isn't then a tendency towards equilibrium, but rather a situation of cumulative inflationary and deflationary spirals. With such an argument one sometimes assumes the existence of fixed prices. It is also often contended that this rigidity as a supposition is not required in order to determine instability in the market process.

For the Keynesians this instability implies that government can - in one way or the other - create the conditions for stability in a capitalistic economy. The neo-Austrians, on the contrary, contend that government intervention which goes beyond the supposed intervention in the minimal state, actually increases disequilibrium. Government intervention changes the price structure in such a way that reactionary conduct from the private sector does not, or at least not until a later stage, lead to a tendency of equilibrium. Thus adaptation processes are delayed and disturbed. An important consideration in this position is the fact that, a government confronted with a situation of disequilibrium, does not have sufficient information at its disposal to intervene in such a manner that would result in stability. In the neo-Austrian's view, participants on the market should be allowed freedom of trade to the end that signals can be generated by the market which will enhance the information regarding external data. In the situation where agents are hampered in their activities by the conduct of government, this information will not come about and the private sector will base itself on wrong expectations.

According to the neo-Austrians, the increase in government interference during the past decades has led to a considerable degree of market perturbation and the development of all sorts of rigidities. Consequently the North-American and West-European economies have undergone stagnation and are confronted with high unemployment rates and government deficits. Sadly enough, politicians reacted to this situation by introducing more regulations. In this context we can speak of policy-addiction, in the course of which failing policy evokes new policy. Neo-Austrians do not fail to point out the creation of vicious circles which are a consequence of this fact. The endogenous character of behaviour within the political sector brings the Austrians to the conclusion that whenever government expands its tasks beyond those normally required in the minimal state, we find ourselves on a slippery slope, sliding further down into the direction of an all-embracing state regulation. In this respect Hayek spoke of "the road to serfdom". Well meant interventions in the domain of macroeconomic policy, sectoral- and structural policy, wages- and price policy and competition policy, are -in the long run-counterproductive. Likewise the redistribution policy, geared at social justice, has not had the desired results. In fact, results have been rather unintended ones which in the long run have thwarted the position of particularly 'the least endowed' of the society; this result being caused by reactions in the markets to this policy. In this context one can define two concepts of freedom. "Freedom in the negative sense" (non-intervention by the government and others) and "freedom in the positive sense" (material freedom in the sense of having sufficient means at one's disposal to be able to develop oneself). Interventions geared at procuring "freedom in the positive sense" for the least endowed in the society do not only destroy the "freedom in the negative sense", but ultimately also destroy the positive freedom of the least endowed due to induced, indirect negative effects on growth and employment.

To a great extent, the political conclusions of the neo-Austrians and the monetarists are concurrent, although, as mentioned before, they differ in terms of analysis. However, there is one particularly important point on which the political conclusions do not always concur. On the matter of monetary policy a number of neo-Austrians differ in opinion from the monetarists. It is well known that monetarists have decided upon the so-called fixed rule of monetary growth through which mere nominal developments are redressed by tuning the monetary expansion to the expansion in the real sphere. This tuning is brought about by a monetary authority (central bank). In the view of a number of neo-Austrians the latter is neither necessary nor desirable. The undesirability stems from the impossibility of what ever authority to produce an adequate tuning. This regulated form of tuning is neither necessary because with adequate competition between money makers, credit expansion will be kept within bounds. The neo-Austrians referred to in this paragraph consider a system of free banking to be a real alternative to the existing situation in which the issuing of money (notes and coins in circulation) is nationalized and the creation of deposit money is regulated by a monetary authority. For, as stated by supporters of a denationalization policy for money, if one assumes that the market operates well, then why should the creation of money not also be left to the market.

When we look over the above-mentioned conceptions of the neo-Austrians, their own place within the international society of economists is evident. A confrontation of these conceptions with those of the mainstream economists does not merely have an intellectual significance that satisfies intellectual needs, but is also of use in the cultivation of opinions regarding the course of the future direction of Western society.

As stated above the neo-Austrian school of thought in economics has persistently predicted the unintended inadequacies of welfare state economic policy. We therefore asked the neo-Austrians Kirzner, Bellante and Salin to present their views both during the conference and in this present volume, supplemented by a Chicago-school economist, Brozen, and an economist from a more mainstream microeconomic position, Vaubel, who both arrive at conclusions with a distinct neo-Austrian flavour. On the other hand we asked economists of various other schools of thought, including those who are in favour of government intervention, to present their views. More specifically, Kregel and Kuipers as Keynesian oriented economists, De Jong with his own position, and Hartog as a neo-classical microeconomist. The contribution of each author is discussed in one or two comments below.

The contributions and discussions, presented in this volume, provide a useful and unprecedented confrontation of insights. On the one hand we observe a lack of communication, which might offer opportunities for a mutually beneficial further exchange of insights. This holds, for instance, for the (im)-possibility of stabilizing the market economy by an adequately institutionalised money market system. On the other hand we notice presumably unexpected (by both parties) congruencies in opinions, e.g. the position on adverse selection discussed below.

The structure of this volume is as follows. First both Kirzner and Kregel give a general introduction on the functioning of the market process. Next the specific functioning of the commodity markets (Brozen and De Jong) and labour markets (Bellante and Hartog) is discussed, from the perspective of the effectiveness of economic policy. Finally the effectiveness of macroeconomic (Salin and Kuipers) and monetary (Vaubel) stabilization policy is analyzed.

In the sequel of this introductory chapter we try to indentify the most important points of discussion and congruence.

2. Markets and Equilibrium: the Functioning of the Market Process

Kregel sums up his ideas on the functioning of markets through a quotation from Lionel Robins: "The pursuits of self-interest unrestrained by suitable institutions, carries no guarantee of anything except chaos." Few economists would oppose this idea. The question remains however: what is the meaning of suitable institutions. The issue at stake with the fundamentalist Kregel is in essence a distinction that should be made between public markets and private markets. On public markets "all exchange is transparent" and "prices ... fluctuate around levels determined by cost of production plus a rate of return which should tend to uniformity for all producers." Private markets "are dominated by expectations of future supplies and prices; the limitations on prices are found in financial factors which determine the costs of holding long or short positions and the alternative returns on financial assets. Here an increase in prices may lead to expectations of a further rise whose extent is only limited by traders' alibity to finance long positions in the commodity. There is no natural self-correcting tendency, and a market reversal, when it comes, is the result of an inability to continue to carry a speculative position or a sudden reversal in expectations. Such market prices express individuals' expectations, the extent to which they influence market prices is determined by their ability to command finance.

In public markets price variations produce changes in producers' incomes, in private markets they also produce changes in capital values so that prices not only influence the direction of productive activities. They may also destroy productive capacity through insolvency and bankruptcy. The constraint on self-interest in private markets is thus linked to monetary factors. The institution of regulations in which competition will act to limit self-interest in these markets is thus very different, as will be the behaviour of prices."

While the neo-classical (the world of Arrow and Debreu) paradigm is a useful description of an economy with public markets only (perfect competition), this model is inadequate for the analyses of the unstable processes in an economy with private markets. (In the Walrasian model of equilibrium agents trade with the famous auctioneer. But in reality agents trade with each other with fundamental uncertainties concerning the conditions on future markets.) Applicable to that situation is the fact that "market action is not constrained by any objective limit of available information about these limits. The constraints are all in the future and depend on whether or not expectations turn out to be correct." Or stated differently: "there were no objective measures for determining prices. ... prices and thus profitability depended on the financial and speculative activities of other entrepreneurs." In such circumstances diverging expectations can destabilize the market process.

Kuipers and Kregel explain this by the functioning of the monetary system. Kuipers states that "unless this process of price increase evokes expenditure restricting forces, there is no reason why this inflationary process will come to an end. Although in a monetary economy these forces indeed exist, for instance restrictive monetary conditions, destabilising forces also exist, for instance the increased attractiveness of making debts or increasing spending as the result of an expected acceleration in the rate of inflation." In a similar vein Kregel states that market "performance was directly influenced by conditions in the money market. The consequence of failure to provide adequate control could be permanent, rather than temporary." And he stresses that Keynes "felt that it was impossible to determine a set of regulations which would assure a financial market environment in which the free play of individual self-interest would always lead to consistent actions." Thus monetary policy is insufficiently effective to prevent the dissemination and the mutual reinforcement of disequilibria. "(Keynes) fell back on an increase in the role of the State in assuring a high and stable level of investment as an equivalent to providing a sufficient amount of security to bring about a permanent reduction in liquidity preference." The institutions referred to in the aforementioned quotation of Robins, are those that relate to the "demand management" of the government. Demand management must now provide an easier predictable future "and to give entrepreneurs the courage of their convictions."

In many respect, neo-Austrians such as Kirzner agree with the views of post-Keynesians such as Kregel. They certainly share the post-Keynesian criticism of the neo-classical thought of equilibrium. If the dynamics in an economy are considered as the result of human action, then, according to Kirzner, the analysis should be moulded in disequilibrium dynamics. According to his ideas, the economic conduct in a general neo-classical model of equilibrium is reduced to optimal conduct under absolute certainty. However, we can in fact talk of utter ignorance. The essence of entrepreneurial conduct in such an environment would rather concern the identification of the limiting conditions under which optimization must take place.

In contrast to the Keynesians, the neo-Austrians contend that the existence of disequilibria does not necessarily warrant government intervention in the market process. The lack of information coupled with subsequent uncertainty, is diminished by the market process itself. Kirzner: "If we want to understand the market's real function, it is necessary to see it not as a computer, but as a mechanism for communicating information - as a social instrument for mobilising all bits of knowledge scattered throughout the economy." It is the "systematic sequence of error, profit opportunity, discovery and correction, which constitutes the market process."

It is precisely this information-generating process which is being disturbed by government intervention. In his contribution to the discussion regarding macro-economic policy (see also section 5 below), Salin voices the neo-Austrians view as follows: "Government intervention, for instance for so-called economic stabilization, interferes with the price system. It is then more difficult for individuals to adjust the changing conditions, since these conditions are made even more unpredictable. Through intervention, government officials destroy the very information individuals need to make relevant decisions ...." And Kirzner: "Given the absence of the public profit incentive, regulators are likely not to notice those opportunities for social improvement which present themselves in the form of potential opportunities."

The general neo-Austrian position, as we can see from the contribution of Kirzner, is that there is an inherent tendency in the market system towards a (temporary) (moving) equilibrium, although equilibrium as such will never be established. Kregel opposes this position when he states that: "Keynes had come to consider full employment not as a result, but as a pre-condition for the full expression of individual freedom" and "Keynes was concerned that government provide the conditions as well as the competitive constraints necessary for the full effectiveness of individual decision making." In Keynesian circles it is customary to draw attention to fixed wages and prices, to support this position. Remarkably Kregel does not refer to this argument. His opinion differs from Kuipers, who also adopts this position -referring to the Patinkin-Malinvaud tradition- in his argument regarding the necessity of a macro-economic stabilization policy (see section 5 below).

The conclusion is that the basic difference in views relates to whether government intervention can improve the functioning of the free market process as an information and coordination generating device.

3. The Impact and Effectiveness of Competition Policy.

In our broad outline of the neo-Austrians trend of thought (see section 1 above) we have stated that the neo-Austrians characterize the market process as monopolistic or monopsonistic competition, due to the permanent disequilibrium and subsequent inherent uncertainties. Alert agents in pursuit of an extra-ordinary "surplus", procure for themselves of a (temporary) monopoly position.

The consequence of the monopoly position for the entrepreneurial monopolist is in the neo-Austrian view a temporary relatively large share of the total benefits generated by a mutually beneficial transaction. The consequence of the monopoly in the mainstream approach is that profits are higher than normal and, as a consequence, monopoly power is thought to be abused. Brozen and De Jong discussed this topic during the conference.

The definition of normal profits may vary: it may be linked, as De Jong observes, to static optimality, to workable competition - in this concept dynamic considerations regarding product and process innovations are thought to be implied -, to general interest or to, as De Jong prefers, "protecting the competitive process." The implied view on competition policy differs accordingly.

Profit is in the neo-Austrian analysis a reward for the discovery of a disequilibrium state and leads to a coordination improvement, which satisfies the Pareto criterion. If entrepreneurial behaviour discovers a profit opportunity by establishing a monopoly position, defined as the exclusive use of a production factor, competition policy may diminish the advantages for the discoverer in favour of the customers. This may seem a wise policy on the short run. However, the neo-Austrians emphasize that a structural policy of this kind diminishes the alertness of the entrepreneurs, leading to a diminished stream of coordination improvements.

Moreover the neo-Austrians consider that thought should be given to the fact that when we talk of "free entry" into the markets, monopoly positions are constantly under pressure. Subsequently, "extra-ordinary profits" are never of a permanent nature. The very existence of government intervention is what hampers the entry into the markets. "Where regulation bars or limits the opportunities for pure entrepreneurial profits ... opportunities may never be discovered..... Freedom of entry ... is relevant to the freedom of potential competitors to discover existing opportunities for pure profits" (Kirzner). As a consequence monopoly positions should never be protected by the government. This is also exemplified by Bellante's statement that: "Union support of government-mandated wage increases are analogous to industry support of protective tariffs: in both cases the demand for government action is best understood as a rent-seeking activity - as protection from competitive conditions."

Given the variety in definitions of normal profits, it is not surprising that there is not much consensus among mainstream economists and politicians under which circumstances there is abuse of monopoly positions. Hence the evaluations and recommendations regarding competition policy differ and are rather vague. This is acknowledged by De Jong when he states: "The authorities have not tried to define what competition is or should be, nor have they tried to serve such vague criteria as the general interest, or the consumer interest, or to limit the size of enterprises, or to strive for the realization of particular types of market structures." Despite the obvious lack of a clearly defined competition policy goal, one observes an active competition policy in both the United States and the EEC. According to De Jong "The policy to protect competition has become an integral part (and one of the

strongest points) of the Common Market's institutional arrangements." De Jong agrees in particular with regulations to prevent or battle:
- the abuse of a dominant position, indicated by rebates to loyal customers, refusals to supply, price discrimination, etc.,
- the creation of mergers leading to dominant positions,
- certain types of agreements and concerted actions among firms and, last but not least:
- the existence of state barriers to impede free entry.

Obviously the neo-Austrians and School of Chicago-economists agree with the last point, but not with the first three points. Actually their position is that the costs of such regulations probably exceed any possible returns. In particular Brozen emphasizes these costs and even refers at great length to literature corroborating this position. Moreover, he doubts whether monopoly positions do lead to higher prices, as is frequently claimed by both neoclassical and Keynesian economists. And he concludes on the basis of empirical studies: "This information suggests that where horizontal mergers and rising concentration occur in open markets, competition increases in the sense of falling costs and prices, and buyers benefit."

Focussing upon monopoly positions on the labour market we observe more concurrent opinions. We return to those opinions in the next section.

4. Labour Market Policy in the Welfare State

The discussion of market failures can have a very broad scope. It includes a discussion of information and uncertainty, economic power in the labour market as well as discussions on the distribution of income.

According to Hartog the labour market parties are not well informed about the market conditions without some collective arrangement - reaping economies of scale in gathering information - and if such an institution does not develop spontaneously, the government should correct this "failure." This line of reasoning seems to be related to Kregel's public market concept: A market needs some form of institution, either given by government or by the market participants or some part of them, to facilitate coordination towards equilibrium.

Hartog is apparently aware of the fact that "the knowledge of the circumstances of which we must make use never exists in concentrated or integrated form, but solely as the dispersed bits of incomplete and frequently contradictory knowledge which all the separate individuals possess." But he might not wholly agree with the neo-Austrian position that "If we want to understand the market's real function, it is necessary to see it not as a computer, but as a mechanism for communicating information - as a social instrument for mobilising all the bits of knowledge scattered throughout the economy." (Kirzner)

According to the neo-Austrian view individuals may agree voluntary to combine their efforts in gathering information on market conditions. And to the extent that Hartog's "collective arrangement" and Kregel's "public market" can be understood in this sense, there is no dissension. However, when Hartog states that "perhaps some gaps may be left for the government to be filled, but they are hard to predict", the neo-Austrian position simply is that it is impossible to make any sensible predictions in this respect. As a consequence there is no argument for government intervention. In contrast, Hartog's position is that "it is well known that the Invisible Hand cannot deal adequately with uncertainty. ... The problems of moral hazard and adverse selection prevent the market from providing optimal insurance packages." Therefore there is "a potential for efficiency enhancing government intervention."

The position on uncertainty will be deepheartedly denied by neo-Austrians and many others: entrepreneurial decisions must be taken in an environment full of fundamental uncertainties [regarding present and future scarcity relations on the basis of possibly erroneous expectations -the acknowledgement of the existence of disequilibria throughout the economy reflects nothing else but an environment full of uncertainties.] This does not prevent an adequate functioning of the market process in generating coordination improvements, as is explained above.

Regarding adverse selection, one is tempted to conclude: most neo-Austrians would presumably agree with compelling individuals "to insure (or otherwise provide) against those common hazards of life [old age, unemployment and sickness]...Similarly, we require motorists to insure against third-party risks ... it seems reasonable enough that the state should also assist in the development of appropriate institutions."(Hayek) One might also consider moral hazard as a market failure, as Hartog does, in the sense that it is a problem which cannot be solved through the market. The question is, however, whether there are other mechanisms which can deal with this problem more adequately. The neo-Austrian position in this respect is that since moral hazard is costly for private insurance companies, it provides an incentive for them to develop an adequate monitoring system. State-organized insurance leads easily to a softening of the budget constraints because of political pressure. Moreover, the incentive to develop an adequate monitoring system is weaker for state-organized insurance in the neo-Austrian view.

In addition, the neo-Austrians hold the view that welfare state interventions provide general security which worsen the problems they intend to cure. Brozen gives several examples of distortions resulting from these interventions: agricultural policy aimed at income security for farmers, import restraints aimed at protecting domestic jobs and policies regarding the right to fire at will in order to provide job security. He concludes: "The interventions aimed at providing security have created insecurity in many cases. Those supposedly aimed at reducing the costs of externalities have been used to protect firms in some sections of the country from competition of firms in other sections ... ." In a similar vein Bellante concludes: "The cross-employer subsidization [through equal unemployment insurance premiums] that takes place, lowers the relative prices of goods produced in industries with unstable and seasonal demand, providing a clear example of how welfare state policies can be the cause of, rather than the cure of market failure." Underlying these conclusions lies the view expressed by Kirzner: "Since government regulation often takes the form of barring entry by potential new competitors, such regulation acts directly to discourage private discovery of existing maladjustments."

According to Hartog, one of the peculiarities of labour is that it is very difficult to assess its quality beforehand. "Only after experience, i.e. after the acquisition the true qualities [of labour] are revealed." The problem then is that "in some cases the costs [of not knowing the true quality] may be quite high (such as with errors by unqualified medical specialists)." As a typical market solution to this problem Hartog mentions the internal labour market. In other cases the suppliers "may unite and create a labelling organization" designed to reveal and control quality levels. These ideas parallel the neo-Austrian position. The only difference is that Hartog thinks that "the regulatory effect of reputation or on product (and service) liability upheld by the legal system" may be in some cases "too costly and then [government] enforced quality standards may be an efficient shortcut." He acknowledges, however, the implied risks of government enforced monopolization or cartellisation. For that reason he advocated an arrangement in which government "set[s], control[s] and inspect[s] the standards and to have otherwise free entry."

The neo-Austrians evaluate the costs of the above mentioned regulatory effects differently: As we have already stressed several times, in their view the costs of government enforced standards are always too high. Bellante states, for instance, in the case of work place safety - which is analytically equivalent to the above problem of labour quality - that "a dynamic process of technological change and improvement ... can be frustrated by the bureaucratic imposition of rules that tend to freeze the technology of safety and reduce the incentive to entrepreneurial alertness to new safety possibilities."

Focussing upon monopoly positions on the labour market, we observe more concurrent opinions. Hartog develops a static model, which leads to the conclusion that "Introducing a union as a countervailing power to dominant firms leads to Pareto improvements and thus seems worthy of government support. (However,) (t)he result is crucially dependent on the assumed behaviour of workers and unions." And Hartog concludes with respect to "the key question of government policies" that: "Whereas support for unions, as a countervailing power to monopsonistic firms, enhances efficiency, support for monopoly elements in the union position (exclusivity) is not warranted, and might even be banned on account of efficiency losses." But he stresses that, in particular in a dynamic context, the analytical framework is not sufficiently developed. Bellante formulates the neo-Austrian position as follows:"...workers might combine with one another to affect wages and restrict output is not per se seen as a problem. Objections arise only where coercion is involved, as when government restricts competition through the ... legal enforcement of the monopoly power of unions." Neither of the authors oppose the emergence and existence of labour unions, but they also do not support government enforced monopoly positions of these unions.

Hartog also mentions distributional arguments for government intervention. The dilemma between equity and efficiency is elaborated by him within the framework of neo-classical economics. This dilemma exists because "the lump sum redistributions necessary [to correct for inequities in the initial distributions of wealth]... are barely feasible and hence usually insufficient to establish the desired welfare distribution." The notion of equity refers to the distribution of wealth as outcome of the market process, the notion of efficiency refers to the concept of Pareto optimality.

Pareto optimality (according to Kirzner "the workhorse of mainstream welfare economics") is not accepted as a normative criterium to evaluate the market process by the neo-Austrians. Pareto optimality might be the outcome of the market process in a stationary situation, but such a situation bears no relevance in the neo-Austrian view. Although the neo-Austrians will probably never use the term efficiency in this context, an economy would be more 'efficient' in their view to the "extent to which an economy possesses a capacity to induce discoveries upon which we must depend for the identification and correction of uncoordinated sets of decisions."

Although we observe an important difference between the concepts of 'efficiency', both parties agree on the existence of a trade-off between 'efficiency' and equity - at least in the sense that more equity can only be achieved at the cost of 'efficiency' loss. Hartog sees as one of the 'neo-classical guidelines on economic policy in general and labour market policy in particular: ...[to] strike a balance between ... efficiency and equity." He concludes for the Dutch situation that:" equity has been bought at an efficiency cost that is now considered too high by many ... Insight in the trade-off between efficiency and equity that is relevant in those situations is still very sketchy, however." For the neo-Austrians these insights are less sketchy. Bellante states, for instance with respect to nation-wide minimum wages in the USA "the primary manifestation of the legal minimum wage is unemployment", which particularly affects minority groups and non-union members. Or more generally,"minimum wage legislation certainly must be seen as a frustration of the coordinating tendency of a free labor market. Minimum wage legislation has also frustrated the entrepreneurial tendency to rectify the problem of regional disparities in the distribution of labor." Although he will not put it this strongly, Hartog agrees with this criticism.

As to progressive income tax Brozen is highly critical of its effects: "Such levies favor the consumption of leisure and the direct consumption of the services of ones own resources (rather than going through the market to sell goods to obtain the funds to purchase other goods). One of the consequences of this diversion of resources to tax-exempt uses is an increase in the tax burden on lower income groups. Also such a tax structure creates a large non-revenue yielding burden of taxation by forcing resources out of more productive into less productive uses." Hartog also acknowledges that "high dead-weight losses" exist as a consequence of high and progressive income taxes, referring to several empirical studies for the USA. As a consequence he considers it "worthwhile to start thinking" about taxing earnings generating characteristics (e.g. education, age, and occupation).

One might conclude that although both from the neo-classical and from the neo-Austrian point of view more equity can only be achieved at the cost of 'efficiency'-losses. Both views differ with respect to their estimations and expectations of these losses. In the neo-Austrian position one expects that these losses will be substantial, according to the standards of the policy makers. The effects of equity-enhancing measures will often be counterproductive due to unintended and unrecognized side effects. In the neo-classical position one usually is less pessimistic.

5. Macroeconomic Stabilisation Policy

The notion of macroeconomic stabilisation policy presupposes the notion of macroeconomic equilibrium. The neo-Austrian position can be found in Salin's paper: A macroeconomic equilibrium exists if and only if all individuals in a society are in equilibrium. And one should realise that "individual equilibrium is a continuously moving equilibrium, and acting individuals are continuously changing their preferred positions." From these considerations it follows that macroeconomic equilibrium is a "moving equilibrium." This brings Salin to the question how to define macroeconomic stabilisation policy. Since this policy aims at "the minimization of the gaps between the actual and the desired values of certain so called 'macroeconomic' variables." However, "who can define the desired values of the variables?" Obviously, from Salin's point of view this question cannot be answered without referring to the moving individual equilibrium. Optimal individual stabilisation is "thus obtained when the marginal utility of the expected diminution of the gap between desired and actual positions is equal to the marginal subjective costs of the necessary actions. (...) Hence optimal individual stabilisation can not be defined by an external observer." As a consequence macroeconomic stabilisation is best achieved in an environment of a decentralised decision-making process: the free market. "There is no justification for macroeconomic policy."

A Keynesian position - albeit a reconstituted reductionist one - is defended by Kuipers. Adhering to the tradition of disequilibrium economics, macroeconomic equilibrium is only related to individual equilibrium by means of the notion that an economy consists of identical individuals with known preference structures. Given these assumptions macroeconomic equilibrium can be observed in principle by an external observer. Moreover, in this tradition one emphasises, that "even in the case that prices are perfectly flexible, capitalist market economies are not necessary stable. Errors in expectations may give rise to cumulative deflationary and inflationary processes." Hence "a capitalist market economy needs to be stabilized."

Kregel derives his Keynesian position from a fundamentalist tradition. In his view "Keynes had come to consider full employment not as a result, but as a precondition for the full expression of individual freedom." And "Keynes was concerned that government provide the conditions as well as the competitive constraints necessary for the full effectiveness of individual decision making." He elaborates this by stating that in private markets "there were no objective measures for determining prices, ... prices and thus profitability depended on the financial and speculative activities of other entrepreneurs. Thus instead of proposing that the escape from market regulation should be made easier, he recommended that policy action should be taken to render the future more easily predictable."

To prevent cumulative deflationary or inflationary developments, one might consider the possibility to constrain speculative positions on future prices by adequately regulating financial markets. However, as we have already mentioned in section 2, Keynes "felt that it was impossible to determine a set of regulations which would assure a financial market environment in which the free play of individual self-interest would always lead to consistent actions. He ... fell back on an increase in the role of the State in assuring a high and stable level of investment as an equivalent to providing a sufficient amount of security to bring about a permanent reduction in liquidity preference."

It appears from the above that, both Kuipers and Kregel defend the Keynesian position that macroeconomic stabilisation policy is necessary. This position rests on two arguments: institutional barriers to the flexible functioning of the market process (wage and price rigidity) and the instability of the market economy resulting in cumulative inflationary and deflationary tendencies. The insight that the occurrence of price and wage rigidities as an institutional feature of most western European countries which hampers the functioning of markets and prevents developments towards equilibrium is not at variance with the neo-Austrian, monetarist or new-classical position, although Kuipers seems to suggest this.

In the neo-Austrian and monetarist point of view most government enforced institutions create rigidities which hamper the functioning of the market process. This leads to structural problems, e.g. structural unemployment. Hence, in order to solve these problems one should remove these rigidities by no longer adhering to an enforcement of such institutions - i.e. no legal monopoly position of trade unions or enforced collective wage-agreements, no rent control, no investment subsidies, no import restrictions and so on. Removal of these rigidities makes macroeconomic stabilisation policy superfluous, under the condition of an adequate monetary system. As Salin puts it: "Government intervention, for instance for so-called economic stabilisation, interferes with the price system. It is then more difficult for individuals to adjust to changing conditions, since these conditions are made even more unpredictible. Through intervention, government officials destroy the very information individuals need to make relevant decisions..."

In the Keynesian tradition one is inclined to take substantial parts of the institutional setting for granted or even as desired. Therefore the solution of structural problems is not primarily sought in changing the institutional setting, but in macroeconomic stabilisation policy. Kuipers is obviously aware, however, of the problems involved with this solution. He stresses the importance of "avoiding that stabilization leads to the distortion of the market mechanism. ..., the danger is certainly not just hypothetical that stabilization leads to rigidities in the wage and price structure, thus impairing the flexibility and by this the growth perspectives of the economy." But he is slightly optimistic that it is possible to create "an institutional structure which makes it possible to prevent the allocational distorsions to a considerable extent."

6. Monetary Policy

According to Kregel, the capitalist economy is inherently instable due to the ubiquity of private markets and it is impossible to determine a set of regulations which would assure a proper financial environment that prevents cumulative, destabilising tendencies.

Monetarists and neo-Austrians disagree with both the inherent instability and the inability to design an appropriate institutional setting. As is well-known, monetarists advocate fixed rules with respect to money growth. In their view monetary policy (alone) is a sufficient institutional setting to stabilise the financial markets. They see this as the only way to make sure that the monopoly position of government with respect to money supply is not abused and that government action is predictable for individuals. Moreover, this policy limits the possibility of financing diverging speculative positions and hence prevents the development of cumulative processes.

The fixed money rule is in the neo-Austrian view a second-best solution: "Although preferable to a discretionary monetary policy, because the latter is liable to inflationary pressures from politicians, a monetary rule is inspired by the same sort of prejudice, namely the idea that external observers are able to decide what ought to be the 'true' value of a market variable" (Salin). Furthermore,"historical experience... shows that monetary authorities often freed themselves from the rule of contract, ..." (Salin), frequently leading to periods of inflation.

They are amended in the sense that secondary conditions in the optimal conduct of economic subjects, operating under conditions of disequilibrium, differ in the short- and middle run from those that exist in the general equilibrium model. Thus government intervention for the short- and middle run is justified.

In spite of the choice of disequilibrium as a premise for the analysis, neo-Austrians come to the conclusion that government intervention in order to redress this disequilibrium is counterproductive. This is what puts these economists in a special position

Although not dealt with in an extensive manner during the conference and in the contributions presented hereafter, there is still a distinct element which concerns the use of mathematical economic and econometric models. Generally speaking, neo-Austrians are rather cautious in the use of these models. This is certainly true when it concerns models that reproduce the relations between macro-economic variables.

As is known, Keynesians as well as monetarists and certain neo-classical economists, frequently use these models. However, approximations based on models are frequently criticized today. In times of great disequilibria, the predictive and diagnostic value of the models have proved to be rather limited. While many consider Keynesian macro-economics as the premise for the building of models and for econometrics, Keynes proved himself to be extremely sceptical here. In this context he spoke -in a reaction to the work of Tinbergen- of black magic and statistical alchemy. To this he immediately added: "But Newton, Boyle and Locke all played with alchemy. So let him (Tinbergen) continue."

In this introductory chapter, we do not wish to express an opinion on either this issue or on the above-mentioned moot questions. Undoubtedly, the reader of this book will be satisfied by the better arguments.

The Market Process

ISRAEL M. KIRZNER

The Market Process: An Austrian View

The modern Austrian view of the market economy, based on the insights of Mises and Hayek, is one that differs significantly from the standard view of economists. This paper surveys this Austrian view, and points out some of its implications for public policy.

For Austrians, the success of a market economy is not to be assessed in terms of the optimality of the equilibrium conditions relevant to its given underlying characteristics. Rather success is to be assessed in terms of the ability of the market in fact to generate equilibrating tendencies. Austrians see such tendencies as arising out of the dynamics of entrepreneurial discovery. Such discovery identifies opportunities for pure profit, which express, in turn, errors stemming from "utter ignorance" (i.e. errors in which the agent is blissfully unaware of his lack of information).

The market economy consists of an institutional framework that transforms such errors into discovery-stimulating profit opportunities.

For this system to work, the prime prerequisite is freedom of entry for fresh entrepreneurial competition. And it is here that the Austrian view sees potential dangers arising out of well-meaning interventions in the market system. Such regulatory intervention typically bars or limits entry into specifies activities. Such limits are then likely to upset the delicate discovery procedure constituted by the market. Because such regulation is unlikely to express any discernible non-market discovery elements, it must be judged, in this sense at least, a threat to the spontaneous discovery process of the market.

Introduction

Modern Austrian Economics has, building on the work of Mises and Hayek, developed an understanding of the market economy as a process of competitive-entrepreneurial discovery[1]. This paper will survey this way of understanding the market economy, and will emphasize some of the more important implications of this view for purposes of public policy. To illustrate the distinctiveness claimed for the Austrian perspective, we shall draw on some recent work in the modern history of economic thought that has presented a strong case for revising the standard account of the celebrated interwar debate on socialist economic calculation.

We shall proceed by first introducing the Austrian view insofar as it provides a distinctive positive way of understanding the market economy. This will then enable us to appreciate how this positive view strongly suggests the adoption of criteria for normative evaluation that differ sharply from those treated as standard in mainstream welfare economics. This discussion, in turn, will lead to an unorthodox approach to the appraisal of much of the economic regulation to which modern market economies have grown accustomed.

How markets work

Many writers (including many economists) have held, of course, that markets do not "work" at all, or that they do so only occasionally (or under conditions unlikely to be fulfilled in many real-world contexts). For these writers, markets are seen as likely to generate sub-optimalities, irrationalities, disappointments, or just plain chaos. (Often the experiences of market economies during periods of economic depression are cited as exemplifying such asserted market failures). But throughout the history of economic thought the core of economic thinking has consisted in the analysis of how, or the extent to which, markets do work. With some significant reservations the Austrian view shares with the main current of modern economics an acceptance of the conclusion that, to an important extent, markets do work. Disagreement with mainstream microeconomic thought centers on what one is to understand by the assertion that markets work, and on how one is to explain and account for this systematic functioning by the market.

---

[1] The ideas in this paper have been, for the greater part, presented at greater length in various of the writer's works especially, *Competition and Entrepreneurship* (Chicago: University of Chicago Press, 1973), *Perception, Opportunity and Profit* (Chicago: University of Chicago Press, 1979), *Discovery and the Capitalist Process* (Chicago: University of Chicago Press, 1985) In those works detailed references are provided to the earlier Austrian economists, particularly Ludwig von Mises and Friedrich Hayek, whose writings provided the intellectual source for the development of these ideas.

For mainstream microeconomics markets are held to work in the sense that they are, on standard assumptions, believed to achieve rapid market-clearing. Prices are held to respond swiftly to changes in demand and/or supply conditions, so that excess supply or shortages are rapidly eliminated. To caricature this view somewhat, one may assert that for mainstream economics the market economy is at all times at or close to, the situation corresponding to the general equilibrium configuration relevant to the respective underlying supply and demand conditions. The Austrian view, on the other hand, considers it most unlikely that the market economy is close to the general equilibrium position at any time. Moreover it is highly critical of the mainstream view (that markets are at all times in approximate balance) not merely as being descriptively inaccurate, but more importantly because this emphasis on the assumed continuous approximation of equilibrium states has tended strongly to deflect analytical attention away from the question of how, if at all, do market economies achieve tendencies *towards* equilibrium.

For most Austrian economists (including this writer) markets do typically generate significant tendencies towards equilibrium. For these Austrians the core of economic understanding consists not in the description of equilibrium states (the relevance of which all Austrians would seriously question) but in the explication of the systematic market processes set in motion, at all times, by the disequilibrium features likely to characterize markets at any give date.

From this perspective the answer to the question: "How Do Markets Work?" is briefly as follows: Markets work by providing incentives for the discovery of overlooked opportunities for mutually gainful exchanges. Markets fail to correspond to equilibrium situations because, and to the extent that, market participants have erred in their assessments concerning the presence of exchange opportunities. Such errors become translated, in turn, into opportunities for pure entrepreneurial gain; such opportunities tend to attract attention. As these opportunities are successfully noticed and exploited, the market is nudged *in the direction of* equilibrium (which is itself, in a changing world, never attained). This tendency is not a guaranteed one, since entrepreneurial endeavor may itself introduce new, additional, errors into the system. Moreover, even successful entrepreneurial endeavour proceeds against the background of spontaneously changing underlying conditions of supply and of demand; such change may not only alter what needs to be learned; it may frustrate the very learning process. Nonetheless, most Austrians would argue, markets do seem to work, and their working is to be understood in terms of the competitive-entrepreneurial discovery process here outlined. What follows represents an elaboration of this outline. We commence this outline by discussing what would be required for markets to be in the imaginary state of full equilibrium.

The equilibrium market

We can imagine a market in equilibrium only by imagining a situation where each participant is, in effect, aware of the full extent of the willingness of every other participant to engage in exchange transactions, under all conceivable terms of exchange[2] - and has proceeded to take advantage of such willingness to the fullest possible extent. Such a market would generate a pattern of exchanges such that no conceivable opportunity for mutually gainful exchange had been passed by. If one could imagine absence of change in underlying daily conditions of demand and of supply, we could be sure that this attained array of exchanges would be repeated each day. The market would be in equilibrium; today's pattern of production, exchange, and consumption activities would be identical with those of yesterday and with those of tomorrow.

The "full-awareness" interpretation of market equilibrium itself calls for a certain degree of interpretation. To effect exchange transactions frequently calls for the expenditure of resources. The equilibrium market must then be defined in the context of the relevant transactions costs; some otherwise gainful exchange may not be worthwhile after all. In particular, an important part of the costs of transacting may consist of the costs of acquiring relevant information. So that the "full-awareness" interpretation of equilibrium need not mean full knowledge of all relevant information; it may mean merely full knowledge of how to acquire (costly) relevant information. Ignorance may thus be consistent with market equilibrium to the extent that it is known that removal of this ignorance is not worth the cost of such removal.

What is not consistent with market equilibrium is ignorance, the costs of removal of which *would* be well worth while. That kind of ignorance would imply, (as would the continued existence of any other unexploited profitable opportunity), in turn, utter ignorance of the fact that the cost of ignorance-removal is indeed worthwhile, or utter ignorance of how to proceed to remove it. It is thus "utter ignorance" that is inconsistent with market equilibrium, since it implies an unexploited opportunity for mutually gainful exchange.

---

[2] F.A. Hayek, "Economics and Knowledge", *Economica*, 1937; reprinted in *Individualism and Economic Order* (London: Routledge and Kegan Paul, 1949).

Notice that what is assumed, in our discussion of equilibrium, is that the existence of an unexploited opportunity for mutual gain cannot be consistent with a calmly continuing state of affairs. Sooner or later such opportunities will be grasped, utter ignorance will dissipate, stirring up the apparently placid water (which were rendered placid only by that utter ignorance).

The meaning of market disequilibrium

But this latter observation concerning equilibrium is at the same time the clue to what we must mean by the term "market disequilibrium". At first glance it may appear tempting to deny the possibility of market disequilibrium altogether. It is tempting to say that changes in outputs, prices and adopted methods of production need not - even against the background of given tastes and conditions of production - spell disequilibrium (in the sense of a market displaying or correcting its lack of adjustment); instead it might be held that such changes arise out of the systematically changing pattern of transactions or other costs which the market experience itself generates. At each and every instant, it might be held, each market decision is the optimal one, in the light of current costs (including the costs of acquiring relevant information). As however, completed transactions operate to lower subsequent costs (including especially the costs of transacting), the pattern of optimal market transactions itself changes - even with unchanged underlying conditions of supply and of demand. The sequence of market events thus determined need contain no surprises. At each and every instant, it might be held, all achievable, worthwhile exchange opportunities are being correctly - and predictably - grasped.

Our identification of equilibrium with the absence of unexploited opportunities for gainful exchange throws light on what we are to mean by disequilibrium. Austrian emphasis upon the possibility (in fact, upon the extreme likelihood) of market disequilibrium thus corresponds to the conviction that, in the ordinary course of market events, we can almost invariably expect there to be great numbers of genuinely unexploited market opportunities. So that observed changes in outputs, prices, and adopted methods of production are likely to express the continual discovery of such hitherto overlooked opportunities (quite apart from any systematic changes generated by market-altered costs of transacting and information-acquisition). As suggested above the possibility of such overlooked opportunities' existing rests on the phenomenon of what we have called "utter ignorance"; the likelihood that overlooked opportunities will generate market agitation arises from the propensity of utter ignorance to become spontaneously dissipated.

The nature and consequences of "utter ignorance"

"Utter ignorance" differs from the kind of ignorance which, as discussed earlier, is consistent with the imaginary state of market equilibrium. Utter ignorance involves not the recognized lack of information, but the state of affairs in which the agent is blissfully unaware of such a lack. Where an agent is aware that he lacks information, we can assume that, in the agent's judgement the acquisition of the missing information is either impossible or not worthwhile; continued ignorance is thus consistent with optimizing behaviour. Where an agent is "utterly ignorant", there is the strong possibility that his ignorance is distinctly sub-optimal ; that is, that, when it indeed dawns upon him that he has lacked an important piece of intelligence, he will "want to kick himself" for having overlooked an obvious fact (or an obvious implication of recognized facts) staring him in the face. Much of the distinctiveness of the Austrian approach to understanding markets rests on Austrian insistence on the possibility - and ubiquity - of utter, sub-optimal, ignorance (in the face of mainstream refusal to consider this possibility, in the context of economic theorizing).

We should take note of the extraordinarily far-reaching implications of the possibility of "utter ignorance". It is not merely that utter ignorance may involve sub-optimal failure to acquire available information. Once we recognize sub-optimality in the context of information-acquisition, we are brought face-to-face with the possibility of *sub-optimality in each and every department of human decision-making*. What permits economists to place heavy reliance upon individual rationality, upon the assumption that individual decision-makers are choosing optimally in the context of given constraints, is the insight that human beings will never consciously forgo a superior option for an inferior one. Our recognition of the possibility of utter ignorance, however, compels us to consider the limits of the rationality assumption. We are confronted not simply with "bounded rationality", but with the apparently ubiquitous phenomenon of sheer sub-optimality, grounded in the open-endedness of utter ignorance.

For Austrians, however, realizations of these disturbing consequences of utter ignorance does not at all spell a sense of analytical helplessness. Quite the contrary; the phenomenon of utter ignorance turns out, for the Austrian view, to be the very foundations for our confidence in the systematic quality of market processes. This apparently paradoxically assertion draws our attention to the role of *discovery* in the market process.

Surprise, discovery and the market process

As noted, the phenomenon of "utter ignorance" may correspond to an overlooked opportunity for information-acquisition. We saw that this phenomenon was not to be explained in terms of the costliness of such information-acquisition. So that one could not assert that any subsequent reduction in the costs of information-acquisition ("search-costs") might be expected to lead to any narrowing of the range of utter ignorance. It was not cost that deterred learning; it was sheer ignorance that anything existed that was waiting to be (economically) learned. From this it might appear that utter ignorance is utterly invincible; no conceivable changes can be expected to eliminate it. Were this the case one might well pronounce such ignorance to be utterly irrelevant to human affairs. What people do not know, to the extent that they will never know, and never know that they do not know, need simply not be considered. Even more to the point, were this to be the case, the Austrian perspective on market processes would have lost its foundation.

The foundation for the Austrian perspective consists in the insight that utter ignorance is the source of the phenomena of surprise, and particularly of *discovery*. It is simply not the case that the range of utter ignorance, for any given human being, remains static over time. The fog of utter ignorance has the propensity to be spontaneously dissipated. To be human is to be subjected, continually, to a stream of undeliberate, surprise learning experiences. To be human is continually to discover things that one had not noticed before. For the more alert among us such discoveries are likely to occur earlier than for those of us who are less alert. But for all of us our utter ignorance is being continually eroded by undeliberate discovery (while at the very same time, of course, the relevant range of utter ignorance may be undergoing continual spontaneous *expansion*, along other dimensions, as the result of the continually changing market environment).

While discovery is undeliberate, it is not necessarily accidental. Discovery is inspired by the prospect of gain. We are alert human beings because we are hopeful (or, which is not greatly different, because we are fearful) of what might befall us if we doze. In the market context discovery is inspired by the prospect of pure profit. The market process consists, then, in the sequence of entrepreneurial decisions that reflect the profit-inspired discoveries (or supposed discoveries) of market participants. The market process consists, thus, in a continual stream of transactions expressing newly-discovered insights on the part of market participants concerning the attitudes and plans of their fellow participants. In this discovery process, as noted, pure profit provides the incentive; it is, moreover, an essential element in the notion of pure profit, that its possibility is generated precisely by that kind of utter ignorance which we have seen to constitute the basis for the phenomenon of discovery.

Pure profit and the market process

If the notion of utter ignorance has been excluded from economic analysis, the idea of pure entrepreneurial profit must present insuperable difficulties. Pure entrepreneurial profit can occur only if a given item can be sold at a price higher than that for which it (or the entire complex of factor services needed to produce it) can be purchased. But it should be apparent that, absent the possibility of utter ignorance, such an occurrence cannot even be imagined. Pure profit must simply be incomprehensible. To imagine that an item can be sold for a price higher than that at which it can be bought, is to imagine that some prospective buyers are prepared to pay more for that item than they need to. Such a situation must, absent utter ignorance, be an absurdity. Ordinary ignorance (deliberately maintained in the light of careful cost-benefit calculation) cannot account for such a situation. (If search costs are required, say, in order deliberately to ascertain the lower price at which the item can be purchased, then this means that such costs must be included in the complex of outlays needed to acquire the item). If utter ignorance is excluded, pure entrepreneurial profit has been assumed out of existence. (Those who, already in possession of the knowledge of the price differential and of how to take advantage of it, do so take advantage would, in the absence of utter ignorance, merely be receiving the implicit rent on their superior endowment of information). The phenomenon of pure profit, and the inspiration it provides for entrepreneurial innovative activity, rest entirely on the possibility of utter ignorance.

Buyers pay the pure entrepreneurs higher prices for given items than the latter themselves have paid, simply because those buyers have no inkling of where to obtain those items for less. Utter ignorance is completely able to account for the phenomenon of pure profit.

But, at the same time, the recognition of utter ignorance, precisely because it renders possible the concept of pure profit, provides the key to understanding what it is that markets do, and how they work. Markets are the scene of continual error, of decisions being continually made on the basis of "utter ignorance". These erroneous decisions generate continually emerging opportunities for pure profits. Since it is the lure of pure gain which activates entrepreneurial antennae, it thus turns out that it is the utter ignorance expressed in market activity that becomes translated into that market phenomenon (pure profit) which inspires discovery and correction of error. It is this systematic sequence of error, profit opportunity, discovery and correction, which constitutes the market process, It is a process which, in the light of continually changing supply and demand conditions, never ceases. It is responsible for whatever coherence and order that a market economy displays.

Not only does this market process generate systematic movements of prices and of short-run production decisions, it is also responsible for the much celebrated capacity of market economies to display spectacular long-term progress and growth. It is the entrepreneurial response to the lure of longrun pure profit that is responsible for such progress and growth. From the perspective developed here these entrepreneurial responses represent alertness to as yet untapped opportunities for technological invention and innovation, involving both scientific discoveries and the perception of new possibilities for long-term (capital) investment. Before turning to develop parallel Austrian insights into appropriate normative criteria, we pause to take note of the *competitive* character of this entrepreneurial discovery sequence that makes up both the short and the long-run market process.

Competition and the market process

Our account of the market process has, thus far, emphasized its entrepreneurial character. We have underlined how each step in this process expresses an entrepreneur's hunch that he has discovered an opportunity waiting to be grasped - whether by underselling the competition, introducing a more effective method of production, or whatever. What we wish now briefly to point out is that such an entrepreneurial market process constitutes, at the same time, a *competitive* process. It is in this sense that the market works, in the Austrian view, through the powerful agency of competition. But a certain terminological confusion, now fairly widely recognized, must first be mentioned.

For mainstream microeconomics the term "competition" has for many decades meant the state of affairs associated with the conditions of the perfectly competitive equilibrium market. That state of affairs is the one in which, for each market participant, market price is given, not subject to modification by any one agent's bids or offers. As is by now fairly generally understood, such conditions imply that the market price is *already* assumed to be the equilibrium price. This is not the place to review the "Austrian" reasons for being less than satisfied with this notion of competition as an analytical tool. Suffice it to say that the part played by competition in the above discussed entrepreneurial market process, refers to a notion of competition that is totally different from that of so-called perfect competition. For us competition refers not to a state of affairs but to a dynamic process.

The entrepreneurial market process is a competitive process in the sense that it relies on the freedom of potential entrepreneurs to enter markets in order to compete for perceived available profits. Were incumbent firms arbitrarily protected against competitive entry by government measures, the market process would be hampered or halted. Later in this paper we shall return to appraise the consequences of governmental intervention in markets, against the background of our understanding the competitive character of the unhampered market process. For us a market is competitive only insofar as it expresses the discoveries of entrepreneurial market participants each of whom is aware that, unless he stays on his toes, others may steal a march on him, and that he is himself free to take advantage of any market opportunity that he believes himself to have detected. In order to be completely competitive, in this sense, we do not require that there be many firms in any one industry; all we require is that there be complete freedom for entrepreneurial entry. No market participant enjoys the privilege of being protected against competitive entry.

In particular it will be clear that in order to be competitive we do not require that knowledge be perfect (as is, of course, required for the mainstream notion of perfect competition). Quite the contrary, we are depending on the competitive process itself to generate a flow of new entrepreneurial discoveries. It is in this sense that Hayek has referred to competition as a "discovery procedure": it is not a process in the course of which existing knowledge is brought to bear on production and market decisions, but one in the course of which new knowledge concerning market possibilities is discovered.

The evaluation of economic performance

The approach we have been discussing, viewing the market as a process of competitive-entrepreneurial discovery (rather than as expressing the fulfilment of attained equilibrium conditions), offers a correspondingly distinctive approach to the *appraisal* of a market's performance. Throughout the development of modern welfare economics, economists have sought to evaluate the performance of an economy by asking, in effect, whether the allocation of resources within it corresponds to that pattern which an omniscient (consumer-oriented) central planner would select for that economy. Since Hayek's seminal work in the early 'forties[3], Austrian economists have understood that this may not in fact be the relevant criterion for such evaluation. The economic problem facing society, Hayek taught us, is not primarily or directly that of the global allocation of society's resources, but first that of mobilizing the dispersed bits of knowledge available in a society so that decision-making can take advantage of them. In terms of our emphasis on the competitive-entrepreneurial discovery process of the market, we may build on Hayek's insights in the following way.

Were a market to achieve instantaneous equilibrium, it would be appropriate to evaluate its performance, as mainstream welfare theory seeks to do, in terms of a comparison between (a) the allocation of resources constituting the equilibrium state, and (b) the allocation of resources that would be selected by the omniscient central planner. Equilibrium would however require the absence of what we have called "utter ignorance", whereas such utter ignorance is perhaps the most characteristic feature of the human condition; such a comparison is thus of little relevance. A more relevant normative criterion thus suggests itself as relating to the degree to which the system is able to mobilize its knowledge resources and, most especially, able to inspire that spontaneous, undeliberate discovery process upon which we must rely for the containment and constriction of such utter ignorance.

It is consistent with these insights, therefore, that Austrians in recent decades have focussed attention on the concept of *coordination* as a relevant normative criterion. The social tragedy arising out of utter ignorance is surely that market participants have failed to take advantage of the opportunities awaiting each of them as a result of the attitudes and abilities of others. Utter ignorance is responsible for individual activities which are uncoordinated with

---

[3] See particularly F.A. Hayek, "The Use of Knowledge in Society", *American Economic Review,* 1945; reprinted in *Individualism and Economic Order, op.cit.*

each other. Coordination, therefore, offers a relevant normative standard. But a linguistic ambiguity needs to be warned against.

The term "coordination" can connote (a) the state of affairs in which decisions *are* coordinated decisions; or the same term can connote (b) the *process* in the course of which initially uncoordinated decisions come to be revised in the direction of greater mutual coordinatedness. The first of these two meanings of the term does not provide a normative criterion that differs substantively from the criterion of Pareto optimality - the workhorse of mainstream welfare economics. To judge whether a particular set of decisions are or are not fully coordinated, is to judge whether a reallocation of resources or goods could be unanimously considered an improvement (since a potential improvement implies scope for mutually benficial exchange). It is to the second of the above two meanings that we are referring when we state that from the Austrian perspective coordination emerges as a significantly relevant normative criterion. We are interested in the extent to which an economy possesses *a capacity to induce discoveries* upon which we must depend for the identification and correction of uncoordinated sets of decisions.

These observations will be helpful in understanding the social usefulness of the market process, and in evaluating the consequences of governmental regulation of that process. An excellent introduction to these issues can be provided by a brief consideration of the celebrated controversy that raged during the 'twenties and 'thirties concerning the possibility of economic calculation under socialism.

The Austrian approach and the socialist calculation debate

It will be recalled that Mises argued in a 1920 article[4] that central planners must necessarily lack tools by means of which to compare the efficiency of alternative methods and patterns of production. Such comparisons can be made in the capitalist market economy by calculating comparative costs. But such calculations rely on the availability of market prices for factors of production. Under socialism such markets are excluded. Without factor prices planners have no basis for calculation. Central planners have no way by which to rank the desirability of alternative production projects. Mises' position was vigorously contested; in particular a line of argument developed in

---

[4] Translated in F.A. Hayek, ed., *Collectivist Economic Planning: Critical Studies on the Possibilities of Socialism,* (London, Routledge and Kegan Paul, 1935).

1936 by Oskar Lange came to be widely regarded as the definitive socialist response to Mises' challenge.

A recent study by Professor Lavoie[5] has shown that that the commonly accepted history of the debate has erred in several important respects. That history considers the Lange response to have decisively refuted the Misesian argument. Lavoie shows (a) that Mises (and Hayek, who strongly supported Mises' contention) never considered Lange's reasoning to have dealt seriously with the original challenge; (b) that Lange (and other socialist writers of his time) failed to realize the Austrian, market process provenance of that original challenge; so that (c) the socialist response to that challenge, which was conducted strictly within a mainstream understanding of markets, was based on premises commitment to which precluded appreciation for the Mises-Hayek insights. Let us see briefly how this was indeed the case.

Lange's position was that socialist decision-makers can make use, for purposes of economic calculation, of *non*-market prices for factors of production. Such non-market prices can be announced periodically by the central economic authorities, and can guide the socialist managers of state enterprises in exactly the same way as market prices guide the owners of private enterprises under the market economy. And, just as market prices adjust continually to take account of excess demands and supplies (generated by inappropriately low and high prices), so too can the socialist authorities periodically adjust the announced non-market prices to take account of revealed inadequacies in the prices announced previously. Whatever the market can achieve through market prices, the socialist economy can do through non-market prices.

As Lavoie (and others) have shown, Lange was viewing the function of market prices strictly in terms of the perfectly competitive market model. That is, his understanding of the market was built firmly and narrowly upon the comprehension of its equilibrium position. For this reason he was able to assert that the role of market prices is a "parametric" one, that is, that market participants (and, by analogy, plant managers in the socialist context) treat prices strictly as data to which they must adjust their own decisions, and over which their own decisions have no influence. But the way in which Mises and Hayek understood the role of prices in markets (and the basis for their contention that no "non-market prices" could fulfil a similar function under socialism) was altogether different.

---

5 D. Lavoie, *Rivalry and Central Planning* (Cambridge: Cambridge University Press, 1985).

For Mises and Hayek prices are not given features of the environment to which market participants adjust. Prices are, instead, at each moment the expressions of the active, current entrepreneurial decisions of market participants, and are continually inspired by the hunches that market participants have concerning the availability of pure profit opportunities. To argue that non- market prices under socialism can perform the same role as equilibrium prices in the market economy, is to ignore the role which the competitive-entrepreneurial market process plays in the discovery of the information required in order for market equilibrium to exist. To imagine that the central economic authorities under socialism can periodically adjust non-market prices in the same way as, in models of equilibrium markets, excess demands and excess supply lead to appropriate price adjustments, is to ignore the Hayekian knowledge problems that are completely begged in equilibrium models. To imagine an announced arrray of non-market prices that could stimulate the set of equilibrium market prices, is to imagine that the announcing authorities somehow already possess all the information which it is the function of the market process (under *dis*equilibrium conditions) to begin to reveal. These Austrian insights into the problems of socialist calculation hold important implications also for the analysis of governmental regulation of and intervention into the market economy.

The market process and the perils of regulation

The Austrian insights that emphasize the discovery function of the market process, do not challenge the more traditional arguments raised by economists concerning the potential dangers inherent in government regulation. These insights do, however, add a new dimension to these arguments. The traditional economist's critique of regulations generally cover the following points: (a) government regulation may involve a paternalistic substitution of the preferences of legislators or officials in place of the wishes of the consuming public; (b) these "official" preferences may in fact be inspired by personal interests of officials, rather than by concern for the public weal; (c) apparent shortcomings in market outcomes may in fact merely express genuine social scarcities (so that the alleged need for regulation may be highly questionable); (d) even where intervention may address a genuine need, and even where its immediate objectives are in fact met, there may be unanticipated side-effects of the intervention that render it, all things considered, undesirable. The Austrian approach is in basic agreement with these criticisms; but it identifies an important *additional* line of reasoning one that offers a serious fresh criticism of government intervention. Quite apart from - and even in the absence of the formentioned criticism of intervention, the "discovery" approach to understanding markets suggests a potentially significant problem arising out of government regulation. This problem has to do with the propensity of government regulation to inhibit discovery. That is, we must address the question of how regulation may impact upon the incentives upon which the market depends for its functioning.

The most serious example of how this influence may be distinctly harmful occurs where regulation bars or limits the exploitation of opportunities for pure entrepreneurial profits. This is likely to take the form of a regulatory barrier to entry. Freedom of entry, for the Austrian approach, is relevant to the freedom of potential competitors to discover (and to move to grasp) existing opportunities for pure profit. Where entry has been blocked opportunities may never be discovered.

From this perspective, regulation introduced to create or maintain competition is no less harmful to the competitive-entrepreneurial process than are other forms of entry-limiting regulation. Entry of competitors need not, in the dynamic sense of the term, mean entry of firms of about equal size. Entry might, for example, refer to the *replacement*, through merger, of a number of high-cost producers, by a single, low-cost producer. Anti-trust activity designed ostensibly to maintain competition, might block this kind of entry. Such activity would thus block the capture of pure profit (in this case available through the discovery of cheaper ways of producing, through economies of scale).

Standard economics frequently draws attention to the harmful consequences of imposed prices. By fixing prices above or below their equilibrium levels, government price regulation generates artificial surpluses or shortages. But, quite apart from the discoordinating consequences (generated by such imposed prices) in the markets for *existing* goods and services, price constraints may also inhibit the discovery of wholly *new* opportunities. A price ceiling does not merely erase the upper portion of a given supply curve. Such a price ceiling may, in addition, slow down the process through which wholly unsuspected sources of supply might be discovered. (In the absence of the price ceiling, such discovery might eventually have shifted the entire supply curve to the right, or might have created wholly fresh supply curves, for products hitherto unknown and unimagined.) It is the lure of pure profit that tends to draw attention to such as yet unglimpsed opportunities. It was this kind of beneficial by-product of the free market system that the late Professor Machlup had in mind when he referred to the "fertility of freedom".

The basic insight that emerges from the foregoing relates to the unstated and profoundly false assumption underlying more traditional (and favorable) treatment of economic regulation. That assumption was that these well-meaning efforts at improving economic resource allocation can be conducted against a background of given information (including, especially, information concerning the feasibility and potential usefulness of information-increasing search). As soon as this assumption is dropped, as soon as it is recognized that economic efficiency depends on continual alertness to (i.e. the discovery of) hitherto unknown information (i.e. the very existence of which had not been suspected), the picture becomes drastically different. The writer has elsewhere identified four ways in which "discovery problems" may hamper appropriate governmental regulation.

(a) *Undiscovered Discovery* - Simply because an apparent problem manifests itself in the market, does not justify the assumption that regulatory correction is called for. After all, the market process is not instantaneous; regulation may merely frustrate the discoveries which markets might have stimulated.

(b) *Unsimulated Discovery* - The discovery process of the market cannot be simulated by regulatory activity. Given the absence of the pure profit incentive, regulators are likely not to notice those opportunities for social improvement which present themselves in the form of potential profit opportunities.

(c) *Stifled Discovery* - Since government regulation often takes the form of barring entry by potential new competitors, such regulation acts directly to discourage private discovery of existing maladjustments.

(d) *Superfluous Discovery* - Government regulation itself is likely to open up new avenues for entrepreneurial gain. Many of these avenues may not necessarily be socially beneficial. One thinks in this regard of enterprising bribery or other criminal activity, where entrepreneurial ingenuity is ("superfluously") channeled into grasping pockets of potential pure profit generated (undeliberately) by the regulatory constraints.

It should be noted that the "perils" of regulation identified in this section, have been introduced primarily for their microeconomics relevance. We have not attempted to discuss the rationale for, or possibly perilous consequences of, government intervention designed to serve as macroeconomic stabilization measures. To a certain extent such stabilization policy is likely to involve the danger we have identified in this section. Such policies characteristically exemplify what we described above as "undiscovered discovery" (i.e. the belief that macro problems perceived are unable to stimulate spontaneous market solutions). For a critical discussion of marcrostabilization policies, see the paper in this volume by Professor Pascal Salin.

The market process: an Austrian view

Our survey has sought to establish the distinctiveness of the Austrian understanding of the market economy. This understanding offers an important alternative to standard positive theory, particularly in its understanding of how capitalism works. In addition, we have seen, the Austrian view offers of novel angle for a critique of the regulated market economy. This novel angle, it turns out, affords some interesting analogies with the now-classic debate on socialist economic calculation. There are grounds to believe that a fresh round in that debate may be in the offing; for any such episode, the full appreciation for the view of the market as a competitive-entrepreneurial discovery process will surely be an important prerequisite.

Comment by Angus Maddison (University of Groningen)

Kirzner's paper presents a rather low profile. Most of it is an elegant and abstract exposition of his view of how markets work, backed up almost entirely by references to himself and Hayek. Those who differ from Kirzner in their view of market processes are treated as an anonymous mainstream. There is no reference to contemporary economic problems of a kind you might find in an OECD report, a budget speech, or a central bank report. There is no empirical evidence. There is no reference to the main differences between Austrian and Keynesian theories. The only really explicit element of controversy is not over mainstream policy issues for capitalist countries but concerns the Lange-Mises debate of the 1930s about the feasibility of running communist economies on a quasi-market basis.

As the Lange-Mises debate is not very relevant to current or even to past policy issues, I felt tempted, after reading Kirzner, to simply repeat Wittgenstein's good old Austrian advice: "Worüber man nicht sprechen kann davon muss man schweigen".

However, I will take issue with Kirzner on two points, and in order to stimulate debate I will provide some materials for a full colour identikit picture of Kirzner so that I can pin him down like a butterfly in a showcase, and, by way of contrast, display my own mainstream characteristics. I do this because Kirzner's reference to "mainstream" economists is very vague, and his specification of what Austrians are, or are not, is too narrow.

My taxonomic scheme identifies 13 more or less contemporary schools of thought on economic policy and market processes, and it enables one to identify their position on 13 points concerning policy. The specification of rows and columns is not meant to be exhaustive. In this listing, I call my own mainstream position a "market Keynesian" one. Market Keynesians distrust politicians and bureaucrats and therefore accept the virtues of the market process on most microeconomic issues, where bureaucratic action is difficult to monitor, but they believe that governments should engage in some rough macroeconomic tuning with discretionary fiscal and monetary policy instruments in order to achieve five macroeconomic goals to which they attach some importance. I have also listed some of the quantitative yardsticks they think are important in judging performance. In my table, market Keynesians get 13 ticks to indicate what they think is relevant to policy.

In trying to portray what I believe to be the Austrian position I have made only four ticks. This is based mainly on my reading of Mises and Hayek, who seem to believe that governments should make some minimum effort to maintain law and order, and leave most other goals to be attained by spontaneous market forces. I would, by way of confirmation, like to ask Kirzner three questions:

Do Austrians admit that there are any valid macroeconomic objectives apart from minimizing inflation?

Do they think you can have any valid macroeconomic yardsticks apart from price indices?

Do they think that the divergence between their objectives and the way the real world functions is so great that we can legitimately call them utopians?

In the past, Hayek's reluctance to take major problems to the real world seriously led Lionel Robbins to defect: "I shall always regard my dispute with Keynes as the greatest mistake of my professional career, and the book, *The Great Depression*, which I subsequently wrote, as something I would willingly see forgotten.... I let my judgement of possible remedies be distorted by an inappropriate sense of proportion... Fluctuations of aggregate demand must not be left to look after themselves.... it is an important function of government, national or international, to pay attention to such matters". (see his *Autobiography of An Economist*, Macmillan, 1971, pp. 154-5 and 188). Hayek's indifference to real world problems was also criticized by Machlup in his survey of Hayek's contribution to economics for the Nobel prize committee (*Swedish Journal of Economics*, 1974, p. 506):

"after several years of the Great Depression, it had become clear that Hayek's prescription of "waiting it out" was inopportune. Only a few students of the depression were willing to give earnest consideration to hypotheses from which so unacceptable policy recommendations were derived. In those years of "secular" stagnation and unemployment, a model for which full employment was the starting assumption could not compete with one that was based on unemployment equilibrium".

The second point I want to make is that Kirzner's description of the market process is somewhat extreme or even mystical, even by Austrian standards. Schumpeter makes a distinction between circular flow (Kreislauf) situations of a routine character, and dynamic developmental situations where there are new products, new processes, new outlets, new supply sources or new organizations. Thus the range of ignorance is much smaller for producer, merchant or consumer if you are talking about bread or beer than it is if your are talking about the Channel Tunnel. Kirzner does not accept Schumpeter's dichotomy and stresses "the possibility of sub-optimality in each and every department of human decision making".

Even in markets where there is a high degree of ignorance, it is rarely "utter ignorance", and the typical way of reducing ignorance is not a stream of "undeliberate, surprise learning experiences". Is there not room in the Kirzner view for organized education and research as a source of learning and innovation?

A Non-Exhaustive Taxonomy of Schools of Thought on Economic Policy and Market Processes in Diferent Kinds of Economy

	Utopia?	Communist Countries		Advanced Capitalism							Utopia?		
	1	2	3	4	5	6	7	8	9	10	11	12	13
	Market Communism	Nepmen/Magyars/Deng	Dirigiste Communism	Supply and Demand Planners	Supply Planners	Keynesian Demand Planners	Market Keynesians	Reaganomics	Monetarism	Gladstonians	Rational Expectations	Austrians	Anarchists
Macroeconomic Objectives													
1. Enhancing/Realising GDP Growth Potential							✓						
2. Enhancing/Realising Employment Potential							✓						
3. Simple and Transparent Redistributive Policies							✓						
4. Enough Payments Equilibrium to permit Freedom of Choice in domestic Policy Objectives							✓						
5. Minimising Excess of Inflation above zero							✓					✓	
Microeconomic Objectives													
6. Reducing political-burocratic favours for rent seekers							✓					✓	
7. Limited Action to Remedy Market Failure in Asset, Goods and Factor Markets							✓					✓	
Instruments													
8. Discretionary Fiscal Policy							✓						
9. Discretionary Monetary Policy							✓						
Quantitative Macro Yardsticks for Assessing Performance													
10. National Accounts							✓						
11. Labour Market Accounts							✓						
12. Growth and Productivity Accounts							✓						
13. Inflation Accounts							✓					✓	

J.A. KREGEL

Market Design and Competition as Constraint to Self-Interested Behaviour

the pursuit of self-interest unrestrained by suitable institutions, carries no guarantee of anything except chaos (*Robbins*, 1952, p. 56)

This paper argues that most economists have mistaken the force of competition for the man-made institution called a market when they argue in favour of a free-market mechanism which is supposed to coordinate self-interested individual action. Once it is recognized that a market is a man-made institution it is possible to indentify different market configurations composed of specific institutions which act to use the forces of competition to provide a constraint on self-interested behaviour such that it is channelled into a limited number of acceptable outcomes which are then considered as coherent or mutually compatible. If the outcomes are not acceptable to the market participants they soon act concertedly to change the institutions which form the market and to allow the forces of competition to operate.again.

The evolution of different market configurations, here generalized under the form of "private" and "public" markets following Braudel, can then be explained in terms of countervailing periods in which self-interested individuals recognize that they can increase their profits by acting outside of the regulations of the market, eventually destroying the existing market structure which is, however, replaced by a new set of regulations governing exchange and competition which controls this private activity by rendering it more transparent. This new set of regulations creates the required coherency, but also creates new profitable opportunities for those acting outside the new market institutions. Much of what today passes for an increase in competition due to deregulation is thus identified as being a simple recognition that greater profits can be made outside the existing regulations which confine the market institution; their elimination eventually produces a new set of regulations and a new market institution. Neither market can be considered as more competitive, they simply channel the forces of competition in a different way. The paper thus seeks to support Lionel Robbins dictum that "the pur-

suit of self-interest unrestrained by suitable institutions, carries no guarantee of anything except chaos" by showing that institutions that restrain self-interest and produce coherent market outcomes are historically specific.

1. Introduction

It has become common to link Keynes' name with the emergence of the Welfare State during the period of rapid growth of the Western industrialized countries which followed the second world war, yet there is no evidence that Keynes was in any way involved in, or approved of, the social role taken on by governments in this period. If anything, he was highly sceptical of such activities (cf. Kregel, 1985). Indeed, Keynes' own philosophical position was anchored in a particular type of Cambridge individualism (cf. Keynes, 1949). By the time of writing the *General Theory* Keynes had come to consider full employment not as a result, but as a precondition for the full expression of individual freedom. There is thus a similarity of view between the economic liberalism of the Classical and post-Keynesian economists on the operation of markets which differs from that of neoclassical economics, some neo-Austrians and most neo-Ricardians who consider unbridled self-interested action as the only means of achieving full employment. What follows suggests how these similarities and differences concerning the role of the market have led to differences in economic policy.

2. What is a "market"?

Markets are institutions; they are not part of the natural environment, but are created by man. Market form indicates the behaviour of man within the institutions called markets, while competition is a mechanism or process which operates more or less effectively in determining market form by constraining individual self-interest. For the Classical liberal, which Robbins is describing in the quotation given above, the "suitable institutions" refer to markets and the regulations governing behaviour in them: "it was the central contention of the Classical Economists that, when the market conformed to the conditions which they postulated, then interference with its working was harmful and self-frustrating. They did not conceive the self-acting mechanism to be self-created" (Robbins, 1952, p. 57).

The forces of competition, acting in a suitably defined and regulated market, provided the constraint on, or the guidance of, self-interest:

"The invisible hand which guides men to promote ends which were no part of their intention, is not the hand of some god or some natural agency independent of human effort; it is the hand of the law-giver, the hand which withdraws from the sphere of the pursuit of self-interest those possibilities which do not harmonize with the public good" (Ibid, p. 56).

For the Classical economist it would thus be misleading to speak of an harmonious "market mechanism" which co-ordinates individual actions, or even of a "market economy", for the market is not a mechanism, and every economy known to man has been based on markets of some form. More correctly, what is usually intended by these terms might be described as a particular set of institutions circumscribing a market in which competition acts to guide self-interested behaviour in such a way as to produce a limited set of acceptable outcomes which are thus classed as coherent or mutually compatible.

Mistaking the location of action for the action itself, or the location of action for the constraint on the action does, however, create difficulties when it comes to the formulation of economic policy. To the Classics it was self-evident, as it was to Keynes, that policy could only concern the location, or the framework, of action. While policy could "withdraw" certain possibilities for action and attempt to channel action in particular directions, it could not be expected to control the action of the individual on his own behalf (cf. Samuels' 1966, excellent extension of Robbins' position).

If Keynes differed from the Classics in this respect, it was over the specification of what should be included in the institutional framework, or in what Bentham called the "Agenda", which determined the market within which self-interest could be left free to operate (cf. De Brunhoff, 1985). For Keynes "The most important Agenda of the State relate not to those activities which private individuals are already fulfilling, but to those functions which fall outside of the sphere of the individual, to those decisions which are made by no one if the State does not make them. The important thing for government is not to do things which individuals are doing already, and to do them a little better *or a little worse*; but to do those things which at present are not done at all" (JMK;IX, p. 291, emphasis added).

Different socio-economic circumstances will require different "frameworks" or "Agenda", producing "markets" which will allow competition to act in very different environments in order to produce coherent independent individual behaviour. All this is far from the neoclassical rendering of "the" a-historical market as producing order out of chaos by providing perfect information about individuals' self-interested actions. The Classical-Keynes view is rather that active policy intervention is required to assure the existence of institutions which produce a market which renders order out of chaos by eliminating the possibility of chaotic, unacceptable and incompatible behaviour.

In the neo-classical conception the action required for coordination is all vested in an anthropomorphic "market", in the body of the mythical "auctioneer". Market participants are passive observers who maximize utility functions using prices as parameters rather than as the objects of action. Since such action is forbidden, this conception leads to the innocuous question of who sets and changes prices in actual markets in which there is no anthropomorphic representation of "the" market. It also leads to the requirement that competitive markets should be crowded by an infinite number of buyers and sellers thereby increasing the difficulty of the formation of a group of individuals who should usurp the function of the auctioneer in setting prices.

This presentation has been criticized because it leaves no place for the independent, voluntary actions of individuals to determine prices. The auctioneer is more damaging to our understanding of markets, however, because it takes the place of the required specification of the institutions which determine the market. In this way it lends credence to the idea that there is only one possible conception of a market, when in fact there are an infinite variety.

3. Public and private markets

Historians have documented the evolution of markets in a way that economists have yet to fully exploit. The early urban markets and trade fairs which organized exchange in medieval Europe seem to have resembled what the neoclassical conception attempts to represent. They were what Braudel (1979, 1985) has called "public markets"; all exchange was transparent and the markets were subject to objective regulations. The bargains struck in public produced information about the intentions of buyers and the availability of supplies. For any trader it appeared as if the determination of prices was beyond his control, it was determined "in the market". But this should not be interpreted to mean that traders had no role in setting prices. In any bilateral exchange relationship prices are determined by the parties to the exchange. However, the transparency and centrality of exchange constrained the self-interested action of the seller to charge the highest possible prices and buyers to hold out for the lowest possible prices, for the action of each is limited by the fact that other buyers and sellers would be quick to make more attractive offers if the bilateral discussions looked like being concluded at prices above or below the minimum for any supplier and the maximum for any buyer. It was thus not so much the crowding of the market, making coalition and usurpation of the price setting function impossible, as it was the necessity of providing a number of buyers and sellers facing different objective productive conditions and having different consumption requirements which would produce the "competition" in the market, or what the Classics would express in terms of freedom of entry into any market.

Despite the fact that exchange in these markets took place in public, prices and bargains were not free from manipulation by those attempting to trade outside of the confines of the regulated market and to thus escape the discipline of competition. The function of efficient dissemination of information about prices in the trade-fairs and city markets was thus crucially dependent on the legal regulations which centralized exchange in time and space and on the uniformity of the regulations governing the settlement of exchanges concluded. Indeed, these "markets" usually required the express permission of the Sovereign who imposed date, duration, location, commodities to be traded, etc., thereby assuring that exchange did not escape government surveillance and control. When economists talk about "the" market, they are usually implicity referring to one single market place for a limited range of commodities occurring periodically and predictably which produced information about prices used in making decisions linking the world of consumption and production. The relation of these markets to the agricultural cycle seems obvious, although as trade became more widespread they became cadenced throughout the year.

As already mentioned, there were always strong incentives for self-interested individuals to attempt to avoid the regulations that were imposed on exchange by trading outside the limits of the market. By seeking profitable advantage in this way, an activity which is today often described as the "market process", agents are in fact engaging in the subversion of the organized market, or in an anti or "counter-market" process. It is always profitable to escape regulations, whether it is by fraudulent means, e.g. short weights, or by engaging in activity that was not previously foreseen and thus conflicts with existing institutions and regulations.

This second type of activity might be better represented as a force for change in the configurations of the legal institutions of the market because those in existence no longer succeed in allowing competition to produce a constraint on self-interest. The history of the development of capitalism is punctuated by such "anti-market" processes bringing about changes in the market, usually by an alternation of the decentralization of market activity or what Braudel calls the dominace of the "private" market, which is in its turn centralized and controlled as a public market. As trade becomes an increasingly private activity, taking place in furtive rendezvous between consenting adults on the margin of the town markets and trade fairs, exchange ceased to be carried out primarily in order to join producer and consumer, but became dominated by the merchant or profit seeking intermediary who bought and sold in order to profit from his ability to determine prices sheltered from competition.

Since bargaining took place in "private" there was no longer complete dissemination of information, indeed the very essence of exchange was to hide information about both prices and quantities. The growth of financial wealth which accompanied the ability of merchants to avoid competition also meant that they could always meet competition by buying out (the modern "take over") the competition. As these merchants or negociants came to specialise in particular lines of activity the very conception of the "market" shifted from the trade fair in which a wide range of products were exchanged, to an interconnected network of individual commodity "markets" identified by the goods traded in them.

The decentralization of exchange that was brought about by escaping from the large, regulated market fairs thus eventually led to disintegration of the single market into specialized trading markets centred on particular commodities, grains, metals, etc. These markets in their turn became centralized, regulated and controlled, but at a lower level of aggregation; they differed in that they were controlled and dominated not by suppliers and final users, but by specialized traders who bought in order to sell; by what we would call either market makers or speculators according to ideological inclination. These were no longer markets linking producers and consumers, but markets which traded promises to buy and sell commodities which in general did not exist. In these markets anticipation and speculation dominate and they might best be conceived of as places where information concerning expectations about potential supplies and demands at future dates were exchanged. Here the type of information that was provided to traders by the public markets is concealed if it exists; more often than not it does not exist at all. Trade is primarily in future performance contracts.

Now these "private" markets were also subject to regulation, just as the public markets had been; with regulation came increasing centralization and control, and exchange more "public". As before, regulation was to attempt to eliminate incoherent behaviour concerning price movements and to re-establish the constraint of competition in all other cases. Neither were these regulations perfect, as the history of speculative bubbles, manias and panics demonstrates. While these markets are no more, nor less, subject to the operation of the force of self-interest, the constraining force of competition operates differently because market action is not constrained by any objective limit of readily available information about those limits. The constraints are all in the future and depend on whether or not expectations turn out to be correct.

The history of capitalism might then be summarized as a process of alternating centralization and decentralization of public and private markets as self-interested individuals attempt to profit by evading the force of competition channeled through the customs and regulations that constitute the institution of the market. It seems that this generalization also holds if we look at the side of production, from guilds, to putting out systems, to factory labour and division of labour, the specialization of product lines to mergers to divestiture and so forth.

The important point here is that competition as a constraint on self-interest is always associated with the regulations and institutions which circumscribe the market; competition is not unbridled self-interest nor the complete absence of controls over exchange. Neither can such complete freedom of individual actions describe the market mechanism. At best it is the escape from competition and the market and the process by which under capitalism new market institutions are developed. Those who accuse regulations and controls of bridling entrepreneurial initiative are often only objecting to the operations of the market in attempting to assure the constricting forces of competition in limiting self-interest.

4. Public and private markets and the policy agenda

It is this difference between public and private markets that provides an insight into the different ways in which the Classics and Keynes viewed the content of the Agenda appropriate to economic policy. It also provides insight into the difference between the neoclassical conception of the market as possessing self-equilibrating tendencies, the Austrian idea of spontaneous order, the neo-Ricardian centre of gravitation and the Keynesian rejection of such a position except with reference to an Agenda which includes either full employment or monetary policy which saturates liquidity preferences.

In the operation of the centralized public markets, such as the trade fair, prices are held within strict limits by the fact that all exchange is transparent and that effective market supplies can be objectively defined. Within the duration and location of the market, prices above equilibrium will bring effective offers to supply existing goods at lower prices and vice versa. The general run of prices established in the market generates information which traders and producers use to prepare themselves for the next market meeting by turning their production or trading activities toward those commodities which yield highest returns at those prices. Over a series of such markets prices should then fluctuate around levels determined by costs of production plus a rate of return which should tend to uniformity for all producers.

On the other hand, private markets are dominated by expectations of future supplies and prices; the limitations on prices are found in financial factors which determine the costs of holding long or short positions and the alternative returns on financial assets. Here an increase in prices may lead to expectations of a further rise whose extent is only limited by traders' ability to finance long positions in the commodity. There is no natural self-correcting tendency, and reversal, when it comes, is the result of an inability to continue to carry a speculative position or a sudden reversal in expectations. In such markets prices express individuals' expectations, the extent to which they influence market prices is determined by their ability to command finance.

In public markets price variations produce changes in producers' incomes, in private markets they also produce changes in capital values so that prices not only influence the direction of productive activities, they may also destroy productive capacity through insolvency and bankruptcy. The constraint on self-interest in private markets is thus linked to monetary factors. The institution of regulations in which competition will act to limit self-interest in these markets is thus very different, as will be the behaviour of prices.

It is interesting that while the Classics were primarily concerned with the public market in their representation of the operation of the invisible hand, they did make an exception in their treatment of money and fluctuations. It was not generally accepted that regulations could be introduced allow in the creation of money which would produce the same competitive mechanism to produce coherent individual actions. These problems were discussed at length in the argument over general gluts, then in the divisions between the Currency and the Banking Schools. Here we have an especially interesting application of the idea of the policy maker attempting to exclude undesirable behaviour in order to allow the operation of competition within the market as circumscribed by regulation. Clearly the issue of paper money is an example of that process evoked above in which self-interest leads to attempts to escape from the regulations of the market; it is, if you like, an entrepreneurial activity by which bankers recognized the possibility for profit by moving outside the traditional monetary regulations which gave to the Sovereign the sole right to coin money. Here is Adam Smith's view on such entrepreneurial activity: "To restrain private people, it may be said, from receiving in payment the promissory notes of a banker, for any sum whether great or small, when they themselves are willing to receive them; or, to restrain a banker from issuing such notes, when all his neighbours are willing to accept of them, is a manifest violation of that natural liberty which it is the proper business of law, not to infringe, but to support. Such regulations may, no doubt, be considered in some respect a violation of natural liberty. But those exertions of the natural liberty of a few individuals, which might endanger the security of the whole society, are, and ought to be, restrained by the laws of all governments; of the most free, as well as the most despotical. The obligation of building party walls, in order to prevent the communication of fire, is a violation of natural liberty, exactly of the same kind with the regulations of the banking trade . . ." (Smith, 1976, p. 324).

The difference in the position between Keynes and the Classics over control of private markets, and in particular, money and financial markets may thus be found in the assumptions over which type of market will dominate. For the Classics, "private" markets were the exception which could be limited to the creation of money; failure to control it directly would lead at worst to temporary cyclical fluctuations. For Keynes, on the other hand, private markets were ubiquitous and their performance was directly influenced by conditions in the money market. The consequence of failure to provide adequate control could be permanent, rather than temporary. We thus find Keynes recommending a more extensive Agenda than the Classics while maintaining the Classical presumption that is was the Framework or Agenda that was the objective of policy, not the substitution of government actions for individual action. Keynes was concerned that government provide the conditions as well as the competitive constraints necessary for the full effectiveness of individual decision making.

The reason for the dominance of the money market over other markets was because of its effects on the entrepreneurial decision to invest. Keynes' conception of entrepreneurial activity was not radically different from the activity of seeking out profitable advantage as it was represented by Schumpeter or the Austrians. His concern with the role of the entrepreneur was not, however, in breaking the constraint of competition in order to earn profits, but rather with the difficulties in identifying and justifying profitable opportunities within a private market in which there were no objective measures for determining prices, in which prices and thus profitability depended on the financial and speculative activities of other entrepreneurs. Thus, instead of proposing that the escape from market regulation should be made easier, he recommended that policy action should be taken to render the future more easily predictable.

This is perhaps the appropriate place to refer to the "Concluding Notes" of the *General Theory*. These are often interpreted as Keynes' acceptance of the validity of traditional theory in conditions of full employment, when in fact he was referring to the traditional philosophical values of economic liberalism: "The result of filling in the gaps in the Classical theory in not to dispose of the 'Manchester System', but to indicate the nature of the environment which the free play of economic forces requires if it is to realize the full potentialities of production. The central controls necessary to ensure full employment will, of course, involve a large extension of the traditional functions of government. . . . But there will still remain a wide field for the exercise of private initiative and responsibility. Within this field the traditional advantage of individualism will still hold good" (JMK:VII, p. 380). Keynes then goes on to recommend individual liberty, while recognizing that it can only be realized if appropriately limited: full employment must become the central tenet of the Agenda for a democratic society that wishes to preserve individual freedom. He recognizes that this goes beyond Smiths' "party walls" and therefore "would seem to a nineteenth century publicist or to a contemporary Amercian financier to be a terrific encroachment on individualism. I defend it, on the contrary, both as the only practicable means of avoiding the destruction of existing economic forms in their entirety and as the condition of the successful functioning of individual initiative" (Ibid.).

Keynes was just as impressed as Hayek with the threat of Fascism and Socialism to individual liberty; he believed that they could be fought more effectively by measures to stabilize the economic environment in which liberty was exercised, rather than reinforcing unbridled freedom of individual action. "The authoritarian state systems of to-day seem to solve the problem of unemployment at the expense of efficiency and of freedom. It is certain that the world will not tolerate the unemployment which, apart from brief intervals of excitement, is associated - and in my opinion, inevitably associated - with present day capitalistic individualism. But it may be possible by a right analysis of the problem to cure the disease whilst preserving efficiency and freedom" (Ibid, p. 381) The "right analysis" should lead to the right design of the market framework.

It is one thing to identify economic security and full employment as a necessary part of the economic Agenda and the framework describing the market, rather another to carry it out. Keynes saw possibilities in two areas. The first was in the organization of financial markets. This he eventually abandoned because he felt that is was impossible to determine a set of regulations which would assure a financial market environment in which the free play of individual self-interest would always lead to consistent actions. He thus fell back on an increase in the role of the State in assuring a high and stable level of investment as an equivalent to providing a sufficient amount of security to bring about a permanent reduction in liquidity preference. I have spelled out these problems at greater length in another place (cf Kregel 1985, 1986). It should by now be clear why these issues of the appropriate framework or Agenda imply Keynes' implicit rejection of the majority of the "welfare state policies" carried out in his name in the 1960's.

5. The entrepreneur in the public and private market

A more important point for the purposes of our discussion is the difference in the role of the entrepreneur and of entrepreneurial activity. In a public market the entrepreneur is rewarded for seeking out unexploited profitable activities. But, as we have seen, profitable advantage may be of two types. One is within the confines of the market, the other is in initiating "counter market" activities. Classical liberalism argued against unnatural restrictions on action of the former type, against monopoly rights granted by the Sovereign, for example, while seeking to eliminate by law activity of the second type. This second type of activity could not be eliminated, however, and capitalism has seen a never-ending struggle between unbridled self-interest attempting to circumvent the market regulations which assure competitive constraints on activity and the creation of new regulations and market institutions in order to establish them. For the neoclassical, the neo-Ricardian and some neo-Austrians the second type of entrepreneurial activity is implicitly assumed not to exist; indeed counter-market activity would be a contradiction in terms within these approaches. The denial of such activity allows the affirmations of a process by which prices produce the information required for the compatibility of plans or a process of gravitation to natural prices or a tendency towards spontaneous order in market relations. It is this second type of activity, however, that produces the tendency to disequilibrium, to the chaos of which Robbins spoke, and which requires the continual refinements of the market framework in which competition operates. It is the responsibility of man to assure that the institutional design of markets is such that these spontaneous gravitational forces are centrifugal[1].

For the post-Keynesian, however, capitalism is characterized by the dominance of private markets in which the second type of entrepreneurial behaviour will always be more rapid than the attempts to find market forms in which competition can restrain it. The implication of this is that the system will be tendentially producing below its potential, leading to chronic unemployment which will jeopardise the system's existence. The problem of full

---

[1] In order not to be misunderstood it should be pointed out that this is not an external process of imposing regulations on markets, but a spontaneous internal process generated by the experience of agents who populate markets. Consider the regulation which limits the maximum upward and downward movements in prices which may occur in any trading session in many commodity and financial markets. This is a regulation which can be traced to the traders' desire to provide stability as a form of self-preservation expressed in *Schelling's* explanation of the motives of the party-goer who the day before the party asks his friends to make sure that he does not drive home after the party.

employment thus becomes part of the Agenda in which market forces are allowed to work.

Further, for Keynes the kind of entrepreneurial discovery process which characterises the public market is absent in the private market because of the change in the operation of the market from dealing with objective, transparent exchange to the operation of the market as the expression of individual expectations. It becomes difficult, if not impossible, to identify profitable opportunities with certainty, and policy is required to give entrepreneurs the courage of their convictions: "For if effective demand is deficient, not only is the public scandal of wasted resources intolerable, but the individual enterpriser who seeks to bring these resources into action is operating with the odds loaded against him. The game of hazard which he plays is furnished with many zeros, so that the players as a whole will lose if they have the energy and hope to deal all the cards. Hitherto the increment of the world's wealth has fallen short of the aggregate of positive individual savings; and the difference has been made up by the losses of those whose courage and initiative have not been supplemented by exceptional skill or good fortune. But if effective demand is adequate, average skill and average good fortune will be enough" (JMK:VII, p. 381). Thus the Agenda requires specification of the proper full employment environment for sucessful entrepreneurial activity.

In conclusion I should like to reiterate the post Keynesian position concerning the relativity of the market process to the market as a man-made institution which will have different characteristics at different points in the development of the economy. Differences concerning policy are closely related to different conceptions of markets. Likewise, different conceptions of the market lead to different conceptions of the role of entrepreneurial activity within the market, in particular between the Austrian emphasis on the discovery of unexploited opportunities for profit and the idea of the entrepreneur as the active force in the creation of profitable opportunity which has been so forcefully put by Professor Shackle (cf. Kregel, 1988). These differences will also imply different policy recommendations and different assessments of the success of policy.

Bibliographical references

Braudel, F. (1979) *Civilisation materièlle, économie et capitalisme, XVe-XVIIIe siècle*, Paris: Armand Colin.
--- (1985) *La Dynamique du Capitalisme*, Paris: Arthaud.
De Brunhoff, S. (1985) "La Critique Keynésiènne du 'Laissez Faire'," in A. Barrère, ed., *Keynes aujourd'hui: Theories et Politiques, Paris: Economica.*
*Keynes, J.M. (1949) Two Memoires, London: R*upert Hart-Davis.
---- (JMK:VII) *The General Theory of Employment, Interest and Money*, Vol. VII of *The Collected Writings of J.M. Keynes*, London: Macmillan, 1973.
--- (JMK:IX) *Essays in Persuasion*, Vol. IX of *The Collected Writings of J.M. Keynes*, op.cit., 1972.
Kregel, J.A. (1985) "Budget Deficits, Stabilisation Policy and Liquidity Preference: Keynes's Post-war Proposals," in F. Vicarelli, ed., *Keynes's Relevance Today*, London: Macmillan.
--- (1986) "Laws of the Market and Laws of Motion: An Essay in Comparative Social History," in H.J. Wagener and J.W. Drukker, eds., *The Economic Law of Motion of Modern Society*, Cambridge University Press.
--- (1988) "Imagination, Exchange and Business Enterprise in Smith and Shackle," in S. Frowen, ed., *Unknowledge and Choice in Economics*, London: Macmillan.
Robbins, L. (1952) *The Theory of Economic Policy*, London: Macmillan.
Samuels, W. (1966) *The Classical Theory of Economic Policy*, Cleveland: World Publishing.
Smith, A. (1976) *The Wealth of Nations*, Glasgow edition, Oxford University Press.

Comment by K. Groenveld (Telders Foundation)

Kregel quotes L. Robbins to support the view that "the pursuit of self-interest unrestrained by suitable institutions, carries no guarantee of anything except chaos". Few economists will disagree with this opinion. So we can also subscribe to the idea that: "markets are institutions; they are no part of the natural environment, but created by man". Individual behaviour in the market is indeed restrained by a set of rules or institutions. There remains however the important question of how these rules are established. Is there a tendency towards spontaneous order in market relations, or are these relations the outcome of government intervention?

According to Kregel, history shows that market regulation is the result of action by the law-giver and that the institutions that have been created are necessary ones. He also states that the rules "act to guide self-interested behaviour in such a way to produce a limited set of acceptable outcomes". The institutions will have different characteristics at different points in the development of the economy. Rules that restrict the pursuit of self-interest in the private market ought to be different to those that prevent the occurrence of chaos in the public market.

Kregel believes that we should think of competition as being an endogenous variable, since economic agents react to the rules imposed on the market. Agents try to avoid the confines of the market institutions by performing "counter market activity". Due to these counter market activities we can observe a development in the economic order. The economy has developed from one that was dominated by public markets to one that is becoming a private market economy. To meet these changes, the institutions and rules have also had to evolve and "withdraw from the sphere of the pursuit or self-interest those possibilities that do not harmonize with the public good".
Assuming that we now live in a private market economy, Kregel and Keynes advocate "an increase in the role of state in assuring a high and stable level of investment as an equivalent to providing a sufficient amount of security to bring about a permanent reduction in liquidity preference". Kregel's points of view cause me to elaborate on the following questions:

1. Does it make sense to impose government or other restrictions, if agents manage to bypass these obstacles?
2. What kind of behaviour is caused by the imposition of Keynesian institutions? How does "demand management" effect the expectations of private agents?

3. Since Keynesians and Austrians agree on important features of the dynamics of a private market economy, why do the two schools differ on economic policy?

We can quote Adam Smith with regard to the first question, "The man of system... seems to imagine that he can arrange the different members of a great society with as much ease as the hand arranges the different pieces upon a chessboard. He does not consider that the pieces upon the chessboard have no other principle of motion beside that which the hand impresses upon them; but that, in the great chessboard of human society, every single piece has a principle of motion of its own, altogether different from that which the legislature might choose to impress upon it. If those two principles coincide and act in the same direction, the game of human society will go on easily and harmoniously, and is very likely to be happy and successful. If they are opposite or different, the game will go on miserable and the society must be at all times in the highest degree of disorder"[1]

In other words, we cannot play the game of economic policy in the same manner we play the bagpipes. We must proceed with caution, because if agent do try to evade restrictions intervention may be ineffective, and, if policy is effective, the long-term result may be the highest degree of economic disorder.

When considering Kregel's historical analysis, we get the impression that restrictions will not be very effective in the long term because agents try to develop "counter market" activities; government-imposed rules will therefore need to be continuously adapted. Kregel illustrates this fact when he describes the evolution of market institutions (from public market to private market).

We now arrive at the second question. Are Keynesian institutions (to give entrepreneurs the courage of their convictions) really effective? We can see from recent economic-policy history that Keynesian policies cause expectations in the private sector to change and they are therefore not successful. We can refer here to publications issued by the members of the "rational expectations"-school[2]. The political process forms another important obstacle. It is obvious that this process gives the wrong incentives to politicians and Keynesian economic policy cannot therefore be applied in a symmetrical

---

[1] See Adam Smith, *The Theory of Moral Sentiments*, London, 1759, Part 6, Ch.2.

[2] R.E. Lucas, "Expectations and the Neutrality of Money", *Journal of Economic Theory,* 1972, 4, 103-124.

manner[3]. The policies are used to fight deflation, but politicians refuse to use them against inflation. We may therefore conclude that since the Keynesian "Agenda" induces reactions in both the private and political sectors it is of doubtful effectiveness.

To illustrate these considerations, we can note the following. Let us assume that the Keynesian analysis of the way in which our economy functions is correct, which means that the government should guarantee an adequate level of demand for investment goods. But what is adequate in a world full of uncertainties?; How do we manage demand? Does all this mean "fine-tuning"? How does management affect expectations of private agents? What about government budget deficits and what about the consequences of using government loans or money creation to finance collective investment and expenditure? What experience do we have of Keynesian stabilization in the market economy? Kregel refuses to answer these questions, but they nevertheless remain important. I am convinced that in answering these questions, we must conclude on the basis of economic history that adequate control by means of global instruments is impossible, and in fact such control tends to destabilize the economy rather than prevent chaos in the coordination of individual behaviour. As I have stated above, the political process sometimes gives the wrong incentives to politicians. Electoral motives do not always tend to coincide with motives to stabilize the economy. When we discuss the market process we should always bear in mind that the responsibility for intervention lics with the politicians.

There now remains the third question. In the presentation of his analysis Kregel makes a distinction between neo-classical economists on the one hand and classical and post-Keynesian economists on the other. Although Kregel hesitates about the position of the (neo)-Austrians in this dichotomy, he actually places them in the first camp.

I think that this classification results from the fact that Austrians and neo-classical economists agree on many points of policy recommendations. If we penetrate the post-Keynesian view on the operations of the private markets, however, we must conclude that there are numerous similarities between Austrians and Keynesians. Why they disagree on stabilization policy remains an interesting question.

---

[3] J.M. Buchanan and R.E. Wagner, *Democracy in Deficit. The Political Legacy of Lord Keynes*, New York, 1977.

Both Keynesians, for instance Shackle[4], and Austrians argue that:
1. An important element in economic reality is the basic uncertainty of economic agents and disequilibrium in the coordination of supply and demand.
2. A mechanical interpretation of decision-making would be entirely acceptable for a world of perfect knowledge and prediction, but such an interpretation does not make sense in a world characterised by uncertainty and disequilibrium. In such a world, entrepreneurs play a decisive role in finding "new opportunities".
3. It makes a difference whether "goods buy goods" or "money buys goods and goods buy money".

Neo-Austrians and neo-Keynesians are both opposed to the very static representation of a capitalistic economy. They both agree that there is a lack of information on future prices or the possibilities of future markets; there are also great lags in the adaption process in the behaviour of agents in the market. There is a difference of course between a world in which "money buys goods and goods buy money" and one in which "goods buy goods". Indeed, there is a not unimportant incentive to speculate on the markets. Some people can "wait" to see what the future brings, but others cannot and are so in a much more difficult position.

Perfect competition does not exist and in fact never has existed, not even in 1200 or 1400 B.C., and will probably never exist in the future. This view is also one of the neo-Austrians arguments when confronted with the neo-classical world in which agents do not negotiate with each other, but only with the impersonal market or the famous "auctioneer"[5].

In that neo-classical world we can never explain why prices change as a result of "human action". We can never explain how history develops and competition takes place. Of course both the Austrians and the post-Keynesians stress the influence of the lack of information, the existence of speculation, the finite speed of adaption processes and the like. In Kregel's terminology, Austrians study the behaviour of agents in a "private" market economy. Hayek always pointed out that economics is about adaption and dynamics; it is a system in which the enterpreneur plays a decisive role[6]. Jan Kregel therefore has a confused perception of the distinction between Austrians and Keynesians.

---

4 G.L.S. Shackle, *The Nature of Economic Thought, Selected Papers 1955-64*, New York, 1966.

5 See I.M. Kirzner, *Competition and Entrepreneurship*, Chicago/London, 1973.

6 See F.A. Hayek, *Individualism and Economic Order*, London, 1949.

Nevertheless, Austrians are not in favour of demand management in the same way as Keynesians. Whereas Austrians believe that private sector stability is an important feature of economic development, Keynesians believe that the adaption processes are unstable because there are positive feedbacks when the competitive process corrects mistakes and few market agents learn from experience. As Kirzner has pointed out on several occasions, however, when some agents (entrepreneurs) are alert and others merely optimize the result is stability. Kregel makes a distinction between the entrepreneur who takes advantage of unexploited profitable activities within the confines of the market and the one who initiates "counter market" activities. I believe that the Austrians also make the same distinction. Kirzner for instance makes a distinction between the efficiency-seeking behaviour of the economizers and the behaviour of pure entrepreneur, whose entire role arises out of his alertness to possible changes in the data[7].

The question of stability still remains. Is there a clean-cut answer in a world dominated by private markets? I believe the answer is two-fold. Firstly, there is a dominating gravitational force towards spontaneous order in market relations within the so-called corridor. Secondly, there is the issue of destabilizing spirals outside the confines of the corridor[8]. The final question is concerned with the width of the corridor. There can however be no answer to this question, neither now nor in the future.

---

7 See I.M. Kirzner, *ibidem.*

8 See A. Leijonhufvud, "Effective Demand Failures", in A. Leijonhufvud, *Information and Coordination*, New York/Oxford, 1981.

The Commodity Markets

YALE BROZEN

The Economic Impact of Government Policy

The tool of politics (which frequently becomes its objective) is to extract resources from the general taxpayer with minimum offense and to distribute the proceeds among innumerable claimants in such a way as to maximize support at the polls. Politics, so far as mobilizing support is concerned, represents the art of calculated cheating - or more precisely how to cheat without being really caught.[1]

... the government consists of a gang of men exactly like you and me. They have, taking one with another, no special talent for the business of government; they have only a talent for getting and holding office. Their principal device to that end is to search out groups who pant and pine for something they can't get, and to promise to give it to them. Nine times out of ten that promise is worth nothing. The tenth time it is made good by looting A to satisfy B. In other words, government is a broker in pillage, and every election is a sort of advance auction sale of stolen goods.[2]

Many of the government policies in the economic arena aimed at (1) the redistribution of income, (2) moderating the business cycle, (3) curing market failures, and (4) producing a competitive industrial structure can be characterized as government failures. The deadweight loss to the economy of government failures in the United States exceeds one trillion dollars.

In its various policies for redistributing income, such as the use of steeply progressive income tax rates and transfer payments, the government's aim is presumably to increase the income of the poor. The actual effect of the progressive income tax rate structure chosen is an increase in the burden of taxation borne by the bottom half of in income recipients and a decrease in the rate of capital formation. Transfers increase the incentives to be poor. The decreased rate of investment diminishes the opportunity to escape from poverty. Government policies such as "fine tuning" money growth create the

---

[1] James R. Schlesinger, "Systems Analysis and the Political Process," *Journal of Law & Economics*, vol. 11 (Oct. 1968), p. 285.

[2] H.L. Mencken, *A Carnival of Buncombe.*

business cycle instead of moderating it. Policies such as regulation of utility and insurance prices presumably aimed at curing market failures cause inefficient allocations of resources. Industrial organization policies such as the antitrust laws, agricultural marketing orders, automobile dealer laws, and occupational licensing prevent competition in industries which would otherwise become more competitive. The net result of these policies is lower average income and a more unequal distribution of income than would otherwise prevail.

Introduction

The deadweight losses caused by government policies in the United States reach an astonishingly large figure. One trillion dollars is a modest estimate of their sum. Current income would be at least 25 percent higher if we had never instituted some of the programs operating in the postwar period.

Most of the policies causing this loss can be characterized as an application of the welfare state philosophy or of rent-seeking behind the smoke-screen created by the good-hearted seekers of gains for the less fortunate members of our society[3]. Although the policies were often justified on the basis that they would benefit those low on the income ladder, the actual effect was that the poor frequently were made worse off. Some of the programs produced losses for everyone at the low end of the ladder (sugar quotas, for example). Others produced benefits for those at the middle of the income distribution at a cost to both the bottom and top greater than the gains to the middle[4].

---

[3] That rent-seeking is the major determinant of the outcome of the political process is indicated by the fact that "the total welfare bill ... has been estimated ... (at) over $403 billion in 1982. This amounts to ...$46,920 for each poor family of four". Dwight R. Lee, "The Politics of Poverty and the Poverty of Politics," *CATO Journal*, vol. 5, no. 1 (Spring/Summer 1985), p. 18. In addition to the welfare bill, there is a massive transfer of wealth through regulation, tariffs, etc., which goes largely to middle and upper income recipients. Gordon Tullock, *Economics of Income Redistribution* (Boston: Kluwer/Nijhoff, 1983).

[4] State operated highter education, for example, is supported by a regressive sales tax in most states and used by students from middle income families. Since the state education subsidy is obtainable only by attending a state institution, the result is lower quality education than that which would make optimum use of resources. Sam Peltzman, "The Effect of Government Subsidies-in-the-Kind on Private Expenditures: The Case of Higher Education", *Journal of Political Economy*, vol. 81 (Jan-Feb. 1973). Also, see E.G. West, *Education and the State: A Study in Political Economy* (London; Institute of Economic Affaires, 1965); Gordon Tullock, Welfare for the Well-To-Do; George J. Stigler, "Director's Law of Public Income Redistribution", *Journal of Law &*

The government policies harming welfare operate at four levels. At one level, they aim at producing "equity" in the distribution of income. In welfare state terms, that means equalizing income[5]. So welfare state advocates press for nominally disproportionate tax levies on higher income individuals and families and for transfers to those at the low end of the income ladder.

At the second level, the welfare state aims at moderating the business cycle and fluctuations in employment. So activists "fine tune" monetary and fiscal policy. They expand money growth and government spending when evidence of a recession becomes apparent[6]. Also, they tax more heavily those who save and more lightly those who consume. That choice is based on the presumption that recessions are caused by a tendency for saving to outrun investment.

The third group of policies consists of interventions in the market at the micro level to cure "market failures"[7] and to mitigate suffering that arises when people fail to anticipate or to adapt to change or are the victims of accident or illness. The typical "market failure" is the case where externalities (neighbourhood effects) occur. That is, costs are not borne by those causing the costs or benefits are not collected by those whose uses of real estate affect the value of neighboring properties. The reason for patent laws is the benefit conveyed to society at large by investments in research and development that discover valuable processes and products which can then be produced by others at a much smaller cost than that borne by the investor in the discovery of the new knowledge. The activist state regulates the producer of externalities (as in the case of zoning laws and pollution regulation) rather

---

Economics, vol. 13 (April 1970) pp. 1-10.

5 They "indeed, implicitly argue that no other injustice equals in enormity that of large differences of income". George J. Stigler, *Five Lectures on Economic Problems* (New York: The Macmillan Company, 1950), p.1. Marc Plattner draws a distinction between the welfare state and the redistributive society which is not used in this paper. "The Welfare State v. the Redistributive Society", *The Public Interest*, no. 55 (Spring 1979), pp.

6 On average, monetary expansion has begun 3 to 5 months after the beginning of a recession in the postwar period (see table 14), about the length of time required to recognize that a downswing has begun.

7 That "government failure" in activities designed to mitigate "market failure" may make the cure worse than the disease was seldom considered. See Horst C. Recktenwald, "The Public Waste Syndrome: A Comprehensive Theory of Government Failures" in Horst Hanusch, ed., *Public Finance and the Quest for Efficiency* (Detroit: Wayne State University Press, 1984); Charles Wolfe, Jri, "A Theory of Non-market Failures", *Public Interest*, no. 55 (Spring 1979). Also see Deborah Haas-Wallon, "The Effect of Commercial Practice Restrictions: The Case of Opt....", J*ournal of Law and Economics*, vol. 29 (april 1986).

than relying on methods for internalizing externalities (as in the case of patent law).

To mitigate the suffering from change and misfortune, the activist state pursues such policies as agricultural price supports and income subsidies to protect farmers from past follies or the need to change industries. It uses protective tariffs and import quotas to protect workers from the need to change jobs or accept wage cuts. It protects consumers from nominal price increases for water and mass transit services and then assumes ownership and operation of enterprises it has regulated to the point of extinction.[8] It reshapes tort law to force "involuntary good samaritans" to assume the burden of supporting those who carelessly use a product or operate a machine and consequently injure themselves. (In the United States, product liability law has run amok and the contributory negligence doctrine is fading away)[9]. It also enacts *ex post facto* laws which change existing contracts between employers and employees. In addition, it regulates the promotion of workers and the choice of employees, overriding the market which has "failed" to avoid discrimination.[10]

The fourth level is the shaping of the structure of industries, the size of non-governmental enterprises, and the siting of ownership and control of individual enterprises. Welfare activists willingly tolerate huge government enterprises such as the U.S. Postal Service, which employs 756.000 workers, but are unwilling to tolerate a Great Lakes Chemical Company acquisition of another firm which would increase its total number of employees to 3000.[11]

---

8 Steve H. Hanke, "Seizing Assets Slow and Subtle", *Reason,* vol. 17, no. 2 (Nov. 1985), pp. 36-38. Also, see B. Peter Pashigian, "Consequences and Causes of Public Ownership of Urban Transit Facilities", *Journal of Political Economy*, vol. 84, no. 6 (1976).

9 Richard S. Higgins, "Product Liability Insurance, Moral Hazard, and Contributory Negligence, *Journal of Legal Studies*, Jan. 1981; Richard A. Epstein, "Manville: The Bankruptcy of Product Liability", *Regulation*, vol. 6, no. 5 (Sept/Oct. 1982). Walter Olson, "Pandorra's Docket: Dist 2 on Makes All Businessmen Potential Victims of Crime", Barrow's, Feb. 16, 1987.

10 The failure to avoid discrimination is in part due to the government's regulation of entry and prices which reduces or eliminates the cost of discrimination to the discriminator. Free markets make it costly to discriminate. Harold Demsetz, "Minorities in the Market Place", *North Carolina Law Review*, Feb. 1965; Thomas Sowell, *Markets and Minorities* (New York: Basic Books, 1981); Walter E. Block and Michael A. Walker, eds., *Discrimination, Affirmative Action, and Equal Opportunity* (Vancouver: Fraser Institute, 1981).

11 The argument offered against allowing private firms to grow large is that they can then exercise political power. For an analysis of this argument, see Yale Brozen, *Concentration, Mergers and Public Policy* (New York: Macmillan, 1982), pp. 323-327. A large government enterprise, such as the U.S. Postal Service, wields far more political

In the United States, we have stringent anti-merger laws. They presumably aim at preventing private monopoly but they largely serve to restrict the growth of the most efficient firms.[12] Additional anti-merger laws were requested during the 1960s and 1970s to prohibit any merger which would increase the size of a corporation beyond an arbitrary threshold regardless of whether the merger would have any influence on the state of competition.[13]

Welfare state advocates do not oppose monopoly or large enterprises as such. It is non-governmently sponsored monopoly and large private enterprises they oppose.[14] Government monopolies and government sponsored monopolies are accepted and abound. Most cities in the United States operate water supply enterprises and monopolize the supply of water. They operate mass transit systems and monopolize the supply of mass transit services. They sponsor taxi cab and saloon cartels. They monopolize the provision of garbage and trash collection services. Most states grant monopoly status to the providers of electricity, gas, and telephone services whether they are governmentally or privately owned.[15]

The federal government in the United States also sponsors numerous cartels and monopolies and operates many large enterprises. The Postal Service has a monopoly of the delivery of first class mail by law. Until very recently, operators of trucking services were granted monopolies of certain routes or over the carriage of specific commodities on those routes. The only airlines allowed to operate, until recently, were those with "grandfather" rights. The federal government continues to sponsor cartels of dairy farmers, lemon growers, tobacco growers, growers of navel oranges, avocado growers, almond growers and numerous other cartels with a consequent wastage of agri-

---

influence than any large private firm.

[12] James C. Ellert, "Mergers, Antitrust Law Enforcement and Stockholder Returns", *Journal of Finance*, vol. 31, no. 2 (May 1976), pp. 727-728; Dominique T. Armentara, Antitrust Policy: In Case fore Repeal (Washington: CATO In..., 1986).

[13] S.600, introduced into the U.S. Senate in 1979, would have forbade any corporation with assets or sales exceeding $350 million from increasing its size by *merger*.

[14] The U.S. Department of Interior appealed the Federal Power Commission's grant of a license to a private utility to develop a water power site on the Roanoke River, arguing to the court that it would be preferable not to develop the site at all rather than to allow private development. Interior was arguing that the license should be granted to a government agency.

[15] Privately owned firms, even with monopoly franchises, operate more efficiently and are more efficacious in designing services to suit consumers than government owned firms. Sam Peltzman, "Pricing in Public and Private Enterprises: Electric Utilities in the United States", *Journal of Law & Economics*, vol. 14 (April 1971).

cultural products and of resources used in agriculture.[16] It operates the largest electricity generating enterprise and the largest water supply system in the United States.

Equalizing the distribution of income

Those who favor the minimum state do not usually disagree with the goals that the welfare state activists seek to achieve. It is the means by which the goals are pursued that create disagreement. In the choice of means for bringing about a more egalitarian society, for example, the welfare activist chooses a steeply progressive income tax rate schedule and a tax structure that bears more heavily on the income from property than on the income from labor.[17] He chooses to change results rather than opening opportunities for individual initiative and entrepreneurial discovery. The minimalist, on the other hand, chooses a neutral tax structure, the abolition of special privilege, and the establishment of the right for any two informed individuals to freely contract with each other.[18]

The minimalist points to the fact that steeply progressive income tax rates and corporate taxes defeat the very purpose for which they are chosen over other means for raising revenue. Such levies favor the consumption of leisure and direct consumption of the services of one's own resources (rather than going through the market to sell goods to obtain the funds to purchase other goods). One of the consequences of this diversion of resources to tax-exempt uses is an increase in the tax burden on lower income groups. Also, such a tax structure creates a large non-revenue yielding burden of taxation by forcing resources out of more productive into less productive uses.[19]

---

16 For an analysis of the cost of one of these cartels, see "Costs of Milk Regulation", in Paul MacAvoy, ed., *Federal Milk Marketing Orders and Price Supports* (Washington: American Enterprise Institute, 1977).

17 Michael Boskin estimates that the resulting distortion in the terms of choice between consumption and saving caused a deadweight welfare loss of $50 billion in 1977, approximately 2,5 percent of gross national product. "Taxation, Saving, and the Rate of Interest", *Journal of Political Economy,* vol. 86, no. 2, part 2 (April 1978), p. S19.

18 Yale Brozen, "Welfare Without the Welfare State", *Il Politico*, vol. 32, no. 1 (1967); "The Revival of Traditional Liberalism", *The New Individualist Review*, vol. 3 (1965).

19 Y. Brozen, "Foreword" to John Agria, *The Federal College Housing Program* (Washington: American Enterprise Institute, 1971); *Economic Report of the President* (Washington: U.S. Government Printing Office, 1985), pp. 71-73. The Council of

Experience with various tax rate schedules

Examining the experience with the relative burdens of steeply progressive income tax rates as compared to a flatter schedule, we find that the change in the United States income tax in 1932 to a more progressive set of rates increased the relative burden on lower income groups. The 1931 top income tax rate was 25 percent. It was raised to 63 percent in 1932. Anomalously, that decreased the relative burden on the rich. The portion of tax revenues collected from those reporting income in excess of $ 25.000 (1931 dollars) dropped from 79 to 63.7 percent. The income group below $ 25.000 found its share of the income tax burden rising from 21 to 36.3 percent (see table 1).

Table 1
Shares of Tax Revenues Contributed According to Income Groupings 1931 and 1932

Income Grouping (constant 1931 dollars)[a]	Range of Marginal Tax Rate on Joint Return 1931	Range of Marginal Tax Rate on Joint Return 1932	Share Tax Revenues Contributed 1931	Share Tax Revenues Contributed 1932
Less than $10,000	1,5-5%	4-9%	8,0%	21,7%
$10.000 to $25.000	6-12	10-18	13,0	14,8
$25.000 top $50.000	12-18	18-30	16,3	13,0
$50.000 to $100.000	18-24	31-55	18,2	14,1
Over $100,000	25	56-63	44,6	36,4

[a]The parallel constant dollar brackets for 1932 are: (a) less than $8,985, (b) $8,985 to $22,462, (c) $22,462 to $44,923, (d) $44,923 to $89,846 and (e) over $89,846.

Source: James Gwartney and Richard Stroup, "Tax Reductions, Incentive Effects, and the Distibution of the Tax Burden"

Economic Advisers estimates that, at a marginal tax rate of 46 percent, the allocative cost (*non-revenue yielding burden*) of a marginal dollar of revenue is 53 cents. The total allocative cost (deadweight loss) of the income tax collections of Federal, state, and local governments is probably at least $125 billion. Also see Charles L. Ballan, John B. Shoven and John Whallan, "Several Equilibrium Compensations of the Marginal Welfare Costs of States in the United States", *American Economic Review*, vol. 75 (March 1985).

In contrast, the burden on lower income groups fell between 1921 and 1926 when rate progressivity was flattened. A phased decrease reduced the top tax rate from 73 to 25 percent. The portion of the revenues collected from those reporting income in excess of $ 50.000 (1929 dollars) rose, despite the reduced progressivity, from 44.2 percent in 1921 to 70.1 percent in 1926. The share collected from those reporting incomes below $ 25.000 dropped from 40.1 to 14.5 percent (see table 2). Less progressive tax rates produced a more egalitarian effect.

Table 2
Shares of Tax Revenues Contributed According to Income Groupings 1921 and 1926

Income Groupings (1929 dollars)	Range of Marginal Tax Rate on Joint Return		Share of Tax Revenues Contributed	
	1921	1926	1921	1926
Less than $10,000	9-11%	3- 5%	22.5%	4.6%
$10,000 to $25,000	12-19	6-12	17.6	9.9
$25,000 to $50,000	19-31	12-18	15.7	15.4
$50,000 to $100,000	32-56	18-24	16.1	19.2
Over 100,000	60-73	25	28.1	50.9

Source: James Gwartney and Richard Stroup, "Tax Reductions, Incentive Effects, and the Distribution of the Tax Burden".

Similar results occurred in the 1963-1965 phased reductions in income tax rate progressivity. The top 5 percent of all returns (reported gross income in excess of $13.667) paid 35.6 percent of all income taxes collected in 1963 when the top tax rate was 91 percent. By 1965, the top rate dropped to 70 percent (a 23 percent reduction in the top rate and a roughly 16 percent reduction in rates 72 percent and below). The top 5 percent of all returns (reported gross income in excess of 15.000 1963 dollars) paid 38.5 percent of all income taxes in 1965 (see table 3), a one-twelfth increase in the relative burden of the top 5 percent. Again, less progressive tax rates were more egalitarian.

Table 3
Effect of 1965 Tax Rate Reduction
1963 and 1965

Income Group	Adjusted Gross Income Interval		Percent of Personal Income Taxes Collected from Group[a]	
	1963	1965	1963	1965
Bottom 50 percent	0-I$4,704	0-$5,148	10.4	9.5
50 to 75 percentile	$4,704-$7,620	$5,148-$8,426	20.8	20.0
75 to 95 percentile	$7,620-$13,667	$8,426-$15,000	33.2	32.1
Top 5 percent	above $13,667	above $15,000	35.6	38.5

[a]These estimates were derived via interpolation.

Source: James Gwartney and Richard Stroup, *supra*, Table 2.

In 1982, a similar experience occurred with a reduction from 70 to 50 percent in the top rate (a 29 percent reduction in the top rate with a 7.5 percent reduction in the below 50 percent rates). The income tax collected from the top 1.4 percent of taxpayers rose from 20.4 percent of all revenues in 1981 to 21.8 percent in 1982.[20] The burden on the bottom 50 percent of taxpayers dropped from 7.6 percent of all revenues to 7.0 percent (see table 4).[21]

---

[20] Most fo the increase in share of taxes paid came from the top 80,000 taxpayers. Their share rose from 8.5 percent to 9.7 percent. Lawrence Lindsey, "Taxpayer Behavior and the Distribution of the 1982 Tax Cut", (Cambridge, MA: NBER Working Paper No. 1760, 1985). Lindsey calculates that the revenue maximizing top rate is 43 percent. "Estimating the Revenue-Maximizing Top Personal Tax Rate" (NBER Working Paper No. 1761).

[21] James Gwartney and Richard Stroup, "The Redistributionist Tax Reduction", *Wall Street Journal*, June 26, 1984. The share of income taxes paid by the bottom 50 percent rose from 6.5 percent in 1978 to 7.6 percent in 1981 and by the bottom 75 percent from 26.4 to 28.4 as income tax rates on the top 25 percent increased as a result of bracket creep caused by inflation. (Bracket creep had little efffect on the bottom 50 percent compared to its effect on those in the top brackets - see table 1). The share of the top 25 percent dropped from 73.6 percent in 1978 to 71.6 in 1981. "Highest Earning Half of Population pays 90% of All Federal Income Taxes", *Tax Foundation's Tax Features*, vol. 29, no. 5 (May 1985), p.1.

Table 4
Effect of 1982 Tax Rate Reduction
1981 and 1982

Income Group	Income Tax Collected (billions)		Percent of Income Taxes Collected from Group	
	1981	1982	1981	1982
Bottom 50 percent	$21.7	$19.5	7.6	7.0
50 to 75 percentile	59.0	55.6	20.8	20.1
75 to 98.6 percentile	145.4	141.3	51.2	51.0
Top 1.4 percent	58.0	60.5	20.4	21.8

Source: James Gwartney and Richard Stroup, "The Redistibutionist Tax Reduction", *Wall Street Journal*, June 26, 1984.

By 1983 the share of total income taxes paid by the top 1 percent of income recipients grew to 20.64 percent from 17.44 percent in 1981. Although tax rates were less progressive in 1983 than in 1981, tax payments were more progressive. The tax payment Gini coefficient rose from 0.6488 to 0.6560 between 1981 and 1983.[22]

Equalizing income distribution by encouraging capital formation

Reducing the highest marginal tax rates not only led to greater progressivity in tax payments; it also led to a more rapid rate of capital formation. This, in turn, reduced inequality in the pre-tax distribution of income. The more rapid the rate of capital formation, the more rapidly labor's marginal productivity and wage rates rose relative to its average output. That increased labor's share of national income. When wage rates rose relative to average output per worker hour, greater equality resulted (unless the wage rise went

[22] Richard Vedder and Lowell Gallowy, "Soaking the Rich Throught Tax Cuts", Wall Street Journal, March 21, 1985.

beyond market clearing levels).[23]

What is the cause of the more rapid rise in marginal productivity than in average productivity? Capital equipment and labor are complementary. That is, the more capital per worker, the greater the marginal productivity of a worker (and the lower the marginal productivity of capital). With a static set of technological possibilities, a more rapid growth in the quantity of capital than in the amount of labor causes a rise in the marginal productivity of labor and the wage rate relative to average output per worker. It also causes a fall in the marginal productivity of capital and its wage rate (the rate of return on capital).[24]

If the stock of capital in the United States were doubled with no increase in the quantity of labor and no change in the technology available, national income would rise 26 percent. About 4 percentage points of the increase in national income would go to the providers of capital and 22 percentage points would go to the providers of labor services. A doubled stock of capital would increase the total income of property owners by about 20 percent. It would, however, reduce the rate of return on capital by about 40 percent. (That is, if the pre-tax real return on capital were 6 percent before doubling the stock of capital, then after doubling it would fall to 3.6 percent.) On the other hand, the real wage of labor, would rise 27.5 percent. Labor's share of national income would rise by one percentage point.

The effect of an increase in the stock of capital relative to the number of workers can be illustrated using Brazilian data from the 1950s. I worked out the relationship when I was at the Escola de Sociologia e Politica in Sao

---

23 The rise in wage rates relative to average output from 1948 to 1952 raised the employee compensation share from 64.2 to 67.3 percent of national income and decreased the Gini coefficient of pre-tax income distribution from 415 to 408. By 1969, when the employee compensation share reached 72.5 percent, the Gini coefficient dropped to 403. (It should be recognized that the Gini coefficient overstates the amount of inequality because it is based on annual income data. These do not take into account the value of leisure time, the value of training provided to low wage employees by employers, the return in some years at high levels which offsets the low incomes of earlier years spent in training to obtain higher income in later years, or the high returns in some years to employees such as test pilots who occupy dangerous jobs which shorten life expectancy and the period of lifetime earnings).

24 "...a complete abolition of capital income taxation would increase...(the) new steady-state capital/labor ratio some 15-20 percent (and) . . . capital's share of gross income would fall by around 15 percent." Michael J. Boskin, op. cit., pp. S21-S22. The system of taxes and regulation has also had impact on the allocation of capital, causing an overallocation to housing. This causes GNP to be 300 billion dollars lower than it would otherwise be. Edwin S. Mills " eviding Up the Investment Pie: Have we Overinvested in Housing?" *Business Review: Federal Reserve Bank of Philadelphia,* March/April 1987.

Paulo conducting seminars for the faculties in that area. I did the study in response to the accusation that the investment of American capital in Brazil exploited Brazilian workers. Developing a production function for the Brazilian economy, I found that an increase in Brazil's capital stock by $1,000 per worker raised annual production in Brazil by $350 per worker. Of this increase in annual output per worker, $150 went to increase the annual wage per worker, which at that time was a little over $1,000 per year. Brazilian governments collected $100 per year in taxes levied directly on the investment and on dividends, leaving $100 as a return to those who invested their savings. Forty-three percent of the increase in output went to workers who, at that time, were receiving less than 40 percent of national income. So this increase in output raised their share of national income as well as increasing their real wage. Since the investors received their return from the increase in output caused by their investment, their return did not come at the expense of Brazil or at the expense of Brazilian workers. Workers were better off because of the investment[25].

The share of labor and equality

Labor's share of national income in the United States increased in the 40 years from 1929 to 1969, continuing a rise that began long before 1929,[26] and the division of income became more equal. Capital accumulation and capital-saving technological change produced these trends.[27] In 1929, when

25 Yale Brozen, "The Use of Capital in Developing Areas," *Revista Brasileira de Economia*, ano 9, numero 3 (Septembro de 1955); "The Path to Industralization," *Contribucoes a Analise de Desenvolvimento Economica* (Rio de Janeiro: Livaria AGIR Editora, 1957), pp. 69-96.

26 *Labor's share* (including the self-employed) of *national income* rose from 69.9 percent in 1899 to 72.3 percent in 1929. By 1957, it rose to 81.3 percent. The price of capital relative to the price of labor dropped from 1.43 in 1899 to 1 in 1929 to 0.43 in 1957. John W. Kendrick, *Productivity Trends in the United States* (Princeton: Princeton University Press, 1961), p. 121. Labor's share of factor income originating in the private domestic business economy (including the labor return earned by the self-employed) rose from 67.3 percent in 1929 to 72.5 percent in 1966. Kendrick, *Postwar Productivity Trends in the United States, 1948-1969* (New York: National Bureau of Economic Research, 1973), p. 72.

27 Both Schumpeter and Keynes believed that the inherent forces in a capitalist system eventually cause all income to go to providers of labor services. Schumpeter characterized this tendency as the result of the "suicidal stimulus of profits." He believed that the tendency of capitalists to invest in any profitable field caused supplies to increase and prices to drop. As a consequence, he said, profits trend towards zero in the absence

employee compensation amounted to 60 percent of national income, the top 5 percent of all families ranked by income received 30 percent of national income. During the next 40 years, the share of the top 5 percent declined and the employee share rose. By 1969, the employee share of national income reached 72.5 percent. The top 5 percent's share dropped to 16.5 percent, half of what is was in 1929.

Since 1969, the employee share and the top 5 percent share have been relatively stable. From 1929 to 1969, the employee share rose at an average rate of 3 percentage points per decade (labor's share - including the self-employed - rose at a rate of 3.2 percentage points per decade). From 1969 to 1979, the rate of rise slowed to 0.3 of a percentage point (see table 5).

This is also the decade in which the growth of the capital stock slowed. The growth in capital per employee dropped from 3 percent annually in the early part of the decade to zero (see table 6), net national saving dropped from 16 percent of net national product to 12 percent (see table 7), and the growth in average output per worker hour dropped from a 3 percent annual rise to one percent (table 8). It is evident that the 1970s saw a marked change in the trends shaping incomes in the U.S. economy.

Rapid inflation and the resulting bracket creep raised these rates without the enactment of a change in the rate schedule. Part of the reason for the decline in the net saving rate and the consequent slowing of the growth of the capital stock and of the employee share of national income was the rise in marginal tax rates.[28]

U.S. tax policies, coupled with the inflation caused by U.S. monetary policies, bear much of the blame for the slowing of saving and investment and for the consequent slowing of the rise in labor's share of national income. U.S. policies towards trade unions and labor relations regulations carry equal blame for this state of affairs. In the short run labor unions and minimum wage laws can and do win wage increases for a small part of the labor force.

---

of innovation. (Joseph Schumpeter, *Business Cycles* (New York: McGraw-Hill, 1939), p. 105.) Keynes believed that returns to capital would drop to zero in "one or two generations." He spoke of the "euthanasia of the rentier" being the natural consequence of the rentier's propensity to save. (John M. Keynes, *The General Theory of Employment, Interest, and Money* (New York: Harcourt, Brace and Company), p. 376)

28 Robert J. Genetski, "The Impact of *Marginal Tax Rates* on U.S. Productivity Performance," Testimony submitted to the Congressional Subcommittee on Oversight of the Internal Revenue Service, Washington, D.C., April 13, 1984.

Table 5
Employee Compensation Shares of National Income and the Unemployment Rate at Cyclical Peaks and Troughs 1929 - 1982

Cyclical Peaks			Cyclical Troughs		
Year	Compensation share	Unemployment rate	Year	Compensation share	Unemployment rate
1929	60.3	3.2%	1933	75.1%	24.9%
1937	65.1	14.3	1938	66.8	19.0
1948	64.2	3.8	1949	66.0	5.9
1952	67.3	2.9	1954	68.4	5.4
1956	68.7	4.0	1958	69.3	6.6
1959	68.7	5.3	1961	69.6	6.5
1966	69.0	3.7			
1969	72.5	3.4	1971	73.4	5.8
1973	72.4	4.8	1975	73.6	8.3
1979	72.8	5.8	1982	75.7	9.5

Source: *Economic Report of the President* (Feb. 1986).

This causes labor's share of national income to rise. However, wage increases won in this way cause labor's share to be lower in the long run. In addition, wage increases won in this way slow the rise in the absolute real income of labor.

Part of the cause of current unemployment, particularly in the auto and steel industries in the United States, is union victories in the past three decades.[29] In the auto and steel industries, workers were paid 15 to 20 percent more than the average manufacturing worker in the 1940s. They have since won increases raising the premium to 78 and 81 percent (see table 10).

---

29 Marvin H. Kosters, "Disinflation in the Labor Market," in William Fellner, project director, *Essays in Contemporary Economic Problems: Disinflation* (Washington: American Enterprice Institute, 1984), p. 259.

Table 6
Growth in the Capital-Labor Ratio, 1949-79
Percent change, average annual rate
(end of year to end of year)

Period	Net capital stock (nonresidential)[1]	Employment[2]	Hours[2]	Capital-employment ratio	Capital-hours ratio
1949-59	4.0	1.1	0.7	2.9	3.2
1959-69	4.6	1.6	1.2	3.0	3.3
1969-74	4.2	1.2	0.5	2.9	3.7
1974-79	3.0	3.1	2.8	-0.1	0.2

[1]Net fixed nonresidential business capital, 1972 dollars, end of year.
[2]For private business, alle persons. End of year calculated as average of year's first quarter.

Source: *Economic Report of the President* (1981), p. 71.

Table 7
Average Annual Consumption and Saving Rates, 1951-80
Percent of Net National Product (NNP)

Period	Total Government Consumption as percent of NNP	Federal Government Consumption as percent of NNP	Household Consumption as percent of nongovernmental NNP	Net national saving as percent of NNP
1951-60	14.1	8.2	81.0	16.4
1961-70	16.7	8.3	81.7	15.2
1971-80	18.9	7.0	85.5	11.7

Source: *Economic Report of the President* (1982), p. 116.

Table 8
Labor Productivity Growth, 1949-80
(Percent change per year)

	1948 to 1965	1965 to 1973	1973 to 1978	1978 to 1980
Private Business sector	3.2	2.4	1.2	-0.8
Nonfram	2.6	2.2	1.1	-1.1

Note: Data relate to output per hour for all persons.

Source: *Economic Report of the President* (1981), p. 69.

The impact of public policies

In the 1970s, the marginal federal personal income tax rate on those earning twice the median family income rose from 26 to 43 percent (see table 9).

Table 9
Marginal Personal Income Tax Rates for Four-Person Families, Selected Years, 1965-80
(Percent)

	Familiy Income		
Year	One-half median income	Median Income	Twice median income
1965	14	17	22
1970	14	20	26
1975	17	22	32
1980	18	24	43

Note: Excludes social security taxes and State and local income taxes.

Source: *Economic Report of the President* (1982), p. 120.

Table 10
Employee Compensation for Wage Earners in Steel, Motor Vehicles, and All Manufacturing 1950-1983

	Hourly Compensation			Percent Premium	
Year	Steel[1]	Motor Vehicle[2]	All mfg.[3]	Steel[1]	Motor Vehicle[2]
1959	$1.91	$1.90	$1.59	20	19
1966	4.64	4.65	3.29	41	41
1973	7.68	8.10	5.26	46	54
1979	15.92	15.13	9.07	75	67
1983	22.21	21.85	12.26	81	78

1 American Iron and Steel Institute, Annual Statistical Report.
2 General Motors Corporation, GM Annual Report for various years.
3 Bureau of Labor Statistics, Handbook of Labor Statistics, Bulletin 2217, pp. 229, 428, 435.

Unionized employees in the transit industry, who were formerly paid the same wage as manufacturing workers, now receive a 33 percent premium over the average manufacturing worker (see table 11). These wages increases raise the employee compensation share of national income in the short run, but they cause unemployment (see table 12) or displacement and depress wage rates in other industries. They also cause an inefficient allocation of both capital and labor, a slowing of the growth of the capital stock, and a slowing in the long run rate of rise in employee real earnings.

Table 11
Relationship Between Transit Union Wage Rates and Manufacturing Production Worker Earnings 1947-1980

	Local Transit Hourly Union Rate		Manufacturing Production Worker Hourly Earnings		Transit Worker Premium	
	62 cities	Chicago	U.S.	Chicago	U.S.	Chicago
1947	$1.25	n.a.	$1.22	n.a.	2.5%	n.a.
1950	1.50	1.63	1.44	n.a.	4.2	n.a.
1952	1.74	1.87	1.64	1.77	6.1	5.6%
53	1.77	1.86	1.74	1.87	1.7	- 0.5
54	1.85	1.92	1.78	1.92	3.9	0.0
55	1.90	2.06	1.85	2.02	2.7	2.0
1960	2.37	2.58	5.26	2.49	4.9	3.6
61	2.46	2.65	2.32	2.55	6.0	3.9
62	2.55	2.73	2.39	2.63	6.7	3.8
63	2.65	2.84	2.45	2.71	8.2	4.8
64	2.65	2.84	2.45	2.71	8.2	5.4
65	2.88	3.06	2.61	2.87	10.3	6.6
66	3.00	3.17	2.72	2.99	10.3	6.0
67	3.22	3.41	2.82	3.10	14.2	10.0
68	3.44	3.69	3.01	3.28	14.3	12.5
69	3.71	4.10	3.19	3.50	16.3	17.1
70	4.03	4.57	6.35	3.69	20.3	23.8
71	4.38	4.95	3.57	3.97	22.7	24.7
72	4.68	5.09	3.82	4.27	22.5	24.7
73	5.04	5.63	4.09	4.54	23.2	24.0
74	5.62	6.52	4.42	4.94	27.1	32.0
75	6.25	7.12	4.83	5.46	29.4	30.4
76	6.63	7.55	5.22	5.94	27.0**	27.1
77	7.14	8.26	5.68	6.24	25.7**	32.4
78	7.53	8.91	6.17	6.58	22.0**	35.4
79	8.19	n.a.	6.70	6.77	22.0**	n.a.
1980	9.01*	11.48	7.27	7.18	23.9*	59.9

* An additional 41.2 percent in compensation was provided through fringe benefits. This was a rise from 27.4 percent in 1975. American Public Transit Association, *Transit Fact Book*, 90/81.

** In recent year, transit employers and their unions have tended to agree on a larger proportion of compensation increases in the form of increased fringe benefits (paid holidays, pensions, medical insurance, etc.) instead of straight time pay. If the disproportionately large increase in fringe benefit portion of compensation appeared in straight time pay, the premium over manufacturing workers would have been 33.2 percent in 1980.

Table 12
Annual Rates of Change in Key Variables
Before, During and After Recession

Period	Hourly compensation (private business sector)	Demand for goods (GNP)	Net employment efffect	Employment *	Unemployment rate at end of period
	Recession: December 1969 - November 1970				
1967 III-1969 III	7.6%	8.4%	0.8%	2.3%	4.0%
1969 III-1970 IV	7.4	4.2	- 3.3	- 0.5	6.1
1970 IV-1972 IV	6.4	10.2	3.8	2.7	5.1
	Recession: November 1973 - March 1975				
1972 IV-1973 IV	8.2	11.6	3.4	3.4	4.6
1973 IV-1975 I	11.3	5.7	- 5.6	- 2.1	8.5
1975 I-1977 I	8.5	11.6	3.4	3.0	7.4
	Recession: January 1980 - July 1980				
1977 IV-1979 IV	9.3	12.2	2.9	2.9	6.0
1979 IV-1980 II	12.1	6.2	-5.9	- 2.0	7.5
1980 II-1981 II	9.2	13.2	4.0	1.7	7.4
	Recession: July 1981 - November 1982				
1980 III-1981 III	9.3	12.4	3.1	1.7	7.6
1981 III-1982 IV	7.3	2.9	- 4.4	- 1.4	10.7
1982 IV-1985 III	4.1	8.5	4.4	3.0	7.1

* Unadjusted for change in work week.

The record of the employee share of national income shows that every time it is pushed above the uptrend dictated by the increasing stock of capital, the result has been a rise in the unemployment rate (see table 5). Periods of rising unemployment are also periods of a marked decline in the return on capital, and a decreased rate of investment. Between 1929 and 1933, for example, nominal wage rates fell only half as rapidly as nominal GNP. *The* employee share of national income in the United States rose from 60.3 to 75.1 percent, far above the trend figure of 62 percent for 1933. Consequently, the unemployment *rate* rose from 3.2 to 24.9 percent, the return on corporate equity dropped to less than zero, and the rate of net investment fell to negative levels.[30]

By 1948, the employee share of national income dropped to 64.2 percent. From 1933 to 1948 nominal wage rates rose 202 percent while GNP rose 365 percent. Employment rose 51 percent. Unemployment fell to 3.8 percent (and real wage rates increased by two-thirds over their 1929 level - see table 13). But in 1949, nominal wage rates rose 4 percent while nominal GNP fell by 0.5 percent. The employee share rose to 66 percent, a 2 percentage point increase in one year, and the unemployment rate increased to 5.9 percent.[31] And so the story goes. The employee share rose from 72.8 percent in 1979 to 75.7 percent in 1982. The overly rapid rise in wage rates, which produced this rise in the employee share of national income, increased the unemployment rate from 5.8 percent in 1979 to 9.7 percent in 1982.

At this point in time, if the rise in nominal hourly compensation were to slow to less than 2 percent, employment would rise more rapidly and the unemployment rate would drop (and inflation could be ended). Also, the rate of capital formation would increase, real wage rates would rise more rapidly, and differences in income would diminish.

Each period in which nominal wage rates rose above the market clearing level, the employee share of national income rose above the trend dictated by the rising capital stock. Each is also a period in which the division of income

---

[30] By 1937, *the employee share of national income* dropped to 65.1 percent from the 75 percent of 1933. The *unemployment* rate dropped from 25 percent to 14.3 percent (see table 5). The employee share was still above trend - 2 percentage points above the trend value for 1937 - and the unemployment rate remained high, although reduced from its 1933 level. The employee share and the unemployment rate would not have remained so high but for the minimum wage provisions of the National Industrial Recovery Act of 1933 and the new power given to labor unions. Paradoxically, real wage income would have been higher in 1937 if money wage rates had not been pushed up by union and legislative action.

[31] The trend rate of increase in employee share consistent with the maintenance of full employment in this period was 0.4 percentage point. The 1949 rate of return on manufacturing book equity dropped to 11.6 percent from 16.0 percent in 1948 and gross private domestic investment dropped to $35.3 billion in 1949 from $45.9 billion in 1948. This is not to say that the rise in the employee share caused the rise in unemployment. It and the drop in employment are both consequences of wage rates maintained at a level in excess of the *market clearing* rates in a deflationary period. A very small decrease in nominal wage rates in 1949 would have maintained employment (of production capacity as well as labor) and would have resulted in higher total real wage income.

became less equal even though property income's share fell.[32] Rising employee income shares has, over the long run, diminished differences in income, but pushing it up too rapidly in the short run increases inequality. Impatience in achieving higher wage rates defeats itself. It may increase nominal wage rates, but it decreases real wage rates and decreases equality.[33]

If we allowed the market to operate free of government interference (that is, if we removed the power granted by government to unions to influence wage rates, to employers to grant supracompetitive increases in wage rates, and repealed interventions by government such as minimum wage laws, the Fair Labor Standards Act, the Davis-Bacon Act, the Walsh-Healy Act, the Wagner Act, section 13c of the Urban Mass Transit Act, and subsidies to the shipping and mass transit industries), there would be faster progress toward smaller differences in the income status of various ranks.

Even in the face of government efforts to equalize incomes by legislation of the type just listed and by tax and income transfer policies, which have actually slowed the convergence of incomes, there has been convergence in pre-tax, pre-transfer incomes. The major exceptions are in the lower 20 percent of households ranked by income. In this group, there are a larger number of people who have left jobs and taken a one-third cut in income, on average, in order to collect disability pensions, Aid for Families with Dependent Children, general welfare allowances, early retirement pensions under Social Security, and unemployment compensation.[34] This perverse incentive effect

---

32 The index measuring *inequality* in the division of income rose from 415 in 1948 to 421 in 1949 as *employee share of national income* rose from 64.2 percent to 66.0 percent. From 1952 to 1954, the index rose from 408 to 415 as employee share rose from 67.3 to 56.4 percent. From 1969 to 1971, the index rose from 403 to 409 as the employee share increased from 72.5 to 73.4 percent. *Unemployment and Its Effect on Family Income in 1980* (Washington: U.S. Bureau of Labor Statistics, 1982, Bulletin 2148).

33 The employee or labor share of national income is not the key variable influencing employment levels. We have given it some prominence in this discussion because of its centrality among the goals of union leaders and Marxian socialists. See, for examples, Andrew Healy, "Labour's Share and Profitability Crisis in the United States: Recent Experience and Post-War Trends" (Coventry: Warwick Economic Research Papers no. 269, Nov. 1985).

34 Donald O. Parsons, "The Decline in Male Labor Force Participation," *Journal of Political Economy*, vol. 88, no. 1 (Feb. 1980); C.T. Brehm and T.R. Saving, "The Demand for General Assistance Payments," *American Economic Review*, vol. 54, no. 6 (Dec. 1964); Arlene Holen and Stanley Horowitz, "The Effect of Unemployment Insurance and Eligibility Enforcement on Unemployment," *Journal of Law & Economics*, vol. 17, no. 2 (Oct. 1974); James Gwartney and Thomas S. McCaleb, "Have Antipoverty Programs Increased Poverty," *CATO Journal*, vol. 5, no. 1 (Spring/Summer 1985).

has depressed incomes in the lower 20 percent and slowed the rise in its share.[35]

Moderating employment fluctuations

The attempt to "fine tune" monetary policy with the aim of moderating the business cycle and minimizing fluctuations in employment has produced the cycles that give monetary activists their excuse for "fine tuning." Every rise in the inflation rate has been preceded by rising growth in the money stock[36] that was usually aimed at preventing a developing recession. Every rise in the inflation rate has been followed by a slowing of money growth that was usually aimed at restraining inflation[37]. Every *recession* has been preceded by a slowing in money growth which played an important role in producing the recession (see table 14).

---

[35] Edgar R. Browning, *Redistribution and the Welfare System* (Washington: American Enterprise Institute, 1975). Also, see Y. Brozen, "Welfare Without the Welfare State," *Il Politica*, vol. 32, no. 1 (1967), pp. 135-136. For a compendium of the reasons why attempts to redistribute income may have a perverse effect, see J.E. Stiglitz, "Equality, Taxation and Inheritance," in W. Kreble and A. Shorrocks (eds.), *Personal Income Distribution* (Amsterdam: North-Holland, 1978). Also, see Martin Feldstein, "Social Insurance," in Colin D. Campbell (ed.), *Income Redistribution* (Washington, D.C.: American Enterprise Institute, 1977). For a summary discussion of the behavior of income shares, see Richard B. McKenzie, "Taxation and Income Redistribution," *CATO Journal,* vol. 1, no. 2 (Fall 1981).

[36] A rise in the rate of money stock growth is usually followed within two years by a rise in the rate of inflation.

[37] This is not to say that these have been the only goals of central bankers The over riding aim of the Federal Reserve's monetary policy is to please the Congressional banking committees which have oversight over the Federal Reserve. Kevin B. Grier, "Congressional Preference and Federal Reserve Policy," (Working Paper No. 95, Nov. 1985, Center for the Study of American Business, Washington University, St. Louis, MO).

Table 13
Average Annual and Hourly Earnings of Full Time Employees
1900 - 1979

Year	Earnings of Employees: Annual (current dollars)	Hourly (current dollars)	Annual (1914 dollars)	Hourly (1914 dollars)	Consumer price index 1914 = 100
1900	438	0.14	519	0.17	84.3
1929	1,405	0.56	822	0.33	170.9
1948	2,786	1.34	1,163	0.56	239.5
1969	7,095	3.55	1,945	0.97	364.7
1979	14,378	7.37	1,991	1.02	722.2

Source: U.S. Bureau of the Census, *Historical Statistics of the United States: Colonial Times to 1970* (Washington: GPO, 1975), pp. 164, 168; *Economic Report of the President* (1982), p. 291; *Survey of Current Business*, July 1980.

If the money growth rate were simply maintained at a constant, moderate level with no attempt at fine tuning, fluctuations in the employment level would be more moderate.[38] Instability in money growth has cost the United States 15 percent of its real growth since the 1950s.[39] Current real gross national product would be $600 billion higher (in 1986 dollars) if money growth had been moderate and stable since 1950.

[38] Fluctuations in interest rates, the velocity of circulation, and in the inflation rate would also be more moderate. Milton Friedman and Anna J. Schwartz, A Monetary History of the United States: 1867-1960 (Princeton: Princeton U. Press, 1963).

[39] Roger C. Kormendi and George G. Maguire, "Determinants of Economic Growth," *Journal of Monetary Economics,* vol. 15 (September 1985). In addition to the cost of stop-and-go monetary policy, there has also been a large cost caused by the overly rapid growth of the money stock and the resulting inflation. Martin S. Feldstein, "The Welfare Cost of Permanent Inflation and Optimal Short-Run Economic Policy," *Journal of Political Economy,* vol. 87, no. 4 (Aug. 1979), p. 765. Also, see Dennis Carlton, "The Disruptive Effect of Inflation on the Organization of Markets" (presented before the Applied Economics Workshop, University of Chicago, Feb. 24, 1981); Craig S. Hakkio and Bryon Higgins, "Cost and Benefits of Reducing Inflation," *Federal Reserve Bank of Kansas City Economic Review,* vol. 70, no. 1 (Jan. 1985).

Table 14
Peak and trough timing for money growth rates and corresponding velocity of circulation 1947 - 1984

Rates of growth of M1 (with velocity of circulation)				Months from M1 growth peak to cycle peak	Rates of growth of M1 (with velocity in quarter)				Months from M1 growth trough cycle trough
Peak in M1 growth	V	Cycle peak	V		Troughs in M1 growth	V	Cycle trough	V	
5.3%(8/47)	2.07	-0.5%(11/48)	2.38	15	-2.0%(2/49)	2.34	-0.7(10/49)	2.31	8
6.9(12/51)	2.78	2.0(7/53)	2.95	19	0.3(11/53)	2.82	1.6(5/54)	2.80	6
4.9(2/55)	2.91	0.4(8/57)	3.38	30	-2.2(1/58)	3.21	0.7(4/58)	3.20	3
4.7(1/59)	3.40	-1.3(4/60)	3.60	15	-2.8(2/60)	3.60	0.4(2/61)	3.56	12
7.3(1/66)	4.30	0.6(12/66)	4.47	11	-0.7(10/66)	4.47	5.0(11/70)	4.44	7
8.4(1/69)	4.57	1.7(12/69)	4.68	11	1.7(12/69)	4.68	5.0(11/70)	4.68	11
10.7(1/73)	5.03	4.4(11/73)	5.21	10	2.8(9/74)	5.30	4.5(3/75)	5.30	6
10.9(8/79)	6.39	5.7(1/80)	6.53	5	1.3(5/80)	6.61	3.47(7/80)	6.52	2
14.7(11/80)	6.56	5.6(7/81)	6.95	8	-0.2(10/81)	6.92	9.8(11/82)	6.56	13

Timing of cyclical peaks and troughs, National Bureau of Economic Research except 1966-1967.
M1 growth rates are six months changes to date shown annualized.

Sources: Federal Reserve Bank of St. Louis, *Monetary Trends*, vrious monthly issues. *Survey of Current Business*, Octobser 1982 and various monthly issues.

As part of their business cycle strategy, welfare activists have also chosen a tax structure designed to minimize saving in order to prevent saving from outrunning investment. The taxes which minimize saving, however, also reduce the private returns from investment. That blunts the rate of capital formation, causing the condition that the activists are attempting to avoid. Heavy taxes on corporate earnings and high taxes on business property, together with high marginal income tax rates and taxation of capital gains, have reduced the incentives to invest and to discover and create investment opportunities as well as reducing the propensity to save. The net result has been both less saving and less investment. A less rapid rise in capital per worker, marginal labor productivity, and wage rates, and, therefore, a slower approach to the more egalitarian society desired by the welfare state activists, has been the consequence.

Micro intervention and its consequences

Intervention in markets at the micro level in the United States is wide spread. It ranges from price floors set for commodities such as corn and wheat through regulation of the design of automobiles to the determination of the prices of electricity, gas, telephone and water service. Some of the interventions are aimed at providing economic security, some at reducing the cost and insurance of externalities, and some at protecting buyers from paying high prices, or so it is said.

The interventions aimed at providing security have created insecurity in many cases. Those supposedly aimed at reducing the cost and insurrance of *externalities* have been used to protect firms in some sections of the country from the competition of firms in other sections in lieu of internal tariffs which cannot be levied because of a constitutional ban.[40] Regulation of utility prices was an exchange for the grant of monopoly franchises which closed entry and precluded opportunities for entrepreneurial discovery which would have kept utility prices lower than the regulators have.

Interventions to provide security

In their attempts to create greater security for farmers, workers, and the unfortunate victims of unforeseen change and of accidents, welfare activists designed a set of policies that created greater insecurity. Perhaps the foremost example is the 1981 Agriculture Act of the United States Congress. Price supports were set at levels which simultaneously caused an expansion of American agriculture and sacrificed markets for the price-supported commodities.

---

[40] B. Peter Pashigian, The Political Economy of the Clean Air Act: Regional Self-Interest in Environmental Legislation (St. Louis: Center for the Study of American Business, Washington University, 1982).

Agricultural production outside the United States was stimulated by the high prices mandated for U.S. produced commodities. Foreign markets have now been permanently pre-empted by foreign production.[41] American agriculture now has more excess capacity than ever before. It will have to eliminate a large amount to come back into balance with its markets.

In addition to the incentives created by the high price supports set for the 1981-1985 period, farmers were also encouraged to expand by changes in Federal law which inspired some Farm Land Banks to grant liberal loans on land collateral-land whose price was inflated by these easy loans. As foreign markets disappeared, the price of land fell. It is no longer valuable enough to serve as full collateral for some of the loans made. Government policy created a financial disaster for many farmers and for many of the private banks which made agricultural loans.[42]

To provide job security for American workers in import competing industries, the United States negotiated "voluntary restraints" on the export of Japanese automobiles to the United States, on the exports of textiles and steel to the U.S., and imposed tariffs on imported tuna. The reduction of imports decreased foreign dollar earnings. As a result, export industries (including agriculture) found it difficult to maintain their foreign sales, causing job insecurity for their workers.

According to studies done by the Federal Trade Commission, the annual cost to consumers of the restraints on imports of Japanese automobiles was approximately $241,000 per U.S. job saved. Tuna tariffs cost the U.S. consumer $240,000 annually per job saved. The cost to consumers per job saved by steel quotas was $114,000 and for textiles $43,000. In effect, consumers were taxed to save jobs in these industries, but jobs in the industries from

---

[41] John Antle, *World Agricultural Development and the Future of U.S. Agriculture* (Washington: American Enterprise Institute, forthcoming).

[42] This is not the first of government agricultural policies that created unintended results and were counter-productive. It seems obvious that subsidizing the use of fertilizer and machinery would help farmers by reducing their costs of production. What seemed so obviously true turned out to be untrue. The increased output with subsidies drove prices down with the result that farmers were not better off. Those who were tenants, obtaining their return from their labor, were worse off because labor value was decreased by substitution of fertilizer and equipment. Owner-operators were worse off because the return from their land as well as from their labor decreased. Fertilizer and equipment were substitutes for land as well as labor. Subsidizing their use drove down the return to land as well as labor. D. Gale Johnson, "Output and Income Effects of Reducing the Farm Labor Force," *Journal of Farm Economics,* vol. 42 (Nov. 1960); "Labor Mobility and Agricultural Adjustment," in E.O. Heady, H.G. Diesslin, H.R. Jensen, and G.L. Johnson, eds., *Agricultural Adjustment Problems in a Growing Economy* (Ames, Iowa: Iowa State College Press, 1958), p. 170.

which consumers would have bought goods but for the "taxes" they paid were destroyed. For every two jobs saved in the protected industries, three jobs were lost in other industries.[43]

In an attempt to provide job security for workers, judges created ex post facto law eroding the right to "fire at will". Employers who hired workers believing, on the basis of the law prevailing at the time of hiring, that they had this right are discovering that the implied contract into which they thought they were entering has since been changed by government fiat. In some states, laws have been passed imposing new notification requirements or severance pay in lieu of notification--obligations which did not exist at the time of hiring.

Such ex post facto law has introduced uncertainties that are hindering the efficient functioning of the market. The possibility that ex post facto law may be enacted in other states or at the national level causes employers to hesitate in expanding production because of the risk that future unknown costs may be imposed. Employers facing these risks choose to expand employment only if they can obtain workers with a lower wage bid than they would offer if such uncertainties did not exist. In this case, workers are not bid away from alternative pursuits where they are less productive than they would be with a new employer. As a consequence, productivity, wage rates, and national output rise more slowly and the jobless stage for some workers persists for longer periods.

Producers find themselves at risk not only because rule changes with a backward reach may redefine employment contracts but also because sales contracts may be redefined by ex post facto law.[44] The sale of a product thirty years ago when the rule governing the sale was caveat emptor may now create "product liabilities" for the seller in that ancient transaction. A machine may have been remodeled, safeguards removed by subsequent owners who pur-

---

[43] If we subtract from the losses to consumers the gains to other sectors of the economy from automobile import restraints, the sugar import *quotas*, the textile quota on Hong Kong, and the steel quota, the net cost (deadweight loss) to the economy of these quotas amounts to $2.18 billion annually. The total annual cost to the U.S. economy of all tariffs and quotas is $8.52 billion (1983 dollars). David G. Farr and Morris E. Morkre, *Aggregate Costs to the United States of Tariffs and Quotas on Imports* (Washington, D.C.: Federal Trade Commission Bureau of Economics, December 1984), p. 2. In their analysis, the Bureau of Economics staff assumed that elimination of sugar quotas would not be accompanied by the elimination "of a domestic *price-support* program that guarantees minimum receipts to domestic growers."

[44] Richard Epstein, op. cit., p. 19.

chased the machine in the second-hand market, and yet the original producer be held liable for an injury incurred by an operator of the machine. Even the "contributory negligence" doctrine can be, and has been, abrogated. The seller of the machine can be forced to become an "involuntary good samaritan" simply because his means exceed those of an injured user.

The rise in liability insurance costs caused by forcing the "involuntary good samaritan" role on employers is causing insecurity for many employees Firms have gone out of business because they cannot pay the increased premiums. Others have dropped products from their offerings because of the cost of defending themselves in product liability suits even though they win such suits.[45]

Regulation of emissions

Regulatory intervention to reduce the cost of externalities seems to be justified in cases such as the emission of pollutants. Requiring automobile design modifications to minimize emissions damaging to health and to visibility is apparently necessary since it is not worthwhile to any one purchaser of an automobile to choose a low emission model unless in return all are required to purchase such models. The transaction costs involved in constructing a coalition of sufferers from emissions to purchase an agreement from auto buyers to choose cars with emission controls apparently makes this approach impractical.

The United States has chosen to compel manufacturers to design automobiles with low emissions. Automobile design is regulated, but the regulations have become irrational. Reducing auto emissions by 90 percent, as we did in the mid-1970s, produced annual benefits worth about $10 billion. With an annual cost of $8 billion, design regulation produced a net gain, although costs could have been decreased by not imposing identical regulations nationwide.[46]

The tightening of emission standards in 1979 and 1980 added another $5 billion to costs. The tightening produced less than an additional one billion in benefits. What could have been a net positive return has been turned into a

---

45 Michael Brody, "When Products Turn into Liabilities," *Fortune*, March 3, 1986.

46 Most of the effects of emissions occur in a few major metropolitan areas such as Los Angeles and Chicago. By loosening control standards in other regions where no inversions occur, the cost of emission control could be cut in half with no loss in benefits.

loser.[47] The United States is spending about $13 billion annually to produce $8 to $9 billion of benefits.[48]

The 1977 amendments to the Clean Air Act, which require costly scrubbers at new coal using electric power plants regardless of the sulphur content of the coal used, do not have even the virtue of reducing pollution. At least this can be claimed as an accomplishment of auto emission controls. The 1977 regulations on the design of new power plants will produce more sulphur oxide emissions than the less costly alternative approach of allowing the use of low sulphur coal as a means of controlling pollution.

We have deliberately replaced the pre-1977 regulations, which were less costly and which resulted in less pollution, with new regulations which are more costly and which will increase pollution. There is a gain to the owners of land containing high sulphur coal and to the miners of this coal, but their gain is minuscule compared to the cost to users of electricity, which will amount to at least $3.4 billion a year by the year 2000, and the cost to sufferers from more polluted air.[49]

The externalities described in the foregoing examples could be cured by internalizing them. Regulating automobile and electric generating plant designs is the most costly method for accomplishing a specified amount of emissions reduction. Assuming overwhelming transaction costs inhibit voluntary arrangements between producers of these externalities and those affected by them,[50] a tax on emissions could produce the reduction much more economically. A tax imposed locally in the case of automobiles, since auto emissions are a local problem, and nationally on electric generating plants would minimize the costs of achieving any desired level of atmospheric purity. Alternatively, and preferably, transferable emission "tickets" could be issued permitting only the amount of emissions consistent with the desired objectives.[51]

---

[47] Lester Lave and Eugene Seskin, *Air Pollution and Human Health* (Baltimore: Johns Hopkins University Press, 1977), p. 231. The cost estimates in Lave and Seskin are updated in Lawrence White, *The Regulation of Air Pollutant Emissions from Motor Vehicles* (Washington: American Enterprise Institute, 1981).

[48] For an analysis of the politics involved in this decision, see Howard Margolis, "The Politics of Auto Emission," *The Public Interest*, no. 49 (Fall 1977).

[49] Paul R. Portney, "How Not to Create a Job," *Regulation: AEI Journal on Government and Society*, vol. 6 (Nov/Dec 1982), p. 35.

[50] Ronald Coase, "The Problem of Social Cost," *Journal of Law & Economics*, vol. 3 (Oct. 1960).

[51] Charles Upton, *The Economics of Pollution* (Chicago: Graduate School of Business, University of Chicago, 1970).

Industrial organization policies

The cost to consumers and to the economy of government industrial organization policies is even greater than the cost of tariffs and import quotas. Consumers of postal services, a government operated monopoly in the United States, pay $5 billion more than they would if the private express statutes were repealed.[52] The fruit, vegetable, and "specialty" crop cartels organized under the agricultural marketing order system create waste exceeding one billion dollars.[53] Inefficient management of government owned timber lands creates a loss of $2 billion a year.[54] The cost of consumers of mass transit services, electricity, and water provided by government operated enterprises and by private enterprises granted monopoly franchises has not been measured, but the bits and pieces of evidence available indicate that the total is greater than the cost of the postal monopoly.[55]

Antitrust laws in the United States are also costly.[56] Although they are

---

52 Douglas Adie, *An Evaluation of Postal Service Wage Rates* (Washington: American Enterprise Institute, 1980); John Haldi, *Postal Monopoly: An Assessment of the Private Express Statutes* (Washington: American Enterprise Institute, 1974); James C. Miller III, "End the Postal Monopoly," *CATO Journal*, vol. 5, no. 1 (Spring/Summer 1985). Leaving aside the cost of x- inefficiency in postal operations, the deadweight loss comes to approximately $2 billion a year. This is caused in part by supra-competitive pricing of services and in part by use of over-qualified personnel who would be occupying more productive jobs if postal wage rates were set at levels minimizing total personnel costs (including turnover costs).

53 Thomas M. Lenard and Michael P. Mazur, "Harvest of Waste: The Marketing Order Program," Regulation, vol. 9, no. 3 (May/June 1985).

54 Thomas M. Lenard, "Wasting Our National Forests," *Regulation,* vol. 5, no. 4 (July/Aug. 1981), p. 30.

55 Gregg Jarrell, "The Demand for State Regulation of the Electric Utility Industry," *Journal of Law & Economics*, vol. 21 (Oct. 1978); Robert Cervero, "Deregulating Urban Transportation," *CATO Journal*, vol. 5, no. 1 (Spring/Summer 1985); Peltzman, "Pricing in Public and Private Enterprises," op. cit. There is an indirect cost to consumers in some instances with no direct cost. Amtrak does not set a supracompetitive price for its services, but it consumes a billion dollars worth of resources in excess of the value it provides causing consumers to do without a billion dollars worth of product that could have been produced but for this waste. Congressional Budget Office, *Federal Subsidies for Rail Passenger Service: An Assessment of Amtrak* (Washington: Government Printing Office, 1982).

H.E. Frech III and Joseph C. Samploone, Jr., The Welfare Loss of exess Nonprice Competition Compelion: The Case of Property Liability Insurance Regulation," *Journal of Law and Economics*, Vol. 23 (Oct. 1980), found a deadweight loss of 600 million is produced by state regulation of insurance rates.

56 The antitrust laws have had macro as well as micro consequences. Shughart and Tollison estimate that each one percent increase in annual enforcement activity over the 1947-1981 period added about 7,000 to the number of unemployed persons. "The Em-

presumably aimed at preserving the benefits of competition for consumers, the fact is that most of the applications made of antitrust laws are anticompetitive.[57] Where the applications are procompetitive, the results are frequently anti-efficient.[58]

Antimerger arguments

Here, let us confine ourselves to the antimerger laws. In the past, two sets of antimerger arguments have been raised.[59] One set says that an increase in the share of any one industry in the hands of a few large firms will lead to oligopolistic behavior. By that, it is meant that if a few companies sell a very large share of the amount produced of any one commodity, they will either conspire with each other to set prices above the competitive level or they will engage in live and let live behavior (tacit collusion).[60] They will, it is said, avoid cutting prices when more numerous smaller, presumably more competitive, firms would set lower prices.

This is the argument for preventing mergers between companies with moderate market shares selling the same product in the same market.[61] Under

---

ployment Consequences of Antitrust" (ms., 1984).

[57] Thomas Hazlett, "Is Antitrust Anticompetitive," *Harvard Journal of Law and Public Policy* (forthcoming); William J. Baumol and Janusz A. Ordover, "Use of Antitrust to Subvert Competition," *Journal of Law & Economics*, vol. 28 (May 1985); Yale Brozen, "Some Behavioral Consequences of Antitrust", Management Discretion and Antitrust (New York: Conference Board Research Bulletin no. 179, 1985). For an instance in which the application of the antimerger laws cost $20 million and 1,500 jobs, see A.F. Ehrbar, "The Needless Death of Federal Glass," *Fortune*, July 2, 1979.

[58] George Bittlingmayer, "Decreasing Average Cost and Competition: A New Look at the Addyston Pipe Case," *Journal of Law & Economics*, vol. 25 (October 1982), pp. 201-229; Donald Dewey, "Information, Entry, and Welfare: The Case for Collusion," *American Economic Review*, vol. 69 (Sept. 1979), pp. 587-594.

[59] A third set of arguments raised against mergers is their effect on aggregate concentration. I have dealt with that set in *Concentration, Mergers, and Public Policy*, op. cit. pp. 309-338. Also, see Y. Brozen, *Mergers in Perspective* (Washington: American Enterprise Institute, 1982).

[60] The "evidence" for the existence of collusive behavior in concentrated industries has been shown to be faulty. Harold Demsetz, "Economics as a Guide to Antitrust Regulation," *Journal of Law & Economics*, vol. 19 (Aug. 1976), pp. 375-382; Y. Brozen, "Concentration and Profits: Does Concentration Matter?" *Antitrust Bulletin*, vol. 19, no. 2 (Summer 1974), pp. 381-399.

[61] The Committee of Experts on Restrictive Business Practices of the Organization for Economic Cooperation and Development apparently adopts this view of aggregate as well as market concentration. Also it confuses the concept of barriers to entry with the cost of entry and attractiveness of entry and does not recognize that advertising is a

the current U.S. Justice Department guidelines, for example, the Antitrust Division may challenge any merger of two businesses in an industry with 10 firms each selling 10 percent of the product produced.

The second set of antimerger arguments contend that the borrowings used to make acquisitions would do more for the economy if used by acquirers to build new plants, to do more innovating, or to find new oil rather than to acquire already discovered oil and already built plants. These arguments are based on the belief that the use of capital for acquisitions denies capital to real capital formation and reduces the amount of new assets created.

That belief is wrong. The acquisition of old assets is not a process in which spending on existing assets diverts capital from the creation of new assets.

The simple correlation of spending on the purchase of existing assets by manufacturing and mining firms with spending on the creation of new assets is very high. The correlation coefficient is 0.85. The reason for this high correlation is that an increase in the demand for old assets encourages the creation of new assets. We recognize this in the case of housing, yet we do not apply the same reasoning to other assets. That an increase in the demand for old houses will increase the construction of new houses is a part of the conventional wisdom.[62] The same principle applies to other assets.

The fact that a refining firm finds it cheaper to buy the title to already discovered oil (which does not divert real resources from alternative uses) instead of applying additional real resources to a discovery effort simply says that it is less efficient at discovery than others or that added effort would be less efficient. (By acquiring Gulf, Chevron obtained reserves for $7.40 a barrel. Additional exploratory effort was expected to yield reserves at a cost of $10 to $12 per barrel.) Or it says that the buying firm can use the reserves more efficiently than the selling firm.

Buying already discovered oil increases the demand for discovery effort. Those who have discovered oil and are more efficient in discovery or less efficient in exploiting their discoveries sell their reserves and are provided

---

means of entry or that expansion of capacity by established firms is entry as well as by firms new to an industry. Merger Policies and Recent Trends in Mergers (Paris: OECD, 1984), pp. 7-8, 65. For the distinctions concerning entry conditions, see Y. Brozen, "Competition, Efficiency, and Antitrust," *Journal of World Trade Law*, vol. 3 (1969).

62 Edward J. Mitchell, "New Ideas About Oil Mergers," *Regulation*, vol. 8, no. 2 (March/April 1984), pp. 13-14.

with the capital to engage in additional discovery. Those who earlier invested in companies that discovered oil are, when their companies are acquired, provided with the capital to invest in more discoveries of oil. The result is additional investment in new discovery whether the capital is invested directly by Chevron or Texaco or indirectly by the purchase of already discovered reserves. Even if those who sell their positions in already discovered oil do not themselves reinvest in more discovery, others are encouraged to invest by the demand for discovered oil.

To put this another way, an acquisition does not consume the real resources required for the creation of new assets. The purchase of one company by another simply transfers title. It does not divert the real resources used to create new assets to noncreative uses. If anything, acquisitions of existing assets attract additional real resources into creating more new real assets. (Remember the correlation between the purchase of existing assets and the creation of new assets.)

When firms choose to buy existing assets, such as already discovered oil where that is cheaper than discovering their own, the process of creating new assets, such as newly discovered oil, is encouraged and made more efficient. Those who are most efficient at discovery will engage in it and sell to those who are either less efficient in discovery or more efficient in exploiting and using reserves. To bar such acquisitions would make the discovery process less efficient. It would reduce the amount of oil discovered both for this reason and because of the forced reduction in the demand for discovery effort.

The mergers undertaken by Texaco, Chevron, and Mobil were an adaptive response to the fact that their domestic exploration effort, despite the billions they spent, were not sufficiently successful to develop enough reserves to protect their investment in transportation, refining, and distribution. From 1973 to 1982, during a period when domestic reserves of all oil companies in the United States dropped by 16 percent, those of these three companies dropped by 65, 32, and 25 percent. Their acquisitions were undertaken to restore their reserve position and to provide the insurance they needed to minimize the risk that the value of their other assets could be hurt by a future oil shortage.

Mergers improve productivity and efficiency

Mergers increase efficiency in the use of assets and the efficiency and productivity of the economy.[63] On average, acquirers have offered premiums to shareholders of target companies of 50 percent over the market price of their shares[64]. We should ask ourselves the reasons that buyers find the assets of the acquired companies to be worth more to them than to the current shareholders.

What Shell Oil did with its purchase of Belridge is an illustration of what makes a firm worth more to its buyers than to its sellers. A 1982 Federal Trade Commission (FTC) study found that Shell's 1979 purchase of Belridge Oil allowed Shell to apply its superior oil-recovery technology to Belridge's heavy oil reserves. Belridge's output was doubled. Shell bid 75 percent more than the best alternative offer for Belridge stock and it more than doubled Belridge's earnings from its oil reserves. That was a good deal for both Belridge and Shell stockholders and for the economy. Total output was increased by transferring Belridge to Shell ownership and management.

Using the example of the Chevron-Gulf combination, Professor Edward Mitchell argues that

There is evidence that Chevron's acquisition of Gulf Oil has the potential for significant efficiencies . . . . Gulf earned only an 8.2 percent return on its assets in 1983, compared with 10.5 percent for the integrated petroleum industry as a whole and 11.2 percent for Chevron. This suggests that there is room for improvement in the utilization of Gulf's assets.[65]

That these examples of less efficient firms being acquired by more efficient firms are typical in the merger movement is confirmed by an FTC study. In its analysis of mergers occurring in the 1960s, the FTC found that the corporations acquired by the nine leading conglomerates were only 70 percent as efficient as the average firm in their industries. That is, the average returns earned by the acquired firms were only 70 percent of the average return earned by all firms in their home industries.

---

[63] See Brozen, *Concentration, Mergers, and Public Policy*, op. cit., pp. 56- 75, 350-358. A recent example of an efficiency increasing merger blocked by a U.S. government agency is the proposal opening of the Santa Fe and Southern Pacific railroads. The merger would save 293 million in costs and eliminate newly 1200 million in deadweight loss.

[64] From 1955 through 1976, premiums averaged 25 percent on the price prevailing before each merger or tender offer announcement. Premiums have trended upwards since 1976, reaching 50 percent by 1979. In 1984, premiums averaged 38 percent.

[65] Mitchell, op. cit.

The fact that premiums are paid for the stock of target firms suggests that the acquirers expect to use the acquired assets more efficiently. Premiums are offered only if the buying firms expect to produce returns of greater value to their stockholders that the value to the target firms' stockholders of the expected returns under the old managements. Since the acquirers' stockholders enjoyed returns after the mergers roughly equal to those of all New York Stock Exchange firms, the expectations were accurate. A marked improvement in returns must have occurred after the acquisitions; otherwise the premiums paid would have produced losses in the acquiring companies. They would have suffered below normal returns, with a consequent loss to their stockholders, if the premiums had not been subsequently justified and their value sustained by improvements in efficiency.

Professor Paul Asquith points out that the findings in his study of all postwar mergers involving New York Stock Exchange listed firms show that *mergers cause a change in real activity, and this change produces a real gain for the combined firm. That is, the firms are worth more when they are combined than when they are alone. . .*

Furthermore, the results suggest that the resource which is being acquired in a merger is . . . (an) inefficient(ly) manage(d) . . . target firm.[66]

Are improved returns the consequence of monopoly power?

Merger opponents concede that the returns to the combined firms may be larger than those before the combination occurred. This, they say, is a consequence of increased concentration and the monopoly power of the combination. The result, according to them, is social inefficiency.

Only anecdotal evidence is offered for this assertion.[67] Systematic evidence points in the opposite direction. The data show that the gains from mergers

---

[66] Paul Asquith, A Two-Event Study of Merger Bids, Market Uncertainty, and Stockholder Returns (Ph. D. dissertation, Graduate School of Business, University of Chicago, 1980), tables 6, 12, pp. 26, 35.

[67] See, for an example of an individual instance, David M. Barton and Sherman Rosen, "The Price and Profit Effects of Horizontal Merger: A Case Study," *Journal of Industrial Economics*, vol. 3, no. 2 (Dec. 1984), pp. 165-177. Also see Richard Zerbe, "The American Sugar Refining Company, 1887-1914: The Story of a Monopoly," *Journal of Law & Economics*, vol. 12 (Oct. 1969).

and from increases in concentration are a result of improved efficiency and productivity, not of output restriction and higher prices.[68]

The National Industrial Conference Board commissioned a study of the turn- of-the-century mergers and their consequences. That study found that the customers of industries with large consolidations benefited relative to the customers of those industries with minor consolidations or none. In twenty-six industries in which important consolidations took place and for which price data were available, prices fell by 13 percent from 1900 to 1913. In twenty industries in which no consolidations occurred, prices rose by 10 percent from 1900 to 1913.

Looking at the period following 1913, when inflation became rampant, prices rose by 49 percent from 1913 to 1925 in the twenty-six industries with major consolidations. But in the twenty industries in which no consolidations occurred, prices rose by 96 percent from 1913 to 1925, double the rise in industries with large scale mergers.[69] Evidently, combinations occurred largely in those sectors of the economy where economies could be realized through the merger process. Buyers benefited from the resulting improvements in efficiency and the more favorable prices made possible by greater efficiency.

The consolidations in the twenty-six industries with this very favorable price experience produced firms whose market shares ranged from 50 to 90 percent. It seems that preventing mergers between firms with market shares of 10 percent or more is far too stringent a policy. Yet that is the current policy of the Antitrust Division and the Federal Trade Commission unless there are extenuating circumstances.[70]

In 1968, a White House Antitrust Task Force actually recommended that the United States prevent mergers in industries where four firms have 70 percent or more of all sales. It also recommended breaking up leading firms in

---

[68] John McGee, *In Defense of Industrial Concentration* (New York: Praeger, 1971); Harold Demsetz, *The Market Concentration Doctrine* (Washington: American Enterprise Institute, 1973); J.R. Carter, "Collusion, Efficiency, and Antitrust," *Journal of Law & Economics*, vol. 21 (1978). Also, see E. Woodrow Eckard, Jr., "Industrial Concentration, Plant Scale Economies, and Multi-Plant Operations: Further Evidence," *Review of Business and Economic Research,* vol. 16, no. 3 (Spring 1981), pp. 90-97; Mischa Gisser, "Price Leadership and Dynamic Aspects of Oligopoly in U.S. Manufacturing," *Journal of Political Economy*, vol. 92, no. 6 (Dec. 1984), pp. 1035-1048.

[69] National Industrial Conference Board, *Mergers in Industry* (New York: National Industrial Conference Board, 1929), p. 146.

[70] See U.S. Department of Justice, Merger Guidelines (1982), for a description of the extenuating circumstances.

those industries - a leading firm being defined as one selling more than 15 percent of the product produced by the industry.[71]

Breaking up large firms in such industries would reduce efficiency and cause higher prices. Professor Sam Peltzman demonstrated this in his study of industry experience between 1947 and 1967. He found that, on average, those industries in which concentration (the share of the leading four firms in an industry of the industry's output) increased, productivity increased and prices decreased relative to the industries whose concentration remained unchanged. The data from the Census of Manufacturers showed that if industries in which the leading four firms produced more than 50 percent of domestic output had their leading firms broken up to reduce concentration to less than 50 percent, cost would rise by 20 percent, on average, and prices would rise by 10 to 15 percent.[72]

The conclusions of Peltzman's study have been confirmed by two other studies using different bodies of data. Professor Steven Lustgarten came to the same conclusion using 1954 and 1972 data.[73] The second study, by Professor Woodrow Eckard, found that among industries more than 50 percent concentrated, those in which concentration changed by more than 10 percentage points had price increases averaging only 89 percent of the overall price increase in all industries. He also found that in industries more than 50 percent concentrated, whether concentration did or did not increase, price increases were only 93 percent of the average price increase for all industries.[74]

The bromine industry provides a dramatic example of the benefits associated with increasing concentration. Mergers and the growth in size of one firm in the industry increased the share of the four leading firms of all bromine produced in the United States from 80 percent in 1958 to 95 percent

---

71 Some members of the White House Antitrust Task Force refused to sign the recommendation and others have retracted their 1968 recommendation. See Brozen, Concentration, Mergers, and Public Policy (1982), pp. 388-389.

72 Sam Peltzman, "The Gains and Losses from Industrial Concentration," *Journal of Law & Economics*, vol. 20 (Oct. 1977). Also, see E. Woodrow Eckard, Jr., "The Role of Efficiency in Changing Industrial Concentration: An Empirical Analysis," (Working paper, University of Colorado at Denver, Nov. 1985); Michael Smirlock, Thomas Gilligan, and William Marshall, "Tobin's q and the Structure-Performance Relationship," *American Economic Review*, vol. 74, no. 5 (Dec. 1984), pp. 1051-1060.

73 Steven Lustgarten, *Productivity and Prices: The Consequences of Industrial Concentration* (Washington, D.C.: American Enterprise Institute, 1983).

74 E. Woodrow Eckard, Jr., "Concentration Changes and Inflation: Some Evidence," *Journal of Political Economy*, vol. 89 (Oct. 198-0), table 2, p. 1049. Also, see William J. Lynck, "Interpreting Rise Concentration: The Case of Beer," *Journal of Business*, vol. 57, Number 1 (1984).

in 1979. During this period of increasing concentration, the price of bromine fell from 51 cents to 20 cents a pound (measured in constant dollars).

This information suggests that where horizontal mergers and rising concentration occur in open markets, competition increases, in the sense of falling costs and prices, and buyers benefit[75]. This should not be taken to mean that we should force firms to merge. They voluntarily merge when there are benefits that can be created by a marriage among firms. Some industries are more productive when more concentrated; some are more productive when less concentrated. They will move voluntarily to the most efficient structure under the spur of market forces.[76] Policy toward mergers should be one of neutrality.

Summary

The attempt to transfer goods from those who are well-off in pecuniary terms to those low on the pecuniary income ladder by use of steeply progressive income tax rates defeats itself. Tax payments are less progressive when tax rates are more progressive. In addition, steeply progressive tax rates slow the accumulation of capital and slow the rate at which real wage rates rise. Slowing capital formation slows the rate at which the distribution of income becomes more egalitarian.

Progressive tax rate schedules also cause a large non-revenue yielding burden of taxation. They push resources out of more productive into less productive uses. This misallocation costs the economy approximately $125 billion annually. Do-it-yourself activities by people who are more productive (pre-tax) in their occupations than they are in amateurish attempts to do their own decorating and house and automobile repairs with inadequate tools and

---

75 Also, see B. Espen Eckbo, "Horizontal Mergers, Collusion, and Stockholder Wealth," *Journal of Financial Economics*, vol. 11 (1983); Robert Stillman, "Examining Antitrust Policy Toward Horizontal Mergers," *Journal of Financial Economics*, vol. 11 (1983) and B.E. Eckbo and Peggy Wier, "Antimerger Policy under the Hart-Scott-Rodino Act: A reexamination of the Market Power Hypothesis," *Journal of Law & Economics*, vol. 28 (April 1985).

76 Concentrated industries in any one country are usually concentrated in other countries and the unconcentrated in any one country are also unconcentrated in other countries. F.L. Pryor, "An International Comparison of *Concentration* Ratios," *Review of Economics and Statistics*, vol. 54 (1972). This provides strong evidence that technology and markets determine an efficient level of *concentration* in each industry and that *merger* for monopoly has little influence on the level of concentration.

training is one portion of the non-revenue yielding burden of taxation. Another is the use of property to produce services directly for its owners when it is less productive than it would be (pre-tax) producing for the market. Also, more time is spent in search than is economic since the yield from alternative uses of time is taxed.

By imposing direct taxes on property income (federal and state corporation taxes and property taxes on business property) in addition to the income tax on property income, the terms of choice between saving and consumption are distorted. Boskin estimates the deadweight loss caused by property taxes at 2.5 percent of gross national product. That comes to $100 billion a year. They also cause adverse consequences for the recipients of labor income and cause distribution to be less egalitarian than it would otherwise be.

The attempt to directly influence the share of income going to labor by lending the power of the state to cartels of laborers (unions) and farmers has a short term favorable influence on the labor share of income (although it depresses total labor income) by depressing the income of property owners. It also causes the division of income to become less egalitarian and, in the long run, decreases the share of income obtained by labor. Raising wage rates above the market clearing level in some markets causes misallocation and temporary unemployment. Also, it makes some capital resources obsolete. Although the loss is especially large in recession years, the current cost in the United States from the idling of resources is probably less than $50 billion. A greater cost resulting from this policy is the misallocation of resources caused by overpricing labor.

Labor in the United States is most overpriced in the capital intensive industries such as steel, aluminum, brewing, automobiles, and cement. There union power can be exercised most effectively because there are large hostages which can be held for ransom.[77] It is also overpriced in the regulated industries where the state prevents entry and over-payment can be recaptured by over-charging consumers. The prevention of entry also stultifies entrepreneurial discovery of more effective means of satisfying consumers. The loss from the stifling of entrepreneurial discovery is unknowable.

Income transfers have motivated withdrawal from the labor force. This not only creates an economic loss but also increases measured inequality. Many earners of low wages appear to be willing to accept a one-third cut in income in return for greater leisure. Their withdrawal from the labor force probably creates a deadweight loss amounting to approximately $20 to $25 billion.

---

[77] Henry C. Simons, "Some Reflections on Syndicalism," *Journal of Political Economy*, vol. 52, no. 1 (March 1944), p. 7.

The attempt to moderate business cycles by "fine tuning" money policy since 1950, along with whatever other reasons there have been for an erratic growth in the stock of money, is currently causing an annual loss of at least $600 billion. The attempt to moderate business cycles using a tax and transfer structure designed to reduce the propensity to save has a current deadweight cost amounting to $100 billion annually as well as causing the division of income to be more unequal than it would have been if the incentives to invest had not been damped by the tax structure which has driven a large wedge between the social and private returns on capital.

The cost of micro intervention in the U.S. economy would require a catalog of the costs of programs ranging from the $8.5 billion cost of tariffs and quotas and the $4 billion added to the net-of-benefit cost of automobile design regulation to the looming $3.4 billion cost of counter-productive generating plant emission regulation. The cost of governmental mispricing of irrigation water and of electricity from government operated hydroelectric projects has not been detailed here, nor has the loss from inefficient use of resources in government operated enterprises such as schools, garbage collection, mass transit, parking lots, power generation and distribution, hospitals, fire departments, housing projects, water distribution, street sweeping, et cetera. If you want to find x-inefficiency, it is in government operated enterprises that you will find the most egregious cases.[78]

Not only does society lose through government inefficiency in producing the quality of services currently made available but it also loses through poor quality when it would be economic to produce better quality and a greater variety of services tailored to particular needs. If the government produced men's suits, we would probably all be forced to wear size 40 long made of heavy cloth regardless of the shape of our bodies or the state of the weather. Where government subsidizes production as in the health service industry under Medicare, Medicaid, and Veteran's Administration programs, we consume goods worth less to us than the alternative goods that could be produced with much of the resources devoted to the subsidized production.

---

78 For examples, see Kenneth W. Clarkson, "Some Implications of Property Rights in Hospital Management," *Journal of Law & Economics*, vol. 15 (Oct. 1972); Louis DeAlessi, "An Economic Analysis of Government Ownership and Regulation: Theory and evidence from the Electric Power Industry," *Public Choice*, Fall 1974; Robert O'Brian, "Public Policy Toward Electric Utilities: Overtax and Underprice," *Public Utilities Fortnightly*, July 21, 1972; Robert Poole, Jr., *Cutting Back City Hall* (Universe Books, 1980); Richard H. Silkman and Dennis R. Young, *Subsidizing Inefficiency: A Study of State Aid and Local Government Productivity* (New York: Praeger, 1985), p. vii.

The completion of this catalog would add even more to the trillion dollar deadweight loss already detailed. Yet efficiency losses occurring in government operated enterprises have not been estimated! Add to this the losses resulting from government regulation of competitive practices and of mergers under the antitrust laws.

We make the mistake of thinking that the antitrust laws were designed and applied to keep markets competitive or to make them competitive where they are not. On rare occasion they do that. Most of the applications of the antitrust laws, however, serve as a restraint on entrepreneurial discovery and on competition. They serve largely to preserve competitors, not competition.

Conclusion

Welfare state policies operated in the name of producing greater egalitarianism usually produce a less equal distribution of income than would a "hands-off" policy. The special privileges granted to unions are used primarily to obtain higher incomes for high wage workers. This restricts job opportunities and reduces the pay rates of low wage workers.

The price supports and income subsidies aimed at protecting the security of poor farmers do little for poor farmers and a great deal for rich farmers. The subsidies provided for mass transit enterprises go mainly to raise the wages of well-paid transit workers and do little to decrease transportation costs for low paid workers. To the extent that the subsidies hold down transit fares, the benefit largely accrues to the owners of property in the central city.

The regulation of electricity, gas, and telephone rates imposed upon grantees of monopoly franchises has done more for the investors in those enterprises and their managers than it has for rate payers. While these are the monopolies where the return consists largely of a "quiet life" for managers and stockholders, the costs are nevertheless substantial. The lack of opportunities for entrepreneurial discovery leads to inefficiency and slow progress in reducing costs.

The antimerger laws also create a "quiet life" for managers. They prevent the migration of assets out of the hands of inefficient managers into more productive uses. Also they cause the creation of redundant capacity and waste capital.[79] This is costly not only to stockholders but also to workers whose productivity and wages would be increased by a more abundant stock of capital.

---

[79] Charles F. Keithahn, *The Brewing Industry* (Washington, Federal Trade Commission, 1978).

Politics is a negative-sum game. The benefits to the winners in the political process are less than the losses to the losers. As a result, the prosperity of the nation suffers.

Comment by Arnold Heertje (University of Amsterdam)

Those who have read professor Brozen's contribution can only be struck by its emphasis on empirical results. Let me, therefore, start with a quotation of professor Kirzner, that "Austrian economists are skeptical of empirical "proofs" of economic theorems." (See also S.C. Littlechild, The Fallacy of the Mixed Economy, London 1986, page 24). In quoting Kirzner I do not mean to argue that economics should do without empirical research. On the contrary, in my view econometric analysis is very useful in order to be alert and to discuss new possibilities and new theories. We all know that empirical research hardly ever leads to definite conclusions and often provokes new problems and new questions. This can only be applauded by neo-Austrian economists. With respect to Brozen's paper, it should be pointed out that another feature of econometric research is that results are often antagonistic. In other words, it would not be too difficult to produce evidence which just "proves" the opposite of what Brozen likes to indicate.

In Brozen's paper, however, there is much more at stake. It is not only or perhaps not in the first place or perhaps not at all meant to prove economic theorems. His objective seems to be more of a normative character. He points out that on balance the net outcome of the economic impact of government policy is negative. In my view this implies a weighing up of positive and negative welfare effects, according to a certain yardstick. Brozen, therefore, does not restrict himself to a listing of welfare effects, but he imposes his value judgement on us, namely that the negative effects have to be rated higher than the positive effects. The last sentence of his paper illustrates my point: "Politics is a negative-sum game. The benefits to the winners in the political process are less than the losses to the losers. As a result the prosperity of the nation suffers." Here, I think, Brozen is going too far. I can only accept that according to his political opinions his weighing up of pros and cons of government measures leads to a negative conclusion. Economic and non-economic value judgements play a role, which we cannot discuss here.

We must go back to economic theory. A possible attempt to justify to a certain extent Brozen's reasoning would have been a reference to welfare theory, in particular to Paretian welfare theory. In all the cases Brozen dealt with, the welfare effects are antagonistic, i.e. there are positive and negative welfare effects. Some version of the compensation principle could therefore be applied in order to arrive at Brozen's conclusions. In fact, Brozen implicitly argues along the lines of the compensation principle. His yardstick is money, he estimates advantages and disadvantages of government measures in terms of money. A proper interpretation of his analysis would be that according to his yardstick the winners are not able to compensate the losers. This wording would have made clear that no absolute statements can be derived from the empirical analysis.

This can be illustrated by pointing out that Brozen applies a very narrow and restricted view of welfare. He does not actually use the word welfare, in the financial sense. Up to now, I thought that the broad, subjective and formal concept of welfare, which I have learned from my teacher professor Hennipman, has very strong Austrian roots. As is well known, it refers to the level of satisfaction of wants in so far as this depends on the allocation of scarce resources. It is subjective, in the sense that individual preferences determine its content and formal, in the sense, that no concrete specification can be given. The use of the broad concept of welfare would make it more difficult to apply the compensation principle and would, in any case, make it clear that the weighing up of positive and negative welfare effects is a subjective matter.

Let me give one example. A policy of income redistribution is one of the failures of government policy in Brozen's paper. Brozen restricts himself to tax measures and the rather short run effects on income distribution. My feeling is that other empirical material indicates that due to such policies the poor are better off with than without such policies. I am of course aware of the trade-off between equity and efficiency here, but as economists we cannot compare the increase in welfare due to an even small improvement of the equality of the income distribution and the decrease in welfare due to a major reduction in growth. The impossibility to compare remains if both welfare effects are expressed in terms of money. Furthermore, in the long run education policy may help to make the income distribution more equal by opening up more opportunities for those groups in society who suffer by a cultural drawback.

This kind of reasoning gets some support from a welfare theoretical argument according to which a rich man A and a poor man B both attach a positive utility to a transfer of income from A to B. This enables us to apply the criterion of Pareto in the sphere of the income distribution as well.

But then, even if the policy does not lead to more equality, politicians may consider such a policy defendable on the ground that a society that does not try to offer a perspective to those who are in a weak position is not worth living in.

It is concluded that economists would do better producing lists of positive and negative welfare effects of both market results and outcome of government activities. We would already contribute a lot, if we prepare politicians to compare both institutional mechanisms. As economists, we cannot take decisions and must therefore avoid the impression that we provide normative statements. Professor Brozen's paper is a nice example of a non-Austrian piece of analysis, meant to prove the success of Austrian non-policies.

H.W. DE JONG

Competition Policy in Europe: Stimulus, Nuisance, or Drawback?

This essay discusses the usefulness and goal(s) of competitive policy. The first argument is that, as one type of economic policy, competition policy is conceived and executed not only according to economic logic, but also as a function of the values and ideals of policy makers, lawyers, and interest groups. Historical circumstances can also shape the type of policy which is adopted. These facts explain the great variety of competition policies which are to be found in the various countries. Moreover, a survey of the goals of competition policy, as they exist in the various systems, shows that economists themselves are far from unanimous: some want this type of economic policy to serve the public interest, others stress the goal of reforming market structures towards some state of optimal competition (often clothed in the concept of workable competition), still others advocate its role as a servant of the consumer interest, or the containment of size or economic power.

The author underlines the crucial role of competition policy to protect the competitive process in a market economy. This is the goal of the EC's competition policy, and its success since 1962 shows that it is both necessary and feasible.

In the second part of the paper, the main features of the EC's competition policy are reviewed, being directed at both states and firms.

It is apparent that cartels and collusions, like dominant positions of firms, are more effectively dealt with by the Commission than are acquisitions, as a necessary complement. The weak spot in the Commission's record are the relationships with member states, who are very often less than co-operative. The renewed economic expansion may well reduce this problem to smaller proportions.

The relativity of competition policy

Many economists tend to forget that competition policy is policy, and that it is never made on the basis of simple derivations of analytic models. Such policies are the outcome of views expressed by economists, lawyers, and politicians, being based on historically created systems of law and being applied by executive departments or offices, who differ in the vigour of their actions, and in the extent to which they are subjected to pressures by interest groups.

Consequently, every national and international competition policy is distinguished by its uniqueness and also shows shifts over time. There is, for instance, a world of difference between the West German and French competition policies: whereas the latter has been characterized as "an exercise in futility"[1], nobody would venture to typify the former in this way. In some cases (Italy, Greece), countries manage to get along without having a competition law, whereas in others (the UK or the Netherlands), the state has for a long time considered it to be among its tasks to interfere with the competitive process. Moreover, in those countries which practised competition policies, those policies have differed over time in their intensity and in the extent of their application. Examples include the United Kingdom, where, in the early fifties, some 50 to 60 per cent of manufacturing output was regulated by cartels[2] and, in the view of G.C. Allen, monopolies and restrictive practices had become "characteristic of a large part, perhaps the greater part of British industry".[3] When the 1956 Act on Restrictive Trade Practices abolished cartels on the grounds that they were against "the public interest", several of them were condemned by the Restrictive Practices Court and "the overwhelming majority" (well over 2,000 of those registered, many of which had been in operation for 30 to 40 years) were abandoned by the firms themselves. Following this tightening of anti-restrictive practices policy, a merger wave developed among firms in the UK. Some economists argued that this exemplified the futility of competition policy. Agreements limiting competition were simply replaced by a structural shift, the more so, as only 25 of some 800 mergers undertaken between 1965 and 1974 were referred to the Monopolies Commission (3%); of these less than half of those abandoned (three quarters of those referred) were prevented. Instead. other economists[4]

---

[1] F. Jenny & A.P. Weber, French anti-trust legislation: an exercise in futility. In: A.P. Jacquemin & H.W. de Jong (eds). *Welfare aspects of industrial markets*. Nijenrode Studies in Economics. Vol.2. Leiden: M. Nijhoff, 1977.

[2] D.C. Elliott & J.D. Gribbin, *The abolition of cartels and structural change in the United Kingdom*. In: A.P. Jacquemin & H.W. de Jong. o.c., p.364.

[3] G.C. Allen, *The structure of industry in Britain*. Longmans, 1961. pp.80/81.

[4] K.D. George & C. Joll (eds), *Competition policy in the UK and EEC*. Cambridge, 1975, pp.197-205.

argued for stricter control of mergers, because the "dual standard" approach seriously handicapped the effectiveness of competition policy. The assumption underlying the latter position is that dominant positions, resulting from mergers, may increase monopolistic practices.

Experience of the six founding nations within the EC was different: the merger wave developed before (or at best on a parallel with) the dismemberment of cartels. EC competition policy formally took shape after Regulation 17 was issued on 21 March 1962, but began to be effective against cartels only after 1969/70, when the merger wave was already in full swing.[5] In the EC case, the opening of national frontiers by the process of economic integration obviously undermined the stability of many long existing national cartels. Therefore, firms sought to avoid the enhanced intensity of competition by means of mergers, mainly on a national scale.[6] Two Commission proposals for merger control have not so far been approved by the Council of Ministers.

Another example is that of competition policy in West Germany In this country the debates over competition policy have been rather fierce throughout the postwar period. The Law of 1957 was a watered down version of the Josten proposal of 1949, which aimed, for all practical purposes, at prohibition of cartels and a far-ranging merger control with possibilities for dissolution of integrated firms. Prior to World War II, Germany had been going through the phases of cartel freedom since 1897, of the abuse principle since 1923, and of forced cartel creation since 1933. The Josten proposals, which were initially supported by theoretical economists, politicians, and the Allied Occupation Authorities, met with decided opposition from business and from part of the economic bureaucracy. Merger control and dissolution possibilities were withdrawn and the general prohibition of cartels (albeit with some important exemptions) was only just saved by Ludwig Erhard, the Minister of Economic Affairs. However, the main idea remained as the norm for perfect competition.

In the sixties, the concept of workable competition came to the fore, in Kantzenbach's version of "an optimal competitive intensity of wide oligopolies". Both atomized industries and restricted oligopolies or monopolies were considered to be market forms not conducive to optimal competitive in-

---

5 See table 2 in H.W. de Jong, *EEC Competition policy towards restrictive practices.* In: K.D. George & C. Joll, o.c., p.48.

6 This is not to deny - as is also stated by Elliott and Gribbin - that the reduction of cartels and restrictive fractices may open up growth opportunities for efficient firms, which may be seized by means of both internal and external expansion.

tensity. Further concentration and some restraints on competition were to be allowed in atomized industries; in contrast, in tightly organized sectors, concentration and restraining agreements had to be curtailed. Control of acquisitions by large firms re-entered the scene and were incorporated into the law by the second amendment (1973) to the law of 1957. The merger wave of the late sixties and early seventies was probably responsible for the unanimous Parliamentary support. In addition, there was an introduction of a 33% market share as a presumption of dominance, an abolition of vertical price restraint, a tightening of the price discrimination law, and a prohibition of concerted practices (in agreement with art. 85-EC). It was in 1980, that a fourth amendment dotted the i's in several respects.[7]

It should be clear from this limited survey that one cannot speak of competition policy in the abstract. Every country has its own historical record and specific problems, which shape its type of policy. In order to avoid the sterile discussions of economists about an "ideal" or "optimal" competition policy, based on the so-called market failures framework, the relevant problem will be posed in the form of a double question:

(1) Can government interference by means of a competition policy always be considered necessary?

(2) If such a type of competition policy is approved, what justification is there for such a policy, and what goal is to be served?

In thc second part of this paper there will be a discussion of some aspects of EC competition policy, as an illustration of the general thesis: Competition is the best organization principle in a market economy. and, if necessary, should be protected by an effective policy.

Can competition policy be denied?

The general rule is that firms strive for their own maximum benefit, and, in this process, try to escape the competitive pressures exerted on them if these hurt them. Avoidance of competition can be achieved by means of cartel agreements, collusion, concerted practices, joint venture agreements, mergers, vertical integration and several types of abusive practices. This means that coordination between firms and control over firms may replace the competitive rivalry. The long-term drawbacks of the suppression of competition are, as

---

[7] See the survey by W. Kartte & R. Holtschneider, in H. Cox, K. Jens & K. Market (eds), *Handbuch des Wettbewerbs. München*: Verlag F. Vahlen, 1981, pp.193-224.

economists have been pointing out for a long time, firstly, the misallocation of resources, and, secondly, the impairment of dynamic efficiency, i.e. the neglect of innovations and improvements.

One should not make the logical mistake of inferring from what has already been said that all mergers and cartels restrain competition. Indeed, a certain amount of co-operation between firms and some concentration by means of acquisition may promote social efficiency, for example, if tasks to be undertaken are so large or urgent that they can only be tackled by groups of firms.

Competition in a market economy is a pervasive phenomenon, directly flowing from the independent decision making by autonomous firms. As most of the decisions by the various firms do not run parallel, but reflect different views and varying methods of behaviour, companies will compete for results. If the intensity of competition rises, not incidentally, but presumably on a more permanent basis, so will the urge to co-ordinate the behaviour of firms in a market, either through agreements (or collusion), or through merger and take-over. Thus, positions of economic power may be reached during the process, and such power positions may be abused in the sense that competition will be lessened and power will be exploited. The argument that such economic power will not be exploited, given its existence, is not tenable, in accordance with the previously stated general rule. The fact is that economic power requires investments to bring in a maximum return.

Thus, the conclusion can be drawn that economic power will be abused, unless held in check by competition or by governmental control; because in the absence of a rivalry from other autonomous firms, only prescribed behaviour from a supreme authority (e.g. relating to prices) may contain the exploitation of economic power. This conclusion occupies a timehonoured position, which was entertained by Scholastic economists as early as the Middle Ages,[8] and later by Classical economists and those of a different persuasion.[9] It sets the limits for competition policy.

Consider the following cases:

(1) If a small country with an open, low-tariff economy, strong firms and a weak central government, is situated amidst important advanced neighbours, the need for a competition policy is either absent or restricted to the supervision of purely domestic markets. Foreign competition in such cases will dis-

---

[8] B. Gordon, *Economic analysis before Adam Smith*. London and Basingstoke, 1975, Chapters 5, 6, and 8.

[9] B. Gordon, *o.c.*

cipline national firms, which by themselves are able to compete effectively. Moreover, the weak government is not able to carry out an effective competition policy. Indeed, such a policy may be misused for the protection of existing firms if the principle of the so-called abuse system gives the government power to counter too much competition.[10] The cases in point are Switzerland, Belgium, and (to a lesser extent, because the market is larger) the Netherlands.

In countries with open economies, but with less strong firms (like Norway and Denmark), the government confines itself to price control of market dominating firms or groups of firms (for example the prohibition of price increases of the market dominating brewery cartel in Denmark between 1967 and 1970). Such a control of only one action parameter - viz. price - leaves open the question of efficiency. Will the controlled firms reduce the quantity and quality of the goods and slow-down the renewal of production methods? An important qualification for small, open countries with strong firms or cartels also results from international relationships between firms. Multinational firms and international cartels are practically immune from the types of national competition policies carried out by these countries. Capital and business liaisons between firms and the business behaviour of international firms and cartels prove difficult to control, even more so if changes were to be considered desirable.[11]

If a small country is protected by high tariffs and possessing only relatively weak national firms, and, because of a weak central government, is thus unable to practise an effective competition policy, the country's industries will be tightly concentrated and cartellized. Furthermore, such a country runs the risk of losing its market dominating firms to international companies by means of take-overs. This is said to be the case both in Australia and in South Africa.[12]

---

[10] G. Zenk, Konzentration und Konzentrationspolitik in den Skandinavischen Ländern. In: H. Arndt (ed.). *Die Konzentration in der Wirtschaft. Schriften des Vereins für Sozialpolitik*, Neue Folge Band 20/II. 2. Auflage, Berlin: Duncker & Humblot, 1970, p.222.

[11] Zenk recounts the ineffectiveness of the Swedish authorities against the international pulp and paper cartels, which for decades degraded economic efficiency in the Swedish industry (p.220). Similar cases in the Netherlands relate to cement, sugar, and fertilizer, cartels, which were attacked by the EEC Commission, and not by the Dutch Government.

[12] G. Venturini, *Concentration and concentration policy in Australia*. In: H. Arndt, o.c., pp.3-36. Venturini surveys the Australian literature. See especially pp.28-31.

For large countries and integrated areas, competition policy is more of a necessity, however, except for the time during the process of integration. The reason is that the process of integration is accompanied by an intensification of rivalry between the firms of the integrating parts. This was the case in the EEC during the fifties and for most of the sixties; it also occurred in the United States between 1865 and (approximately) 1890, and in the German Zollverein from the start in 1834 to the cartellization movement of the 1880's.

This is a passing phase, however; once the firms have expanded over the whole territory, they start to encroach upon each other's home market and other established interests. Battles for survival will follow, which emphasize price competition. Weak firms will be eliminated, either through bankruptcy or because of mergers and take-overs,[13] inspired by increased uncertainties. Market structures will become more concentrated, approaching trio- and duopolies (and even monopolies) in product markets, as they did in the EEC during the seventies.[14] When such a mature integration phase is reached, competition policy should be at hand to counteract tendencies towards collusion and exploitation of dominant positions.

With hindsight, one could say that effective competition policies came too late in the US (after the Northern Securities case in 1904), and not at all in pre-war Germany. In the late sixties, penetrating US and UK firms also forced continental EEC companies to effectuate take-overs and mergers. In the second half of the seventies, the tables were reversed, with similar effects. Within large market areas, the domestic companies fight each other for control of important firms in desired areas. In other words: mergers are not so much motivated by so-called efficiency considerations (economies of scale, savings on resources, et cetera), but also by market strategic reasons.[15] There

---

[13] H.W. de Jong, *Dynamische concentratietheorie*. Leiden: H.E. Stenfert Kroese, 1972 (1), 1985 (3), pp.116-123. An English version of this theory is worked out by J. Pelkmans, *Market integration in the European Community*. M. Nijhoff, 1984, pp.76-96.

[14] See the EEC Competition Policy reports: Three (1973), No.146; Seven (1977), No.292; and Nine (1979), No.222.

[15] See EEC Competition Policy report 14 (1984). No.300, The motives for acquisition and joint ventures of 150 European-scale manufacturing firms in 1982/83 and 200 such firms in 1983/84 were specified: market strategy (29%), rationalization (28%), R & D (3%). specialization (3%), and a rather large unspecified category (26%). For joint ventures (69 cases), the main motives were said to be: production (29%), R & D (33%), rationalization (17%), and marketing (17%). Though the proportion of rationalization mergers is higher than reported in some other studies (see H.W. de Jong, Theory and evidence concerning mergers an international comparison. In: Jacquemin & de Jong, Markets, corporate behaviour and the State. The Hague: M. Nijhoff, 1976, or

is also an internally driven merger dynamic, which alternatively may be called merger mania, or merger speculation. One of the motivations which is often encountered in the literature is that being big offers protection against being taken over, and, while this may not be waterproof, it certainly raises the barriers which protect a company's uncertain existence. To a large extent, these dynamics explain the recurrent merger waves, which come and go. As Davidson says: "More mergers produced more urgency to merge."[16] While no competition policy by itself can hope to subdue such waves, let alone prevent them, a good policy might be able to act as a wave breaker, preferably in conjunction with other measures.

Why competition policy?

The preceding discussion raises the question of good competition policy and the answer is intricately tied in with the goals of such a policy. What goal or goals competition policy should serve, will now be discussed analytically, taking into account those that are most frequently mentioned, or that are of practical importance.

(a) The general interest criterion. In British and Dutch law, the general interest is the ultimate criterion by which the operations of firms are judged. In the Monopoly and Restrictive Practices (Inquiry and Control) Act 1948, the UK Government incorporated some guidance for the Monopolies and Restrictive Practices Commission on this matter, "although it still left the Commission with a wide measure of discretion".[17] The commission interpreted its task in a pragmatic way, not supporting the view of many

---

(for West Germany) W.P. Möller, Der Erfolg von Unternehmenszusammenschlüssen. München, 1983, pp.69-86), this is understandable from the years taken: 1982-1984, when, as the EC report states, rationalization mergers in the chemical and mechanical engineering industries were frequent (22 out of 44 cases), due to overcapacities in both sectors. In such circumstances, a merger frequently is the way to liquidate a firm, partially or wholly.

16 Davidson, in a discussion of the megamerger trend in the United States. See K.M. Davidson, *Megamergers*. Cambridge (Mass.): Ballinger Publishing Company, 1985, p.239. In comparison with Continental European countries, the larger role played by stock exchanges in the Anglo-Saxon countries may well account for the greater speculative element and the greater role of intermediaries in the merger game (recall the P/E gimmicks of the conglomerate mergers of the sixties).

17 P.H. Guenault & J.M. Jackson, *The control of monopoly in the United Kingdom*. London: Longman, 1974 (2), pp.9, 58. and 123.

economists that competition is preferable to monopoly. However, a tough line was taken regarding one aspect: "that the individual entrepreneur should be free to enter the trade of his choosing and to carry on his business as he thought fit ...". This was of major importance in many of its decisions.[18] There was no occasion when schemes were approved to suppress the individual producer.

The wide formulation of a general interest criterion opens up possibilities of tackling those practices which are new. Examples are conglomerate mergers in the sixties, such as Unilever and Allied Breweries and Rank and de la Rue. However, there are many disadvantages: the criterion is vague, and provides possibilities for lax treatment; divisions of opinion easily occur, and, within such a system, commissions only have an advisory vote. The government, being subject to pressure from vested interests, retains the power not to follow the recommendations. The reference system is not strong, and the onus is on commissions and the government, to prove that cartels, mergers, and monopolies operate against the public interest.[19] In both the UK and the Netherlands, the general interest criterion has remained as the guideline for competition policy throughout the successive adaptions of the system (Acts of 1965, 1973, and 1980 in the UK, and the abortive proposals to introduce per se prohibitions in the Netherlands in 1976). It is small wonder that no one speaks of an important and enduring impact of competition policy in either country.

(b) Another goal of competition policy could be sought from the diffusion of economic power and the correlated desire to limit the size of firms, In long established constitutional democracies such as Britain, the Netherlands, and Switzerland, this motive has never played an appreciable role, although these countries have very large firms. It was in the US and Germany, that arguments of such a populist origin were voiced at particular episodes in their history. Thus the rise and the practices of the trusts led Senator Sherman to state in 1890: "If we will not endure a king as a political power, we should not endure a king over the production, transportation, and sale of any of the necessities of life ... we should not submit to an autocrat of trade, with power to prevent competition and to fix the price of any commodity". Judge Learned Hand refused to discriminate between good and bad trusts: "... Congress ... did

[18] Guenault & Jackson, *o.c.*, p.58.

[19] K.D. George, *Industrial organization. Competition, growth and structural change.* London: Allen & Unwin, 1981- (3). p.303. Also see the article in the Financial Times (11.6.1986) *'Competition policy: how the UK got left behind'*.

not condone 'good trusts' and condemn 'bad ones'; it forbade all, ... We have been speaking not only of the economic reasons which forbid monopoly; but ... there are others, based upon the belief that great industrial consolidations are inherently undesirable, regardless of their economic results". Recently, a former commissioner of the FTC criticized the "exclusively economic approach to anti-trust questions" as follows: "It is bad history, bad policy, and bad law, to exclude certain political values in interpreting the anti-trust laws.[20] He maintained that great concentration of economic power will breed anti-democratic political pressures, reduce private business freedom, and prompt the state into playing a larger and more protective role in economic affairs.

This motivation was also present in Germany. The pre-war experiences with forced cartellization and the role of big businesses in financing the national socialists and their war preparations, have left their imprint. The former President of the Monopolkommission, Mestmäcker, thus concluded that the desire for a free and decentralized social and economic order played an important role (other than that of efficiency considerations) in the formation of the German Law.[21]

Therefore, it was not surprising that in countries where it has long been felt that the size of firms was too small, and where concentration was actually promoted by the state, there was no competition policy (France, Italy). As Weber and Jenny noted, the official term "competition policy" in France mainly represented the price policies pursued by the Ministry of Economic Affairs, fixing maximum prices, ostensibly meant to control inflation, but in actual fact becoming the industry's cartel price.[22]

(c) Another aspect of the goal of competition policy is thought to be that of exclusively promoting consumer welfare.[23] This is the same line of thought

---

20 R. Pitowsky, The political content of Anti-trust. In: University of Pennsylvania *Law Review*, Vol.127, 1979, p.1051.

21 E.J. Mestmäcker, Competition policy and Anti-trust; some comparative observations. In: *Zeitschrift für die gesamte Staatswissenschaft*, 1980, pp.387 et seq. I. Schmidt, *Wettbewerbstheorie und -politik*. Stuttgart, 1980, p.108.

22 F. Jenny & A,.P. Weber, *Concentration et politique des structures industrielles. La documentation francaise*, Paris, 1974, p.163. In the same sense F. Gobbo, *Il controllo dei prezzi in Italia. Bologna, Il Mulino*, 1982, p.151, who states that the fixed price has the tendency to become a collusion price. Another case is that of Dutch cigarettes, where the State's price fixing and cartel agreements went hand in hand. On 10 December 1985, the Court sustained the EC Commission's verdict of 1982.

23 R.H. Bork, T*he Anti-trust paradox: a policy at war with itself*. New York, 1978, p.57. In Europe, Hoppmann and others represent this line of thinking. See for example the survey article and the literature cited by R. Clapham, *Das Wettbewerbspolitische*

as that of Adam Smith and the Classical School of economics. Competition, driven by the self-interest of autonomous firms, forces the producers to adapt themselves to the wishes of consumers. Otherwise, firms will lose profitability and make losses. Such competition is dynamic, and the best it can do is produce temporary equilibrium positions in markets. Disequilibrium results, not only from shifts in the market data, but also from entrepreneurial initiatives, which create change through the lower prices, quality improvements, and better services, etcetera. There should be no artificial barriers to entry, e.g. by state or business action. Where they exist, competition policies should be active, otherwise economic freedom and the promotion of welfare will not be reconcilable. The so-called "dilemma thesis" is unacceptable. This means that the freedom of competitive action does not stand in contrast to economic advantage, because competition is not to be equated with static perfect competition. If that were the case, freedom with an optimal static welfare outcome would not secure progress (or advantage) because progress requires some economic power to innovate. In the case where the dilemma thesis would hold, competition policy would have to decide which goal to serve first: an impossible task.

The concentrations of large firms and even monopolies are not a problem, as long as they can be freely contested. Mergers are merely a strategic device, unless (in exceptional cases) they create a non-contestable dominant position. From this analysis, it follows that a multiple-goal anti-trust law, although attractive to many people, has several drawbacks, such as burdening the Courts with tasks for which they are ill equipped to deal with, introducing arbitrariness in decisions and focussing upon the wrong economic issues.[24] As to the latter, Hoppmann and others are averse to market performance tests; they only want the test of market freedom. The question must be: Is the freedom to compete really and substantially reduced? This is nearly always found to be the case with cartels and in particular with syndicates. However, competition policy should not be used to promote competitive market structures, nor to reform them into "optimal" structures as that tends toward "market form dirigism".

Hoppmann, however, is left with a problem in relation to market dominating firms and mergers: on the one hand, a system-conforming policy should have general rules, which implies per se prohibition; on the other

---

Konzept der Wettbewerbsfreiheit, In: Cox, Jens & Markert, o.c., pp.131-148.

24 R. Bork, o.c., pp.50-57, and pp.81-86. E. Hoppmann, *Fusionskontrolle*. Tübingen, 1972, pp.59 et seq. and pp. 80 et seq. Hoppmann likewise argued that it is impossible to delimit markets in order to establish a market dominating position.

hand, dominant firms and mergers represent ex-ante co-ordination of firms and may sometimes block the working of the market, It is very difficult to formulate exemption categories for such firms and mergers, as is done for the types of cartels (e.g. specialization agreements) which can be fitted into a per se prohibition system. Thus, discretionary policies would have to be introduced, which is abhorrent to this school of thinking. This results in an inability to tackle the problem of economic power and its abuse; some authors "solve" this problem by denying its very existence.

(d) Another European school of thinking is oriented towards the workable competition concept which sees the goal of competition policy as that of making and keeping markets workable and competitive.[25] The theory pretends to steer an acceptable course between the perfectly competitive and highly concentrated market; the first serves the goals of adequate income distribution, efficient allocation of resources, and freedom of action, but not those of technical progress, innovation, and flexible adaptation to changing circumstances. Innovation, it is said, often requires monopolies, duopolies, or other concentrated market structures. However, these are found to be deficient in respect of the first mentioned goals. Therefore, the workability school sees "an optimal intensity" for competition secured by those market structures which reconcile as many as possible of the various competitive functions, that is in wide oligopolies. Markets which are structured in this way, do not guarantee first best solutions, but offer a second best choice, in which the combination of efficient allocation, reasonable income distribution (not too high excess profits or losses), and economic progress are reconciled with a reduced degree of market power. Competition policy should be orientated towards the realization of market structures characterized by wide oligopolies (although difficult to generalize, these markets often qualify in this respect, consisting of 6 to 12 firms, having a moderate degree of product differentiation).

---

[25] Again, there are parallels in US and European thinking: in the US, the workable competition school is mainly centered around 'industrial organization' economists, who follow the trail set by J.M. Clark, E.S. Mason and J.S. Bain. In Europe, the main representative is E. Kantzenbach, whose book 'Die Funktionsfähigkeit des Wettbewerbs' Göttingen, 1967 (2)), provoked an extensive debate and has been influential in West German policy. In the Netherlands, Belgium, and France, the workable competition school also has a number of adherents.

Thus competition policy becomes instrumental in the hands of the state and should command a rich variety of measures in order to achieve its goals. Amongst these are:[26]

- the prevention of cartel agreements and concerted practices in tightly structured markets;
- the permission of cartels in fragmented markets, as long as they do not completely eliminate competition;
- the promotion of more concentration when firms are too small, or too weak, to finance economic progress;
- the dissolution of firms which have market dominating positions which cannot be contested;
- an active merger policy, sometimes stimulating, sometimes preventive;
- the promotion of factor mobility by means of state measures;
- the prevention of serious forms of abusive behaviour such as boycott, price discrimination, and excessive advertising;
- the rationalization of industries which are saddled with overcapacities; and
- the internalization of external effects, e.g. by means of concentration or direct state measures.

The workable competition school emphasizes the economic functions of competition policy and is sceptical of, what they call, vague concepts for policy guidelines such as that of the public interest, freedom for market participants, and the general consumer interest. These are best served as an indirect outcome from the execution of policies orientated towards the achievement of optimal market structures. Questions to be raised here are the following:

- Although many economists would probably subscribe to the idea that wide oligopolistic market structures have much to recommend them, the question whether governments are qualified to devise such structures in actual markets, is thereby not implicitly answered. Frequently, as imitation develops, markets develop from initiating monopolies towards more competition, whereas mature markets show more concentration. Is a government department or a monopolies office sufficiently well informed to choose the right decisions at the right moment for restructuring a market in a wide oligopolistic sense? As dynamic market theory shows, the market could not have such an oligopolis-

---

[26] See E, Kantzenbach & H, Kallfass, Das Konzept des funktionsfähigen Wettbewerbs. In: *Cox, Jens & Markert, Handbuch des Wettbewerbs*, o.c., pp.105-127.

tic structure during every phase of its development.[27] However, the record of government interference in such markets is, to say the least, not convincing with respect to efficiency. Where governments have fostered concentration, more often than not they have taken the wrong decisions at the wrong time; nationalizations have not been economically successful either, quite apart from the political troubles they evoked (France, UK, Italy); government-inspired mergers were mostly of a doubtful quality and where the government permitted cartels, or minimum price agreements (e.g. in order to prevent ruinous oligopolistic price competition) it would have had to secure at the same time the independence of investment decisions to safeguard technical progress. That, however, was an exception.

• Instead of sustaining the above rather negative conclusions by means of empirical material (which is cumbersome and always debatable), a general proposition may be advanced which makes the verdict practically unavoidable. Competition is a public good, which cannot be appropriated by market participants. Consequently, they hope to take a free ride by letting others pay. The costs of competition are specific, visible, and reducible through organized action, at least in the short term. The advantages, in contrast, are diffuse, mostly not locationable, and cannot be secured by interest groups. Most business firms and labour bear the costs because they are hurt by the competition. They have to make costly efforts to adapt to the changed competitive situations, or they lose out. A few firms, which initiate competitive moves by means of smaller or larger innovations, stand to gain, as do the consumers. The latter group, however, is not well informed, mostly unorganized, and in any case not prepared to pay for the costs of competition. The initiating firms, whilst in the minority, are "free riders", in so far that they are not prepared to foot the bill either. Governments have nothing to gain and much to lose from advocating competition: the groups which are hurt will put pressure upon politicians to contain competition.

Under these circumstances, the few individuals, groups or firms who gain from competition can be isolated, and are depicted as "irresponsible", because they upset the established order and are restrained by organized majorities. Sometimes, this is acknowledged in law, e.g. the Dutch Competition Law of 1956 not only allows for the possibility of dissolving agreements, but also of enforcing them on a market sector, as long as the associated firms, having

---

[27] E. Heusz, *Allgemeine Markttheorie*. Tübingen, 1965. H.W. de Jong, Dynamische markttheorie. Leiden, 1972 (1), 1985 (3). E. Kaufer, *Industrieökonomik*. München, 1980.

a large majority of sales, support such a measure and the "general interest" (whatever that may be) is served.[28] Thus, the public good character of competition means that there is only weak support for government policies in favour of competition, whereas policies meant to restrain competition and to support or protect private interest enjoy public acclaim.

(e) The European Community's competition policy aims at protecting the competitive process, and I consider this goal, simple though it may sound, to be the best standard: the direct problem of all policy in this field is for the authorities to ensure that the competitive process is not distorted.

Of course, more extensive goals are served by the competitive process itself. Article 3(f) of the Treaty of Rome is brought into relation with article 2 of the Treaty, which stipulates the goals of integration: a harmonious development of economic activities, a continuous and balanced expansion, an increase in stability, an accelerated raising of the standard of living, and closer associations between the member states. To achieve these aims as much as possible, the Community "will establish a regime assuring that competition within the Common Market is not falsified" (3f). Competition is clearly seen as the guiding principle of economic activity under a regime of free trade between member countries, which is required under article 3(a). If such a basic principle is adopted, competition should be protected against actions which may prevent, restrict, or distort "the workings of such a process" (article 85).

Breaches of the competitive process may come from states or from firms or groups of firms. Two types of state activity are considered: (1) specific distortions, resulting from acts which affect persons, and (2) general distortions, resulting from differences between the provisions laid down by law, regulation, and administrative action within member states. The former distortions are regulated by EC competition rules and are prohibited, unless exempted by the Commission of the EC, whereas the latter have to be eliminated through the harmonization of laws. They can, if necessary, be prohibited by issuing directives[29]. This dichotomy implies that the Treaty provi-

---

[28] This clause of article 24 has been used a.o. to enforce minimum prices for sugar and to freeze bread baking capacity.

[29] Under the Rome Treaty, a directive is addressed to governments and is binding with regard to the results to be attained, but leaves member states free to choose their method of achievement. In contrast, a regulation has general applicability, and is directly binding on nationals (including firms). These regulations have the status of laws. Finally, a decision is binding entirely upon those addressed, be it member states, legal or individual persons.

sions with respect to distortions from competition can be divided according to the following schema:

EUROPEAN COMPETITION POLICY: GOALS AND MEANS

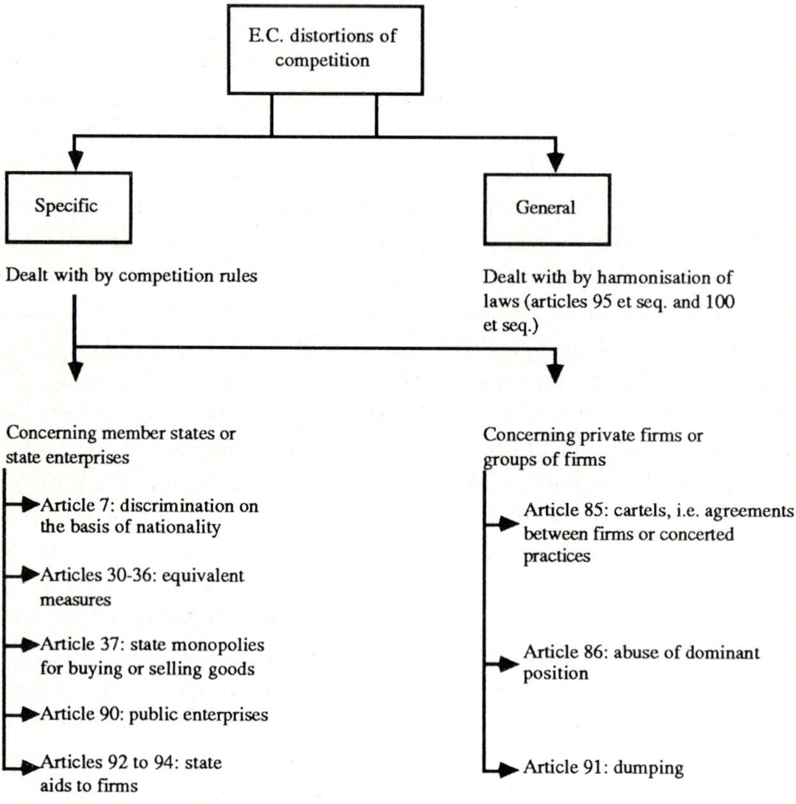

Decisions of the Commission are binding to individuals, firms, and states, and can only be appealed before the Court of Justice, whose judgement is final. In its judgements, the Court has followed the Commission in protecting the competitive process, and doing so, has substantially contributed to the integration of the European economy. Though it may have been critical of some legal, procedural, and substantial aspects of the cases brought before it, the Court has firmly and steadfastly followed the line (a) that competition policy is important; (b) that it serves an integrating function; and (c) that it should protect the competitive process required by the Treaty in article 3(f). In the next section, there will be a brief discussion of a few main topics of EC policy, which will be illustrated by a number of specific cases. Extensive literature exists on EC competition policy.[30]

EC Competition Policy

Many economists have not only tended to forget that competition policy is policy, but also that this type of policy is essential for keeping competition intact. As can be seen in the previous section, competition policy has been burdened by various goals, mostly advocated by various schools of economic thinking. They have projected their ideals about the functioning of competitive markets into policies. Naturally, this only met with limited success, or even none at all. European competition policy has been realistic in this respect, and has worked, right from the start, with Regulation No.17 in 1962, towards the limited goal of keeping competition alive. The authorities have not tried to define what competition is or should be,[31] nor have they tried to serve such vague criteria as the general interest, or the consumer interest, or to limit the size of enterprises, or to strive for the realization of particular types of market structures, However, it was repeatedly stated that competition needs to be maintained by Community policy.[32]

The discussion in this paper will be confined to a few topics, relating to competition policy as directed towards states, public enterprises, national monopolies, and private firms. Some problems have to be neglected, although they are of equal importance, for example property rights.

European integration meant the removal of internal barriers to competitive

---

[30] See a.o. A.P. Jacquemin & H.W. de Jong, *European industrial organization*. London: Macmillan, 1977, Chapter 7; W.C. Schlieder & H. Schröder, Europäische Wettbewerbspolitik. In: *Cox, Jens & Markert* (eds), o.c., pp. 485-532; and D. Swann, *Competition and industrial policy in the European Community*. London/NewYork: Methuen. 1983.

[31] Casual references in Commission or Court Decisions about free, workable, effective or dynamic competition do not mean very much in terms of economic models. These terms were hardly explained, nor was it shown what their operational value was in the cases at hand.

[32] In the ninth report on Competition Policy, the Commission writes: ".... It is an established fact that competition carries within it the seeds of its own destruction. ... Consequently, the second fundamental objective of the Community's competition policy must be to ensure that at all stages of the Common Market's development there exists the right amount of competition in order for the Treaty's requirements to be met and its aims attained" (p.10). (The first objective is to keep the common market open and unified.)

trade, as well as the setting up of an external common tariff and a common commercial policy. The degree of competition within the Common Market depends not only on the former, but also on the degree of protection afforded in the latter sense. In some goods, such as clothing and textiles, the competitive threat from abroad has been restrained by the protective Multi-Fibre Agreements of 1973 and 1978, and the Protocol of 1981, limiting import growth. In other goods, such as ships, a one time price rise with suppliers in Japan was reached (1977), and with cars, the national governments limited imports.

State barriers

The removal of internal common market tariffs and import quotas at the end of the sixties led to the elimination of measures having equivalent effect (articles 30 and 34 of the Treaty), and state subsidies, technical standards, public purchases, and state monopolies became important. Moreover, this was heavily emphasized by the recessions of 1974/75 and 1980/83, and by the stagnation in the Community's economic growth.

Ten years later, the situation shows that the nationalistic sentiments and the various state actions have severely slowed down the integration process, but have not disrupted the functioning of the Common Market. One by one, the steps being taken by the Court and the Commission have laid the groundwork for bringing the national states into line.

(a) As to the equivalent measures, the Court declared in the Dassonville case (ECJ 8/74) that "all trading rules enacted by member states which are capable of hindering, directly or indirectly, actually or potentially, intra-community trades are to be considerations". In Dassonville, it was the issue of certificates of origin, which was decided against the Belgian state, who refused to issue certificates to a Belgian importer of Scotch whisky bought in France. Two official distributing companies of these whiskys joined in, and it was no surprise that the state did not support the Dassonville company. A similar case of parallel imports upheld by the refusal of an authorization was the Cassis de Dyon *case* (ECJ 120/78). A German importer of the French liquor manufacturer Cassis de Dyon was refused, because West German law forbade the sale of liquors with an alcohol content of less than 25%. Cassis only had an alcohol content of 15 - 20%, but the Court decided that the German law was a prohibitive measure of equivalent effect. In 1978, the Commission noted that it had to investigate 400 dossiers of obstructions to free trade of this type; in many cases these were violations of articles 30 to 36. One such typical case was the import of cars into Britain from the continent. The issue of a "certificate of conformity" had been delegated to the official car distributors, who made parallel imports as difficult as possible by various devices: no delivery of right hand drive cars, extra charges, no warranty services provision, withdrawal of credit and discount facilities of dealers who imported, et cetera. Such practices are now illegal, as a result of pressure from the Commission and the recent verdict of the Court.

(b) State subsidies and falsifying the competitive process are equally tough problems illustrating that competition as a public good is in constant danger from obstructive state action, and that there needs to be an independent Commission. Articles 92 and 93 forbid state aids which distort competition, except where the EC Commission is in accord. In the seventies, the Commission asked member states to confirm that they did not make funds available to reduce the cost of export credit in respect of some EC sales. France and the UK acknowledged that they did in fact do this, and, subsequently, terminated the practice. The Dutch Government, however, hid behind the pretext that the Dutch Central Bank was responsible, and had to be forced into line by a threat of Court Action.

States often supply sectoral, regional, and employment subsidies, thus falsifying the competitive process. This practice flourished in the seventies, when economic conditions soured. It was an uphill task to counter this flood of protective measures and the record certainly is not brilliant. But a number of key decisions and rules, among which the regional aid rules (OJ 1979 f), and the Philip Morris decision, upheld by the Court (ECJ 730/79), have brought some order in this chaos.[33] Now that there is a renewed economic upturn, the worst probably has passed. But there have been serious lapses, an example being the "taming of the Bresciani" by means of fines in 1978, because these mini steel mills undercut the ECSC steel cartel. This case shows that so-called industrial policy has a strong tendency to push competition policy to the wall.

(c) State aid to public enterprise and state monopolies. The EC Commission found a lot to do in these areas, because of the extensive role of the state in some countries. State monopolies of goods (Italy vs. Sacchi, ECJ 155/73) are regulated by article 37 of the Treaty. By means of the exclusive powers conferred on these monopolies by the states, they were able to resort to all kinds of restrictions on trade, both national and international. The goods covered a long list, from alcohol and tobacco, to matches, potash, lighters, and

---

33 A useful survey of state aids and subsidies is provided by D. Swann, *Competition and industrial policy*, o.c., Chapter 3.

saccharin. The tactics also varied and centered not only on exclusive import rights, by which these state monopolies used to defend their interests. Marketing, distribution, pricing, subsidizing, and production tactics were also involved, and the Commission had to eliminate these by what has been called "a long drawn out war of attrition".[34] For example, French retailers of tobacco were public servants, so only nationals could be licensed; obviously, they had ties with the Régie du Tabac, and were pressured into not selling imported products. When the German alcohol market was opened up, the monopoly had to face such low prices that its purchase price for spirits could not be covered. The consumption tax on spirits was raised, and the proceeds were used to finance the monopoly's losses. Only when the Court ended the legality of this practice in the German case, the Commission was able to end similar practices in France. Since the Manghera case (ECJ 59/75), where the exclusive import rights were condemned, more headway has been made and France, Germany, and Italy have terminated these rights in respect of alcohol, manufactured tobacco, matches, petroleum, and coal.[35]

Public enterprises are regulated in article 90. Distinctions were made by confronting special rights on public companies and on private companies (examples: railways, gas and water supply firms). National states are entitled to bring companies into public ownership, to retain their nationalized status, but both of the categories mentioned above must conform to the competition rules. The fight against vested interests has been severe, and, in 1980, the Commission felt obliged to take the unusual step of adopting a directive on transparency in the financial arrangements between member states and public companies. It was concerned about the distortions which occurred (for example: subsidies and cheap provision of capital). The countries with substantial public enterprise (France, Italy, and the UK) took the Commission to court, but were defeated.

Agreements between firms and concerted practices

Article 85 covers agreements between firms and associations of firms, as well as concerted practices. Contractual agreements between parties are involved here, both of a horizontal and of a vertical nature; but also the collusion of gentlemen's agreements and the like, and even exchanges of letters between trade associations, as in the French-Japanese ball-bearing case (OJ,

---

[34] Swann, o.c., p.72.

[35] This was the famous Atic case, in which the French coal import monopoly, which even the large French steel companies could not surpass, buying directly in the Ruhr area for example, was finally dismantled. It lost its power to veto import contracts.

L343/19). French and Japanese producers of ball-bearings had concluded an auto-limitation agreement to curtail imports and to raise Japanese prices. Such restrictive agreements within trade associations are not an infrequent phenomenon.

Again, recommended prices which carry no obligation to comply were wronged by the Court in the VCH case (ECJ 8/72). The Court argued that the parties were thus enabled to reasonably foresee their rivals' behaviour.

Concerted practices once were defined by the Court as "a form of co-ordination between undertakings which, without going so far as to amount to a so-called agreement, knowingly substitutes a practical co-operation between them for the risks of competition" (Aniline Dyes case, BCJ 48/69 of 1972), In this case, the Commission discovered evidence of price increases by the main European dyestuffs producers, which were of equal percentages; these were addressed by firms to their subsidiaries at the same moment and in identical phrases, and notified to each other in advance. In the Aniline Dyes case, as well as in the later Sugar case, this was no mere parallelism in behaviour, but demonstrated conscious efforts to evoke a matching response.

Another type of forbidden agreement is the information agreement, in which firms agree to inform each other about their (export) prices, the method of calculation, delivery price systems, discounts, et cetera. In the Glass Containers case (OJ 1974, L160/1), firms in five European countries agreed to fix their export prices on the basis of the price fixed domestically by "the natural market leader".

Common sales syndicates are taken seriously if they handle a substantial share of the relevant market, as was the case in homogeneous mass markets for fertilizers, cement, and sulfuric acid. However, a small affair like *SAFCO* (OJ 972, L13/44), being the sales agency of French exporters of canned vegetables, which supplied only 1 to 2 per cent of the West German output, was granted a negative clearance under article 85-3.

Here, the general principle is encountered: agreements that do not hinder or prevent competition, such as specialization, joint R & D, or rationalization agreements which are only small-scale, were block exempted (a 15% market share being the limit).

In contrast, prices and market sharing agreements, quota agreements, exclusionary practices (on a collective basis), and information agreements on issues other than prices, were regarded as serious offenses and were only barely exempted by the Commission. That is: the Commission's cartel policy has been rather tough with respect to cartel agreements, concerted practices, and similar horizontal restraints of competition. This was demonstrated again in 1986, when European polypropylene producers were severely penalized for their collusionary actions relating to prices, production, market shares, and deliveries of polypropylenes (OJ 1986, L230/1).

Vertical agreements to limit the free movement of goods across frontiers, by means of sole or exclusive distribution agreements, have been forbidden since the Grundig-Consten case (OJ 1964, 2545/64), which was upheld by the Court in 1966, Sole distribution is allowed, but there must be no territorial protection to buttress the dealer's monopoly in distribution. The Grundig-Consten price differences of electric goods between France and Germany, of some 40 per cent, were the result of such a monopoly. When Pioneer Electronic Europe, a Japanese subsidiary, effectuated these export bans, together with its sole distributors in France, Germany, and the UK, in order to uphold appreciable price differentiation, it was fined nearly 7 million ECU (representing 10 per cent of total sales).

Joint ventures

Many joint ventures have been studied by the Commission, and evidence was found to support the economists' view that joint ventures are both pro-competitive and anti-competitive. They may promote innovations, develop new markets, strengthen competitiveness of the firms concerned, but they also may share markets, fix prices, or raise entry barriers.

Late in 1985, Mr. Sutherland, the EEC's Commissar, announced guidelines which normally exempt these ventures if the partners' joint market share does not exceed 15%, or where the partners are not actually or potentially competitors. If the market share is below 5 per cent, they will not fall within the prohibited domain of article 85-1. If it is between 5 and 15 per cent, the joint venture will be assessed both on its structural restrictions of competition, but it will be assumed that no competitive restraints are involved. If a market share of over 15% is concerned, the onus goes against them, and as a rule they will be forbidden.[36] However, a block exemption regulation will not be given "because joint ventures are too varied and multi-faceted to be encompassed in such a regulation".[37]

---

[36] In July of 1986, the Commission approved of a dominating network of joint ventures and licencies concluded by Corning Glass Works (US), inventor of optical fibres used in transmission cables, with several European firms, which, together, gave Corning's joint ventures a 48% share in the EC's production capacity. However, the Commission attached severe informational conditions until the year 2001, stipulating that it must be informed every year about production. sales, clients, and prices (0J1986, L236/30).

[37] D. Sutherland, *Towards positive guidelines on joint ventures,* Brussels, 7 November 1985, p.8.

Dominant Firms

The abuse of a dominant position is forbidden in article 86 of the Treaty. A number of points should be noted:

(1) The Treaty speaks of 'dominance'. and not of 'monopoly'. Of course, monopoly is also market dominance, but in reverse, market dominance is a broader conception, in which some competition may remain. The reason why this term was chosen, can only be guessed, although it is logical within the EC system, which adopts as a norm that competition is the organizing principle of the common market.

(2) However, when the onus is per se against a monopoly, this needs not be the case when up against a dominant position. Temporary power positions are part and parcel of a dynamic market system, and, in many cases, the dominant positions are undermined by competitors, especially in a broad integrated area. In some cases, however, the dominance is unassailable, and may be used to eliminate the competition, or to reduce it to minor importance. This is the abuse aspect: dominance is not only a structural trait (market share, et cetera - see under (3) hereafter), but it also carries behavioural implications, and both are interpreted by their effect on competition.

(3) Thus, the concept of dominance and its abuse are far reaching: horizontal, vertical, diagonal, and conglomerate market power, and a variety of possible practices, all are caught by the prohibition: price discrimination, tie-ins, exclusionary and predatory tactics, seller and buyer pressures, boycott, et cetera. Unlike agreements, market dominance does not have to be notified to the Commission, as this body relies on complaints and on its own investigative powers.

(4) The definition of dominance in the EC is not always easy. The common line in Commission and in Court Decisions, seems to be that a dominant firm enjoys independent power of action - that is: not being constrained by independent competition, whether it be from horizontal competitors, from suppliers, or from buyers. This was most clearly stated in the Continental Can case (ECJ 6/72), and it was repeated in famous cases like United Brands (ECJ 27/76), and Hoffman la Roche (ECJ 85/76), Commercial Solvents (ECJ 6-7/73), and more recently in NBIM (Michelin, OJ L353/33, 1981) and Akzo (OJ L374, 1985). The market share is important, but it is not the only element in the definition of dominance. Market shares in the above mentioned cases ranged from 40% in United Brands, to 85% in Sugar (ECJ 40-48/73), and 100% in GEMA (OJ 1971, L934), which had a monopoly in performing rights in Germany and which compelled its members/composers, authors and publishers, to assign existing and future rights, in all respects and in all countries, to GEMA. Moreover, non-residents were excluded.

Similar decisions were taken with monopoly corporations in France and Belgium in 1974. In addition to the barrier posed by the market share, barriers to entry are considered to be relevant. In Continental Can, according to the Court the Commission had not recognized the fact that food producers could enter the packaging and distribution business and can their own products. Therefore, the decision was reversed, But in the case of United Brands, large investments, vertical integration, scale economies, and high market penetration costs were acknowledged as high barriers, sufficient to speak of dominance where the firm held only 40% of the market.

In the case of Hoffmann la Roche, the technical lead, the surplus capacity, and the power to bind large customers, were considered to be barriers to entry. Other factors, such as the fringe of rivals, and multinationality, have been taken into account, in addition to market share and barriers to entry. As to the relevant market, this may range from parts of larger countries, to entire smaller states.

(5) The concept of abusive behaviour in a dominant position covers a wide variety of practices, and five types are to be discussed in the following examples.

Sometimes, so-called fidelity rebates are involved, as in the cases of Sugar and Hoffmann la Roche. The producers exploited their power positions by means of rebates, which were conditional upon buyers placing all of their orders with them. In the case of la Roche, rebates were aggregated across all vitamins, thus cnabling a transfer of power. Moreover, the use of the 'English Clause' (third party offers to be matched by la Roche on first priority) was meant to close the market. Similarly, Michelin, in the Netherlands, abused distributive bonuses to dealers, by increasing the rate to the proportion of Michelin products sold, and by increasing it in successive years.

A refusal to supply was condemned in the case of Commercial Solvents; that company, holding a monopoly position, refused the supply of a raw material used in a drug to a manufacturer in Italy, since this manufacturer was in competition with Commercial Solvent's own subsidiary. The goal seemed to be a take-over of the Italian firm ICI (and at the same time the elimination of a competitor).

Price discrimination was wronged in several cases, of which United Brands and CSV were leading cases. In the former case, price discrimination was easily proven throughout the Community, with price differences of 2.38 times between countries; CSV's position on the Dutch market was used to effectuate price discrimination between countries and to close off the national markets.

Unduly onerous terms of sale were condemned in the Eurofirma case

(ECPR 1974, 60-1), where Eurofirma, acting on behalf of the continental railway companies, stipulated that they could use designs, patents, and other elements, in tender offers for passenger cars, without any restrictions. The Commission considered this to be an abuse of a dominant buying position.

The EC has also enforced an important change in IBM's market behaviour. The Commission reproached IBM for abusing its dominant position (40% of the mainframes and microcomputer market and 38% of the data processing market) by means of withholding interface information to competitors, by bundling memories and software with central processing units in sales to customers, and by discriminating between users of IBM software. These practices have been given up since August 1984, under an EC-IBM settlement (see J.P. Rainier, Journal of Common Market Studies, Dec. 1985).

Finally, predatory behaviour was condemned in such cases as the German Steel Syndicates (1970), who had tried to eliminate a mini steel producer from the market by means of directed, severe price reductions.

Also there is the case of Akzo (1985), which tried to drive a small British firm, ECS, out of the market of Benzoyl peroxide, which is used in the bleaching of flour and also acts as a catalyst in the production of thermoplasts. When, in 1979, ECS started to make the latter for export purposes, Akzo threatened to eliminate ECS in the former market, by selling below cost. The firm was accused of selective price cutting in ECS's market. The complaint by ECS caused Akzo to suffer the severe penalty of D.Fl. 25 million. EC fines are raised significantly when companies trespass rules which have repeatedly been confirmed in previous cases. Moreover, in such cases the Commission acts swiftly, in order to prevent damage (OJ 1983, L252).

Mergers

In a dynamic view of market development, mergers may create dominant positions, or they may be used to fortify and defend such positions.

Once such actions cross the Rubicon of an anti-competitive impact, they can be tackled by means of article 86. This was initially denied, but in the case of Continental Can (1973) the Court has unequivocally stated that, because in article 86 the concept of abuse is not defined precisely, the goals of the Treaty must be considered. A competitive market structure as such has to be protected and, therefore, a change in the supply structure which virtually eliminates alternative sources of supply appears to be an abuse in itself.[38] Thus, some mergers may be attacked under article 86. This doctrine is only logical, since it abolishes the dual standard which forbids anti-competitive

---

[38] *A.P. Jacquemin & H.W. de Jong*, o.c., p.235.

agreements, but can allow mergers with the same intent and/or effect.

Subsequently, the EC Commission has opposed some mergers or quasi-mergers. One case concerned Pilkington's of Great Britain, which in 1980 intended to take over the flat glass subsidiaries of the leading French glass manufacturer BSN in the Benelux countries and in Germany. This move was thought to unduly strengthen Pilkington's already dominant position in Britain (80% market share) by also giving it over half of the markets in the Benelux, in Denmark, and in the Federal Republic of Germany, two or three times the size of those of its closest competitor.[39] Likewise, the German Federal Cartel Office objected to the transaction.

A solution was found in which (1) Pilkington only took over the German subsidiary of BSN; (2) both companies were decoupled, i.e. no representations on each others boards of directors, and a sale of shares in Pilkington held by BSN; and (3) a severing of distribution networks by both companies. Thus, the competitive structure of the flat glass market in Northwestern Europe was saved by retaining three major companies - Pilkington, BSN, and Saint Gobain.

Sometimes on its own initiative and at other times at the request of companies, the Commission has scrutinized several other intended mergers, since there is no system of notification. Several cases have passed the criteria; in other cases the firm divested itself from a good part of its business during the enquiry (ECPR 1982 No.104-106), and in a few cases the Commission objected. Such was the case in an intended takeover by Ph. Morris of 50% of the shares of Rothmans Tobacco Holding Ltd., which controlled Rothmans International, and which had subsidiaries throughout the EC. In addition, the firms concluded a partnership agreement, linking business behaviour. According to the Commission, this infringed both article 85-1 and article 86, particularly in the Benelux countries, where Rothmans had some 50% of the market before the agreement was reached. Following the objections, new agreements were drawn up, terminating the partnership, withdrawing P.M. from the Board of the holding company, and limiting its stake to that of a minority position (24.9%). During the proceedings, P.M. had claimed that it only desired the shares for "investment purposes" (and had paid a large amount for them), so it got what it "wanted". This decision has been appealed by three competitors (ECPR, 1984, No.98-100).

Whether such controlling operations will in the long run be sufficient to tackle mergers by dominant companies, is questionable. In any case, the Commission twice has asked the Council of Ministers to institute merger

---

39 *Tenth report on Competition Policy*, 1980, No.152.

control. A new proposal for merger control was made by the Commission early in 1988, but at the time of writing this paper, this proposal had not yet been decided upon by the Council. Its main points are the registration of large mergers and the prohibition of mergers constituting or extending a dominant position in het EC (market share < 20%).

Policies relating to the steel and coal markets, under ECSC Law, have generally been permissive. It was felt that this sector needed larger firms to reap the benefits from economies of scale. A ruling by the Commission in 1970 stipulated that steel firms would not be allowed to gain market shares by means of external growth beyond the limit of 13%.

The history of steel mergers and nationalization of coal is such that it cannot be applied to other sectors.

Concluding remarks

This essay indicates that in a large, mature, and integrated economy, such as the EC, competition policy is considered to be both necessary and feasible. The policy to protect competition has become an integral part (and one of the strongest points) of the Common Market's institutional arrangements. It is incorporated in the Treaty, is executed by an independent authority, and is legally controlled by the Court. The process works well, because the political influence on the decisions made is minimal, the goal is clear-cut, procedures are fixed, steadfast, and not unduly lengthy[40], and the decisions of the commission and those of the Court are to be respected and to be taken into account. In substance, cartels are practically outlawed; concerted practices, if detected, are fined, and abuse of dominant behaviour can effectively be opposed. On the other hand, harmless mergers are passed, and a number of business practices (e.g. specialization agreements and R&D agreements) are block-exempted.

Naturally, not all abusive behaviour is detected. No policy can achieve a perfect society. However, it is sufficient that the policy rules are clear and that, if necessary, they can be enforced. The weakest spot has been the nationalistic behaviour of member states in stagnating branches: subsidies and hidden protection had to be traced, exposed, and abolished by means of pro-

[40] Compare, for example, the IBM cases in the United States and in the EEC, In the US, the case was dropped after proceedings lasting more than 12 years. In the EC, the Commission and the Court settled the case - mainly on the Commission's terms - within 4 years.

tracted procedures. Nobody can claim success here, but gradually the rules are tightened and improved economic conditions may attenuate the problem.

The other weak spot is merger control: article 86 (though not article 66 ECSC) probably is too slender a base to be effective in prohibiting all but the most far-reaching monopolization actions. The final conclusion therefore must be that such a type of competitive policy is necessary and worthwhile. It commands support from economists who consider a free market economy, as Churchill phrased it, "the least bad system".

Comment by Yale Brozen (University of Chicago)

European competition policy has made a major contribution to public welfare in the common market by its attack on state barriers to intra-community trade. The Commission and the Court have recognized and acted on not only the obvious internal barriers to competitive trade but also "all trading rules enacted by member-states which are capable of hindering, directly or indirectly, actually or potentially, intra-community trades." They have acted against state subsidies which distort the competitive process, against the restrictions protecting state monopolies such as exclusive import rights, and have begun to act against public enterprises, as Professor de Jong points out with praise for these actions[1].

However, he goes too far in this whole-hearted support of actions by the Commission against exclusive territories, price discrimination, loyalty rebates and vertical restraints. He also supports the Commission in its confusion of barriers to entry with the cost of entry and wishes to give the Commission even greater control over mergers than it now has.

Exclusive territories

Unless an exclusive territory has been extorted from a supplier by a distributor with a threat to use its won monopoly position, which it can possess only if it is the beneficiary of political preferment or state protection, we should rely on suppliers to protect their own interest. Suppliers give distributors territorial protection if they expect that their sales will benefit by according such protection. It is, when freely offered, a trade expanding device and procompetitive for that reason.

Territorial protection is usually given along with requirements on distributors to undertake trade promotion and product support. Requiring a distributor to provide product promotion and support service must be accompanied by protection of the returns on that investment by the distributor if he is to be motivated to render full scale effort[2]. In the absence of protection of his investment, the returns to his investment can be eroded by "free riders", he and

---

[1] H.W. de Jong, "Competition Policy in Europe: Stimulus, Nuisance or Drawback?"

[2] Lester Telser, "Why Should Manufactures Want Fair Trade?" *Journal of Law & Economics,* vol. 3 (Oct. 1960), pp. 86-105.

the free riders will find it uneconomic to provide full sales support, and they will sell less of the supplier's product than would optimally serve consumer welfare.

If interbrand competition is insufficient to prevent a distributor with an exclusive territory from setting prices at a monopoly level of restricting product support to monopoly levels, the supplier may set a ceiling price or impose other vertical restraints or requirements to prevent a distributor from taking advantage of his monopoly position at the expense of his supplier's sales. For this reason, there should be no action against vertical restraints. They are imposed by a supplier to expand his business and are, for that reason, pro-competitive. It does not serve a supplier's interest to impose vertical restraints which are trade constricting unless forced to do so by threats from distributors to boycott the supplier or to take other action against the supplier's interest[3]. Only vertical restraints imposed unwillingly by suppliers at the behest of distributors are anticompetitive with rare exception.

The supplier's interest and the consumer's interest in distributor costs and behaviour coincide. Both the supplier and the consumer are served by the distributor attempting to expand sales, which is the aim of voluntary vertical restraints. If the grant of an exclusive territory does not serve the supplier's interest (and, therefore, the consumer's interest), he will not grant the right to an exclusive territory. If circumstances change after an exclusive territory has been granted and it no longer serves the supplier's interest, he will buy back the right to the exclusive territory. The Coca-Cola Company, for example, granted exclusive territories to the bottlers it franchised to bottle its drink and to distribute its concentrate to soda fountains. With reductions in transportation costs and changes in technology that increased the economies of large scale operation and with reduction in the cost of communicating with consumers (via advertising) to support sales maintenance and expansion, the company urged its most efficient franchises to buy its neighbouring franchises or, sometimes, bought them out itself in order to set up large scale bottling operations supplying larger territories.

Since it is in the supplier's interest to prevent monopolistic behaviour by its distributors, there is no reason for the Commission to attack grant of exclusive territories. Such grants will be given only when they serve the supplier's interest. Serving the supplier's interest will also serve consumer welfare.

---

[3] Robert Bork, "The Rule of Reason and the Per Se Concept: Price-Fixing and Market Division (II)," *Yale Law Journal*, vol. 75 (Jan. 1966), pp. 397-405; Richard Posner, "Antitrust Policy and the Supreme Court: An Analysis of Restricted Distribution, Horizontal Merger and Potential Competition Decisions." *Columbia Law Review*, vol. 75 (1975), pp. 283-288.

Suppliers will impose vertical restrictions to prevent monopolistic behaviour by distributors, with or without exclusive territories, since such behaviour is against their interest[4]. It is, therefore, unnecessary and anticompetitive for the Commission to attack exclusive territories and to attack vertical restraints. It should leave it to suppliers to defend their own interest. It should allow both vertical restraints and exclusive territorial grants.

Price discrimination

The Commission is equally misguided in attacking price discrimination[5]. Any attack on sporadic discrimination simply slows the rate at which price will move toward its long-run equilibrium level. If a supplier, when attempting to attract a customer by offering a lower price to that potential customer than it is offering its current customers, must offer the lower price to all customers, it will hesitate to offer the lower price. It is more costly to offer the lower price to all than to a few. It is likely not to hesitate to offer the lower price to one potential customer or to avoid losing one actual customer if it does not have to reduce the price to all its current customers simultaneously. Since a price cut to one potential customer who accepts the offer soon spreads to others, seeing that the supplier who loses the customer will attempt to refill his capacity by offering a price cut to some other supplier's customer, which in turn causes other suppliers to cut the price to other specific potential buyers if their costs permit, the market fairly quickly moves to the lower price. It would not do so if price cuts had to be uniform to all.

In the case of more unable discrimination, consumers are better served in at least the lower price market. A better allocation of resources results then in the absence of discrimination in most instances. Durable discrimination is possible only in monopoly circumstances with barriers to leakage from the low to the high price market. In the absence of discrimination, the monopoly price will prevail in all markets. With discrimination, a lower price becomes available in some markets (those with a high elasticity of demand)[6].

---

[4] Robert Bork, "The Rule of Reason and the Per Se Concept: Price-Fixing and Market Division (II)," *Yale Law Journal*, vol. 75 (Jan. 1966), pp. 397-405; Richard Posner, "Antitrust Policy and the Supreme Court: An Analysis of Restricted Distribution, Horizontal Merger and Potential Competition Decisions." *Columbia Law Review*, vol. 75 (1975), pp. 283-288.

[5] Thomas W. Ross, "The Costs of Regulating Price Differences," *Journal of Business*, vol. 59, no. 1 (Jan. 1986), pp. 143-156.

[6] There are a few instances in which a price discriminator will raise a price in some markets above the uniform monopoly price it would charge if it could not discriminate.

By attacking price discrimination, the Commission reduces the possibility that at least some consumers obtain the product at less than the monopoly price. It also reduces the return to patent holders, where the monopoly is based on patents, and the incentive to invest in research and development programs, the purpose for which the patent system is erected.

It should also be recognized that price differences are not discriminatory where there are cost differences. Let us suppose that in one market, uninformed consumers must be educated in the use and qualities of the product. Large costs are entailed in building a distribution and sales support network together with sufficient advertising and product promotion to assure consumers that the product is of high quality and that repair services are available to maintain the product. In a second market, consumers are well informed, a dealer network already exists handling similar products and a ready-made network of repair serviced is already available. Much less investment is required in developing the second market and good returns can be earned at a lower price. The lower price, then, is not discrimination in favour of the second market. It simply reflects lower cost. By preventing "discrimination" the Commission will prevent competition in this market and protect competitors, not competition.

Loyalty rebates

The Commission's actions against loyalty rebates is also inappropriate. Suppliers have a choice of many alternative ways for producing a product. If sales fluctuate erratically, they may be forced to choose general purpose, small scale equipment that can be cut back in operation without a large rise in costs or can be readily switched to alternative products. With less erratic sales, they can economically invest in large scale, special purpose equipment that can produce at lower cost and offer their product at a lower price. The purpose of loyalty rebates is to reduce erratic sales fluctuations and provide the security which makes it possible to invest in low production cost technology. Requirements contracts serve the same purposes, but may be inadequate because of opportunistic behaviour by customers or for other reasons.

In these instances, it is appropriate for the Commission to act against price discrimination.

Mergers and entry barriers

As for merger restrictions, the present powers of the Commission seem adequate to the task. Generally, a firm operating with less than 60 percent of an industry's capacity has little or no control over price. A supracompetitive price invites expansion by other firms and entry. A fairly quick loss of market position usually occurs in most cases where firms attempt to take advantage of a dominant position, especially where customers are large buyers who can choose between make or buy. Only if expansion by other firms or entry is barred will a dominant position, measured by share of capacity or sales, make it possible to maintain a supracompetitive price, as the Court recognized in *Continental Can.*

There is confusion in the Commission's mind as to what constitutes a barrier to entry. A large capital requirement is not a barrier to entry. It is a cost of entry, a cost borne by firms already in the industry that is no greater for an entrant, and more likely less because of technical progress in reducing the capital required per unit of capacity. A barrier to entry is something that causes the cost curve of prospective entrants to be higher than the cost curves of firms already resident in the industry and is anti-consumer welfare[7].

The Commission should make distinctions between barriers to entry, cost of entry, and attractiveness of entry. When it argues that overcapacity is a barrier, it is confusing barriers with attractiveness of entry[8]. Entry may be unattractive because of the existence of overcapacity and it should be, since society is in no need of additional capacity and building more capacity would be a waste of capital. Also, when it argues that a technical lead is a barrier, it makes a socially desirable activity - investing in technological progress - grounds for finding an illegality. Again, a technical lead reduces the attractiveness of entry but it is not a barrier[9]. Since technical lead is a result of investment in research or development, it is a cost which has been borne by firms in the industry and will have to be borne by entrants, so it is a cost of entry and more likely to be less for a new entrant than for resident firms in the industry. If items constituting a technical lead are patented, then it is a

---

[7] George J. Stigler, *The Organization of Industry* (Homewood, IL: Richard D. Irwin, 1968), p. 67; C.C. von Weizsacker, "A Welfare Analysis of Barriers to Entry," *Bell Journal of Economics*, vol. 11 (1980), pp. 388, 400; *Barriers to Entry, A Theoretical Treatment* (New York: Springer-Verlag, 1980), p. 13.

[8] Yale Brozen, "Capacity, Advertising, and Entry Barriers" (Working Paper, Graduate School of Business, University of Chicago, 1973); "Entry Barriers: Advertising and Product Differentiation" in H.J. Goldschmid, H.M. Mann, and J.F. Weston, eds., *Industrial Concentration: The New Learning* (Boston: Little, Brown, 1974).

[9] Von Weizsacher, *op.cit.*

legal monopoly and should not constitute grounds for finding an illegality. Vertical integration is not a barrier either. If it is cheaper to produce with vertical integration, then it may be more costly to enter an industry, with an efficient set of capital facilities. But if entry is attractive, firms will enter unless the capital market is imperfect - a difficult argument to sustain since all indications point to a nearly perfect capital market[10].

Practically, the only meaningful barriers to entry are state imposed. Monopoly franchises, limitations on the number of licenses that the state will grant where a license is required for each unit of capacity as in the case of municipal taxicab licensing, limited issuance of certificates of public convenience and necessity as in the transportation industry, limited issuance of marketing certificates as in the case of tobacco growing in the United States, more onerous licensing requirements for new entrants than were imposed on previous entrants as in the case of barbers - all these are barriers in the sense described above since non-licensed entrants must bear the cost of fines or the cost of hiding their illegal operations from the authorities while not hiding from some customers. The state should be attacked in this case, not those who are benefiting from these barriers. The barriers are not removed by an attack on the beneficiaries.

By its confusion of cost and unattractiveness of entry with barriers, the Commission increases the risks to firms of expanding their capacity and the supply of products. Since expansion of supply *is* entry in any operational definition of entry (expansion of supply), the Commission itself has become a barrier to entry, raising cost (risk) to entrants (by expansion) above the cost of existing capacity.

Professor de Jong suggest that the undermined stability of national cartels resulting from the opening of national frontiers was the case of the following wave of mergers which, he suggests were "to avoid the enhanced intensity of competition". He fails to understand the *primary* motive or consequence of mergers[11], downgrading it to a footnote where he speaks of the opening of "growth opportunities for efficient firms", but qualifies his caveat by his later discussion of mergers.

He also suggest that "effective competition policies came too late in the U.S. (1904)". If anything, the merger wave in the U.S. at the turn of the century and its results demonstrate that the non-enforceability of cartel

---

10 Stigler, *op.cit.*, p. 70, Fischer, Mc Gowan, and Greenwood, Folded, *Spindled and Mutilated: Economic Analysis and U.S. v. I BM* (Cambridge, MA: MIT Press, 1983), pp. 183-191; Charles River Associated, *An Analysis of Capital Market Imperfections* (Cambridge, MA: Charles River Associated, 1976).

11 John J. Mc Gowan, "International Comparisons of Merger Activity," *Journal of Law & Economics*, vol. 14 (April 1971).

agreements and the maintenance of open entry is an adequate competition policy. Most American economists did not support the Sherman Act for precisely that reason. Mergers for monopoly mostly ended in bankruptcy or in need of financial reorganization unless they gave up their attempts to monopolize and to exploit what they believed to be monopoly power and began behaving competitively[12].

The National Biscuit Company said as much in its 1901 annual report, stating that monopolizing, or attempting to do so, was the road the ruin. It went on to say that only by efficient production and providing high quality product were profits to be won[13].

Conclusion

European competition policy is well focused when it recognizes that state action is the source of barriers to entry and attacks those barriers[14]. It must be careful not to confuse cost and unattractiveness of entry with barriers. It must also be careful not to confuse the symptoms of monopoly with the means of monopolizing, or with methods of competing which promote consumer welfare. It must be careful to avoid imposing requirements which reduce the incentives for socially desirable activity, as it did requiring firms to disclose their new technology to competitors. When competitors complain about the activities of a rival, that should be taken as a signal that the rival is behaving in socially desirable ways. Otherwise, the Commission will end up protecting competitors instead of protecting competition.

---

12 Brozen, *Concentration, Mergers, and Public Policy* (New York: Macmillan, 1982), pp. 56-59.

13 Ibid., p. 218.

14 The U.S. Federal Trade Commission has also come to recognize this. The head of its Bureau of Competition has stated that, "We have begun investigations of Pharmacists, lawyers, accountants, funeral directors, surveyors - of a great many people who have relied in the past on government or quasi-governmental activities to protect them from competition," Timonthy U. Muris, "Antitrust and the FTC," *CATO Policy Report*, vol. 6, no. 7 (Sept./Oct. 1984) p. 8.

Comment by S.C. Littlechild (University of Birmingham)

Professor De Jong's paper is lengthy and erudite, encompassing several different schools of economic thought and surveying competition policies in many European countries, as well as EEC policy itself. These comments must necessarily focus on just a few specific points.

Is competition policy necessary? De Jong argues that in principle it is not, though in practice it is, except in certain special cases e.g. "if a small country with an open, low-tariff economy, strong firms and a weak Central Government is situated amidst important advanced neighbours" (p. 5). The meaning and significance of weak government is not explained (and it is odd to see Switzerland described as such). But note that whether the economy is open with low tariffs is in itself a government decision. So the decision to erect tariff barriers creates or strengthens the need for competition policy.

This raises the broader issue of why countries adopt competition policies - as a matter of positive rather than normative economics. Professor De Jong emphasizes that "competition policy is policy", and is therefore "subjected to pressures by interest groups" (p. 1) but he does not develop this point. Following Stigler's theory of economic regulation, economists are beginning to ask how far competition policy can be explained in these terms. In the UK, for example, the creation of the Monopolies Commission in 1948 and the Restrictive Trade Practices Act 1956 may have allowed new and expanding firms to throw off more easily the shackles of collusive industry agreements and practices; the Resale Prices Act 1964 (effectively abolishing resale price maintenance) undoubtedly reflected and assisted the growth of supermarkets and discount stores; the Mergers Act 1965 gave some protection from takeover to management and employees of small or under-performing companies, and so on. This is not to deny that some consumers might benefit from some aspects of competition policy. But whether consumer interests have been dominant, or even significant, in the development of competition policy is an open question.

Turning now to mergers, De Jong argues that the possibility of restricting them is one of the major arguments in favour of competition policy. He asserts that mergers are not motivated by efficiency considerations. Nor are they a reaction to other antitrust policy (e.g. against restrictive practices). Rather, "merger and cartel waves are epidemic, feeding upon each other", leading to a "merger mania". This is certainly a frequently heard claim, and there is some accounting evidence that on average mergers are unprofitable (e.g. Meeks,

Disappointing Marriage, Cambridge University Press, 1977). On the other hand, Bittlingmayer asks "Did Antitrust Policy cause the Great Merger Wave?" (*J. Law and Economics*, XXVIII (1) April 1985) and concludes that this is the most plausible explanation. There is some doubt whether subsequent mergers do, in fact, appear in waves (Tollison?). Stock market evidence suggests that most US mergers are indeed profitable and that these profits derive from increased efficiency rather than market power (Jensen and Ruback, "The Market for Corporate Control: The Scientific Evidence", *J. Financial Economics*, vol. 11, no 5, 1983; Eckbo and Weir, "Anti-Merger Policy under the Hart-Scott-Rodino Act: A Re-examination of the Market Power Hypothese", *J. Law and Economics*, XVIII (1), April 1985). No doubt some mergers do not increase efficiency, and others may increase monopoly power. Whether public policy is able to distinguish the good mergers from the bad ones remains to be established.

Finally, consider De Jong's argument in favour of competition policy designed to "protect the competitive process", as embodied in EEC competition policy. Professor De Jong gives many helpful and interesting examples, but how are we to judge whether the decisions taken have been successful? The stated aim is one which most economists would support, but it does beg the question how the competitive process is to be defined, and how it is to be protected.

In his paper, Professor De Jong himself explains the different views which economists have taken. (Another excellent exposition, contrasting the "structuralist" and "competitive process" schools of thought is by K.D. George, "Monopoly and Merger Policy": *Fiscal Studies*, vol. 6, no. 1, February 1985.) Even leaving aside other aspects of "the public interest", different interpretations of the nature of competition have quite different implications for policy.

Merger policy is a case in point. Some economists (including Professors De Jong and George) would place the most emphasis on the degree of concentration in the industry. Others (including Professors Kirzner and Brozen) would place the most emphasis on conditions of entry. Professor De Jong sees the absence of explicit merger control as a prime weakness in EEC competition policy; the second group of economist would presumably oppose its introduction. Who shall be the guardians of the competitive process?

The Labor Markets

DON BELLANTE

Labor Markets and the Welfare State

Government intervention into the labor market is often justified as correcting or mitigating a market failure. In reality many alleged market failures thought to be observed are illusions caused by a failure to recognize the subjective nature of value determination.

Interventionist policy is also flawed by its reliance on the perfectly competitive, perfect information model as the criterion against which the labor market of the real world is evaluated.

From a subjectivist perspective, the following types of labor market policies are critiqued: minimum wage legislation, income security, governmentally mandated or supported collective bargaining, and incomes policies. Minimum wage legislation, besides being a well understood cause of unemployment, is argued to frustrate the coordinating tendency of entrepreneurs operating in labor markets. All three types of income security measures examined-(retirement security, unemployment insurance and workers' compensation) are argued to have consequences that are both unintended and undesirable. Collective bargaining, it is argued, produces a misallocation of labor that in the U.S. has caused a severe shrinkage in the number of jobs in the unionized sector of the private economy. Incomes policies are seen as misguided attempts to reimpose the discipline of the labor market that is eroded by active monetary policy.

1. Introduction

The greatest proportion of government intervention into the free play of supply and demand must assuredly take place in the labor market. The history of intervention is most assuredly of wider scope in the labor market than in all other markets combined. This generalization is appropriate for the entire western world. Indeed, the labor market is the focal point and major instrument of welfare state policy. One could hardly, then, begin an appraisal of the consequences of the welfare state without an appreciation of the impacts of welfare state policies on the functioning of the labor market. The development of such an appreciation is the objective of this paper.

Such development is made difficult by the vast differences in institutional frameworks between the Netherlands and the United States of America. Nowhere are the institutional variations as great as in the area of collective bargaining. I will comment on some of the major difference in historical and current institutional settings as a preface to my discussion.

I shall begin my discussion of the costs of labor market policies from the perspective of the neoclassical static equilibrium model of the labor market. I should emphasize that this model is used only as a starting point from which to gain insight into the forces at work in the labor market. In accordance with all Austrian economists (and a significant number of other economists), I am interested in market processes and not so much with the unattained and unattainable "resting" places suggested by static equilibrium analysis. I will argue that the conclusions reached by mainstream neoclassical economists concerning the costs of welfare policies are sometimes on target but more often flawed or misleading because of their acceptance as reality of the heuristic fiction of perfectly competitive labor markets. Where I differ with some Austrian economists is on the issue of whether the fictional concept of equilibrium is a useful skeleton on which to build a fuller analysis of a world that is constantly in disequilibrium and characterized by incurably imperfect information.[1] But there is no disagreement among Austrians concerning the pitfalls of viewing the qualities of this fictional model as either fully descriptive of the real world or, even worse, as the ideal state toward which public policy should attempt to direct real world markets. As for specific welfare policies, I will discuss the consequences of minimum wage legislation, the social security system and its accompanying taxes, collective bargaining and closed shops, and incomes policies.

2. Labour market institutions in the Netherlands and America

There are quite a number of characteristics of the Dutch industrial relations system that are remarkably different from those of the U.S. system. In both countries, the period from the end of World War II until the mid-1950s witnessed a strong degree of growth in union membership. Whereas growth in union membership, as a percent of the Dutch labor force, seemed to stabilize thereafter, U.S. union membership has declined in absolute and not just in

[1] For a discussion of some issues pertinent to this disagreement among Austrians, see Tyler Cowen and Richard Fink, "Inconsistent Equilibrium Constructs: The Evenly Rotating Economy of Mises and Rothbard," *American Economic Review* (75) September 1981, pp.866-869.

percentage terms. Today less than 18 percent of the U.S. labor force is unionized, although membership was above 25 percent in 1953.

The percentage of Dutch workers who are unionized remains significantly more than double the U.S. percentage. But these statistics can present a misleading picture. The disparity between the two countries in worker coverage by collective agreement is much more dramatic. In the U.S., the percentage of workers whose wages are set by a collectively bargained agreement never varies a great deal from the percent of the work force who are union members. The percentage of workers who are union members is always more than ninety percent of those workers covered by collective agreement. Since World War II, the Dutch experience has been for a much larger fraction of the work force to be covered by collective agreement than the fraction who belong to unions. This covered percentage has in recent years been approximately between three-fourths and four-fifths of the labor force. The most significant differences between U.S. and Dutch collective bargaining systems, however, are not quantifiable. First and foremost is the preeminent role of the Dutch Government in the establishment of wages and working conditions. Only on rare occasions and only for short periods of time has the government of the U.S. exercised any influence over the wage setting process that would even begin to approximate what is the norm in the Netherlands.

Moreover, the labor movement in the Netherlands is highly centralized. Power is unquestionably focused at the top of the three major labor federations, in sharp contrast to the organization of labor in the U.S. Until the 1950s, the two major U.S. labor federations were rivals; the two federations are now merged. However, neither before nor after their merger were the A.F.L. and C.I.O. more than associations than provided organizational assistance to the member unions, and as centralized lobbying offices in relations with the government in Washington. In contrast to the Netherlands, only a tiny fraction of the dues paid by local union members reach the national federation. In no case does the federation involve itself in the wage setting process.

The whole pattern of historical development of unionization is also very different in the two countries. The religious and ideological roots and purposes of Dutch unions, as well as their agendas that go well beyond the employer/employee relationship, contrast with what used to be commonly called "business unionism" in the U.S. The label of business unionism was intended to characterize American unions in their major operations as being largely non-ideological (as compared to their European counterparts) and totally areligious. Unions in the U.S. have traditionally been portrayed as maximizing the pecuniary advantage of that individual union's membership, with scant concern about the impact on non-union labor or even on other segments of organized labor. One manifestation of the decentralized nature of American business unionism is the virtual impossibility of a general strike. Moreover, the philosophy of business unionism does not lend itself to even the appearance of union subservience to some perceived national interest. During one of its flirtations with an incomes policy during the mid-1970s, maximum wage increases were mandated by the U.S. government. The Teamsters Union obtained a contract with truckers that clearly called for wages above the mandated maximum. Americans then were treated to the joint spectacle of Department of Labor spokesmen taking great pains (to say nothing of leaps of imagination) to describe the agreement as being within the "non-inflationary" maximum, while spokesmen for the Teamsters Union steadfastly and emphatically maintained the contract they negotiated clearly violated the guideline maximum. When one understands the political necessity of Teamsters officials claiming to have violated the guidelines, then one has successfully come to understand the nature of business unionism.

Unions in the U.S. are organized either along craft lines (carpenters, printers, etc.)[2] or, to a lesser degree, along industrial lines (auto workers, steel workers, etc.). Bargaining almost always takes place between one craft or industrial union and one firm, with some important exceptions. Bargaining takes place at the industry level, with an association of employers, in almost all of those exceptions. It is never the case that more than one union collectively negotiate an agreement with a firm or employer's association.

Dutch unions, perhaps because of their ideological and religious roots, command a much greater degree of allegiance from their members than their U.S. counterparts. Union security or compulsory membership in unions is thus a serious concern to U.S. Unions, and usually the subject of negotiation. Such issues appear to be of minor concern in the Netherlands; union security arrangements are virtually non-existent. The parochial student of U.S. unionism, such as myself, is struck by the fact that so many Dutch have such a strong and fervent identification with and attachment to their unions. Quite apparently then, the institutional frameworks of the labor markets are so different between the U.S. and the Netherlands that any generalized analytical discussion must proceed with considerable caution, and of course I shall endeavor to do.[3]

---

[2] U.S. craft unions, in large cities particularly, have pursued membership strategies that were aimed at limiting membership severely. I gather that exclusive membership strategies are largely foreign to the Dutch environment.

[3] My understanding of Dutch labor markets is mainly derived from the following sources: Richard T. Griffiths, ed., *The Economy and Politics of the Netherlands Since 1945*, The Hague: Martinus Nijhoff, 1980; John P. Windmuller, *Labor Relations in the Netherlands*, Ithaca, N.Y.: Cornell University Press, 1969; and Lloyd Ulman and

There are, nonetheless, some universal perspectives that can be applied to a discussion of any labor market phenomena. If market processes are seen as coordinating the plans of individual actors in the society, then a cross-cultural discussion of welfare state policies can have as its unifying theme the question of whether particular types of policies or frameworks enhance or impede the coordinating features of the market process.

3. Austrian method and the analysis of labor markets

What sets the Austrian approach apart from mainstream economics is its unflinching emphasis on the individual decision maker as the focus of scientific analysis. If analysis is to be scientific and value free, then the analyst may not substitute his own judgment or values for those of his analytical subjects, with regard to what is desirable, or what are the utility-yielding qualities of objective phenomena. Yet with values and motives of individuals being entirely subjective, it will never be possible for an analyst to pass judgment on the optimality of the individual's chosen set of actions. It would be even more unreasonable to pretend to aggregate over an entire society of individuals in order to evaluate the efficiency of social interactions. Modern welfare economics, with its concept of a social welfare function is of course entirely based on such a pretention, where the gains of some are traded off against the losses of others.

Yet there is much than can legitimately be done in the way of evaluating social institutions in general, and labor market institutions and welfare policies in particular. It is axiomatic that when individuals act of their own free will, they act so as to increase their anticipated utility. When two or more individuals act out a voluntary exchange, they have each exploited an opportunity to gain without imposing a loss on the others. Moreover, the act of exchange brings the desires of the two or more individuals into a pattern of mutual consistency. To a large and complex society, the benefit that accrues from a market form of organization is the coordination of millions of separately constructed plans, all of which are based on values and goals particular to the millions of individuals making those plans.

Any social institution can be examined in terms of whether it facilitates or impedes the process of economic coordination. That is one criterion by which the subjects of this paper will be evaluated. Related to the problem of coordination is the matter of discovery. Austrian economists view competi-

---

Robert J. Flanagan. *Wage Restraint: A study of Incomes Policies in Western Europe.* Berkeley, Cal.: University of California Press, 1971.

tion as a process that brings forth the discovery of potential economic gains from trade. The entrepreneur is the catalyst in this discovery process. His alertness to previously unexploited opportunities to achieve pure economic profits is the essence of the process of value production. It is the entrepreneur who in a free enterprise system provides, through his actions, the coordination of individual plans. In no society will individual plans be perfectly coordinated. But the role of the entrepreneur is to move markets, including labor markets, in the direction of perfect coordination. Governmental planning can be viewed as an attempt to achieve coordination while dispensing with the function that provides that coordinating tendency - the entrepreneurial function. Since this is not the proper forum for reviewing the socialist calculation debate, I will merely assert the conclusion that is universal to Austrian economists - that the informational requirements of central planning, as a substitute for the directions of the market order, are implausible. With reference to the entrepreneurial function of discovery, a reasonable additional criterion for the evaluation of labor market institutions is whether such institutions facilitate or retard the process of discovery.

In general, the views of Austrian economists toward the existence of labor unions and collective bargaining are consistent with their views on product market monopoly. The fact that a producer may make his decisions in concert with other producers is not seen as a problem. Similarly the fact that workers might combine with one another to affect wages and restrict output is not per se seen as a problem. Objections arise only where coercion is involved, as when government restricts competition through the establishment of product market monopoly or legal enforcement of the monopoly power of unions. Of course in both the United States and the Netherlands, the level of power enjoyed by labor unions rests largely on coercion--either the coercive power of government itself, or the willingness of government to tolerate the private coercion that has characterized the history of many trade unions. But in a society of voluntary associations, absent coercive restraints, collective bargaining might well exist, perhaps prosper, and Austrian economists would not be disposed to view such social arrangements differently from any other of the institutions (such as the modern corporation) that evolve in the course of economic development.

4. Minimum wage legislation

Minimum wage legislation is probably the most straightforward example of a government-induced distortion of labor markets. In the U.S., when national minimum wage legislation was first introduced in 1938, the law did not apply to all employment sectors. A large part of the low wage sector of the labor market, most particularly agricultural employment, remained uncovered. Assuming a frictionless market, there need be no permanent loss of employment arising from the minimum wage in such an environment. If we conceive of a model of a labor market in which supply and demand conditions would dictate an equal wage in both the covered and uncovered sector, then the imposition of a higher wage in the covered sector easily can be analyzed. The workers displaced in the covered sector depress wages and become employed in the uncovered sector. Unless there is a significant difference in the demand elasticities of the two sectors, there will not be a significant difference in the average wage level of the two sectors combined. Nonetheless, the productive efficiency of the labor market is diminished. The value of output lost to the covered sector must exceed the value of the artificially stimulated production levels of the uncovered sector. The above depiction had some applicability in the early years of minimum wage legislation, but coverage in the U.S. of the minimum wage by now is nearly universal. Under these circumstances, there is no outlet for the workers displaced and the primary manifestation of the legal minimum is unemployment. The persons who become unemployed are of course not randomly distributed across the worker population, but rather are concentrated among low skill workers with little labor market experience. A 1979 study by Wachter and Kim[4] indicates that a 10 percent rise in the U.S. minimum wage is associated with a loss in total employment of approximately 2.5 percent, or roughly 2,500,000 jobs. Empirical studies vary in their estimates of just how large are the disemployment effects of minimum wage legislation, but they uniformly indicate the loss of employment is borne largely by young unskilled workers, and among these black teenagers are the most severely displaced.[5]

During the 1950s, unemployment rates among black teenagers were roughly equal to those of white teenagers. In the 1970s, the rate among blacks was more than double that of whites. It is not plausible to argue that discrimination against blacks was less of a problem in the 1950s than in the 1970s, so an explanation of the trend in black/white unemployment ratios must be associated with some other phenomena. In fact, between 1955 and 1975 the minimum wage rose from 44 percent to 51 percent of the average manufacturing wage, while the percent of total employment covered by the

---

4 Michael L. Wachter and Choongsoo Kim, "Time-Series Changes In Youth Joblessness, " National Bureau of Economic Research Working Paper No.384, August 1979.

5 An excellent survey of empirical studies of minimum wage laws is provided in Charles Brown, Curtis Gilroy and Andrew Koken, "The Effect of the Minimum Wage on Employment and Unemployment," *Journal of Economic Literature*; (20) June 1982, pp. 487-528.

legal minimum rose from about 60 percent to 85 percent. The increase in the minimum wage and its coverage has made it cheaper for employers to discriminate and more difficult for displaced blacks to salvage employment elsewhere. Employers face a problem of rationing jobs on some nonwage basis. Social connection may be as important as any other rationing mechanism. Perhaps that is why some studies of the minimum wage have found that workers actually employed at the minimum wage tend to be secondary earners in middle- and upper-middle income households. Many of these workers would find work in the market unattractive at the free market wage. Thus whatever argument could be made for the minimum wage as an anti-poverty measure loses its credibility.

Labor unions have been strong and vocal supporters of minimum wage legislation. The costs of lost employment, at least in the U.S., are never in the unionized sector, which is concentrated in the high wage-high skill industries. On the contrary, unions benefit from the distorting effects of minimum wage legislation. In partly unionized industries, rises in the minimum wage may adversely affect production costs for similar products in non-union firms, resulting in reduced intraindustry substitution in consumption. More importantly, interindustry substitution in consumption is frustrated as a result of increasing production costs in non-union industries affected by an increase in the minimum wage. The degree of union benefit from minimum wage legislation would depend, of course, on the elasticity of product demand in the relevant product markets, but the costs to union members, given the conditions that exist in the U.S. are minimal. Union support of government-mandated wage increases are analogous to industry support of protective tariffs: in both cases the demand for government action is best understood as a rent-seeking activity--as protection from competitive conditions. Minimum wage legislation certainly must be seen as a frustration of the coordinating tendency of a free labor market. Minimum wage legislation has also frustrated the entrepreneurial tendency to rectify the problem of regional disparities in the distribution of labor.

Regardless of what arguments are offered in support of minimum wage legislation, the principle of voluntary exchange is thoroughly violated by any legislation which forbids an individual to work if the best option available to him (from his own perspective) is at a wage deemed undesirable by persons other than the worker himself.

Social security and tax distortions

The term social security is used more broadly in the Netherlands than in the U.S. I will use the broader term in the following discussion, which will involve a variety of income security measures: social retirement insurance, unemployment insurance, and what in the US. is called workers compensation. A discussion of the effects of such programs must include consideration of the taxes used to pay for these programs.

Central to my perspective is the contention that the market wage associated with any job reflects not only a return on human capital and raw effort, but a compensation for the relative attractiveness of all characteristics of the particular job in question. In other words, there are implicit markets for job characteristics. These markets, like all others, are never in long run equilibrium, but equilibrating forces are always at work. For example, the entrepreneur in a highly seasonal industry who can divise ways to provide greater employment stability to his work force will find that he can obtain the same quality of work force at a lower wage bill because significant numbers of individuals value the stability more than the difference in wages. Workers whose subjective evaluations of stability and wage income are such that they do not find the tradeoff attractive will, in a world of diversity and free choice, gravitate to other employment situations. The employer who on the other hand provides jobs, such as in high rise construction, where the cost of providing an average level of job safety is very costly, will find that he must offer a significant wage premium. Again, the attractiveness of the total wage is a matter of subjective evaluation, and it is through experimentation and discovery that this premium evolves, with workers effecting their evaluations through job choice.

Unemployment insurance, which is a large part of the Dutch social security system, provides a good example of the distorting effects of welfare state programs. In the U.S., the incidence of unemployment is very uneven across industries, but the payroll tax to support the unemployment compensation system is imposed almost uniformly across industries. Such insurance reduces the size of the premium that must be paid to attract workers into jobs that are seasonal in nature or particularly sensitive to the business cycle. The tax affects not only the overall level of wages and employment, but also the structure of relative wages across occupations and industries, and does so in a way that distorts the processes that maximize individual well-being through subjectively based choices. And as Martin Feldstein has empirically demonstrated, generous levels of unemployment compensation provide firms that experience unstable or seasonal demand with an incentive of use temporary layoffs to a much greater extent than they would in the absence of the program[6]. The cross-employer subsidization that takes place lowers the relative prices of goods produced in industries with unstable and seasonal demand, providing a clear example of how welfare state policies can be the cause of rather than the cure for market failure.

Another common type of income security program is compensation for on-the-job injury or what in the U.S. is called Worker's Compensation. As with the unemployment insurance system, there is a cross-subsidization that takes place through the wage structure. Firms and industries with inherently higher accident rates pay lower relative wages than they otherwise would. However, the tax costs of such programs are not completely in proportion to accident rates and costs. Once again, government induces a market failure - a divergence between private and social cost--where non need exist. Worker compensation also may affect accident rates in an entirely unintended fashion. Because workers are partially insured against financial loss resulting from injury, and are subject to none of the safeguards against moral hazard that can be employed in private, voluntary insurance schemes, workers may be less cautious in the work place[7]. There is some clear evidence, provided by J. R. Chelius among others, that on balance injury rates are higher the more generous are a states benefit levels[8] .

In the United States, the federal government has in recent years tried to affect the safety of the work place through direct regulation, most particularly with the Occupational Safety and Health Act of 1970. The act imposes about 4,000 uniform rules or standards. The rationale for such legislation always ignores the fact that profit motives of employees, combined with the heavy investment of employers in their workers provide substantial incentive for the provision of socially optimal safety conditions, and that market processes produce compensating wage differentials across work environments to account for differences in the costs of providing safety. There simply is not a case that can be made for the existence of systematic market failure in the provision of work place safety. Empirial work by Kip Yiscusi has shown that the Occupational Safety and Health Act, in the five years following its passage, has not significantly increased work place safety[9]. We might expect with the passage of more time that the Act's effect will be detrimental to

---

6 Martin Feldstein, "Temporary Layoffs in the Theory of Unemployment." *Journal of Political Economy* (84) October 1976, pp.937-957.

7 Samuel A. Rea, Jr., "*Workmen's Compensation* and Occupational Safety under Imperfect Information," *American Economic Review* (71) March 1981, pp.80-93.

8 James R. Chelius, "The Influence of Workers' Compensation on Safety Incentives," *Industrial and Labor Relations Review* (35) January 1982, pp. 235-242.

9 W. Kip Viscusi, "The Impact of Occupational Safety and Health Regulation," *Bell Journal of Economics* (10) Spring 1979. pp. 117-140.

work place safety. The phenomenon of work place safety, like all other aspects of the production process, is subject to a dynamic process of technological change and improvement that can be frustrated by the bureaucratic imposition of rules that tend to freeze the technology of safety and reduce the incentive to entrepreneurial alertness to new safety possibilities. The Act specifies many rules that took into account the best technologies available at the time the Act was drafted, but which were obsolete by the time the Act took effect.

In all three cases sighted (unemployment insurance, retirement income security, and workers' compensation), government intervention can be argued to create a market failure. Such interventions, rather than internalizing a market externality, do just the opposite: they externalize a market "internality."

6. Collective bargaining

Unions have the power to raise wages only when they can prevent the substition of non-union labor. The closed shop, wherein only union members can be employed by a particular unionized firm is one such device for preventing substitution. In the U.S., the closed shop has been outlawed for over 30 years. However, U.S. law does permit what is nearly the equivalent--the so called union shop--wherein non-union members may be employed but must become union members within one or two months of initial employment. About 19 state governments, mostly in the south, have outlawed the union shop, but empirical evidence strongly suggests that location of a firm in one of those states does not effect a union's organizing or wage determining abilities[10]. The reason should be no puzzle. The closed shop and union shop may be serious infringements of the worker's right to free association, but even in the states where a worker is not forced to join a union, if the firm has a contract with a union, the worker must be represented exclusively by the Union and must be paid the union wage. It is this exclusive bargaining right that is the legal source of union power.

Empirical studies for the U.S. suggest a considerable degree of variability in the ability of unions to achieve above- equilibrium wages, and such ability also varies by phase of the business cycle[11]. The economy-wide union-non

---

[10] The most recent such study is Walter J. Wessels, "Economic Effects of Right to Work Laws, " *Journal of Labor Research* (2) Spring1981, pp. 55-76.

[11] A comprehensive survey of empirical studies of union impacts on wages in provided in C. J. Parsley, "Labor Union Effects on Wage Gains: *A Survey of Recent Literature*." Journal of Economic Literature (18) March 1980, pp. 1-31.

union differential seems to average about 15 percent over the course of the business cycle. Static equilibrium analysis suggests that workers in the unionized sector who are deprived of jobs because of the higher than equilibrium wage spill over into the larger, non-unionized sector and depress wages there. If this absorption takes place, the gains of unionized workers come basically at the expense of workers in non-union types of employment. There is no necessary effect on average wage levels (union and non-union combined) or on total employment. Nonetheless, a misallocation of labor takes place with greater than optimal employment and output in the non- unionized sector only partly offsetting the lower than optimal employment and output of the unionized sector. This static welfare loss has been estimated to be in the neighborhood of .14 percent of GNP or about $5 billion in current terms[12]. Such estimates must by their nature grossly understimated value of lost output resulting from collective bargaining since they are confined to the most trivial of the costs. Since markets can not immediately respond to disequilibrating wage changes, substantial losses must be associated with the unemployment of labor that successive rounds of collective bargaining bring about. These losses may well dwarf those associated with the misallocation of labor.

The disemployment effects of above equilibrium, collectively bargained wages is masked by the capacity of the non-union sector of the economy to absorb this unemployment. As the accompanying table illustrates, employment in the private sector of the U.S. labor market grew by nearly 34 million jobs between 1956 and 1984. But employment in the unionized sector of the private labor market declined by over five million jobs while employment in the non-union sector much more than doubled. The only reason that the frequently cited figures on total employment of union workers show only a small decline is that unions have been dramatically successful in recent decades in organizing government workers. The steep rise in public employee unionism hides the fact of severe employment loss in the unionized sector of the labor market.

In the Netherlands, where the fraction of the labor force covered by collective agreement (through government intervention) is much larger than the fraction belonging to unions, and is more nearly universal than in the U.S., the coordinating role of entrepreneurship is severely frustrated. Moreover, freedom of entry by workers is grossly inhibited, further frustrating the coordinating tendencies that should exist. One should expect that employment growth would largely be stifled in such an institutional setting. Indeed,

---

12 Albert Rees, "The Effects of *Unions* on Resource Allocation," *Journal of Law and Economics*. (6), October 1963. pp. 69-78.

over the comparable period of time, there has been a substantial decrease in private sector employment in the Netherlands.

Employment by Sector in the United States (in thousands)

	1956	**1984**
Total Employment	51,076	94,156
Total Private Employment	44,254	78,187
Private Employment, unionized	17,189	11,984
Private Employment, non-unionized	27,065	66,203
Total Public employment	6,757	15,969
Public Employment, unionized	915	5,717
Public Employment, non-unionized	5,842	10,252

Source: Derived from U.S. Department of Labor, *Monthly Labor Review* (108)May 1985; U.S. Department of Labor, *Directory of National Unions and Employee Association*, 1979 (Bulletin 2079) September 1980; and U.S. Bureau of the Census, *Statistical Abstract of the United States*, 1986.

The effect of collectively bargained wage gains on unemployment also provides a connection between unions and monetary policy. When a disequilibrating rise of nominal wages in the union sector takes place, unemployment in that sector will result. If the monetary authorities seek to quickly remedy that unemployment, rather than letting the passage of time produce absorption of the unemployed in the non-union sector, they can do so only if they inflate the currency enough to bring the real wage in the union sector down to its former level. Such inflation will temporarily lower real wages in the non-union sector, but the resulting shortage of labor there will cause the real wage in that sector to also return to its original level. All of this can take place without workers having to "spillover" from the union to the non-union sector, but the cost of this battle between the unions and the central bank is the resulting continuing rounds of inflation and the distortions associated with them. Because in the past central banks have acted in this fashion, unions have escaped the discipline that would have otherwise derived from the marketplace in the context of a stable monetary regime.

7. Incomes policies and coordination

In the Netherlands and elsewhere in Western Europe, governments have sought to substitute the more blunt discipline of incomes policy for the discipline of the marketplace and a disciplined monetary policy. Often, incomes policies are rationalized as providing the idealized characteristics of a perfectly competitive labor market in long run equilibrium. Under most terms of incomes policies, uniform wage increases are allowed economy wide, or if percentage changes in wages are permitted to vary, they may vary only within a very narrow range. It is certainly a characteristic of the competitive model that, even in the presence of dramatically different rates of productivity growth, (and in the real world there are extremely dramatic differences) wage growth over the long run will reflect economy-wide rather than industry or firm specific productivity growth. But as demand and supply conditions continually change in a dynamic economy, it is the response of employers and employees to disequilibrium conditions that brings about a more efficient allocation of labor. To attempt through public policy to achieve the end state results of the competitive model deprives the labor market of its devices for coordination in a changing economy. In practical terms, this deprivation means the coexistence of labor shortages in some markets and labor surpluses in others, relative product prices that do not reflect society's changing marginal evaluations, and the frustration of entrepreneurial tendencies to induce workers to move from employments where their marginal products are low to where they are higher. The retardation of efficiency that takes place may seem small in any one year. But if the policies continue to be effective, the stagnation they induce will be cumulative, as will be the stresses put on those sectors of the economy for which the dictates of the policy are most inappropriate.

8. Concluding remarks

When economists try to justify the restrictions on economic freedom that are associated with the welfare state and government sponsored monopoly unionism, they often argue that such policies are in response to market imperfections or failures. The major point of this paper is that most aspects of the welfare state thwart the socially desirable workings of free markets in labor-- that welfare state policies create failures that in the real world are more serious than those that they are imagined to cure.

Comment by P. Keizer (University of Limburg)

Introduction

In this comment I shall first discuss the Austrian view of society in general and of market and labour market processes in particular. Austrians tend to base their judgement of government performance mainly in respect to its negative effects on the market processes. In doing so, however, they also tend to disregard the beneficial effects of welfare state policies. To understand these benefits it is necessary to know why people strive for a welfare state. In the next section I shall discuss the implicit Austrian theory of the state. It turns out to be rather an extreme political philosophy, one which has its roots in Anglo-Saxon liberalism. The history of labour relations in Western Europe shows a growing popularity for those political philosophies that allow some government coercion in the allocation and distribution of scarce resources. A cost-benefit analysis made by economists who have adopted a different value system than that of Anglo-Saxon liberalism, however, puts this development in a different light. In the following section some welfare state policy measures, as discussed by Don Bellante, will be viewed from this different perspective. The final section of this comment includes a short summary and some conclusions.

A closer look at the Austrian view

According to Don Bellante's contribution to this volume the Austrian economic theory is mainly concerned with the description of market processes. Key concepts in these descriptions are 'competition', 'entrepreneurship' and 'discovery processes'. The theory's analytical starting point is the individual decision maker acting of his own free will. The best judges of the individual's preferences and capacities are the individuals themselves. If they act autonomously in deciding the use of their own scarce resources, i.e. each individual bears his own costs but receives all the benefits, the use will be optimal. If individuals decide to act in groups, their activities must be considered as the optimal solutions to economic problems as long as free entry to and exit from the groups in guaranteed, i.e. every person is free to join another group, in which case the procedures for dissolving contracts are extremely important. This implies that in the labour markets individual or collective labour contracts will be drawn up, which will prescribe the tasks, responsibilities, job description and the conditions of wage levels and of resignation and discharge.

These principles are the hard core of what Hayek has called Anglo-Saxon liberalism[1]. In this liberalism the government plays an important but very small role. The evaluation of welfare policies nearly always stresses the negative effects, as the Austrians do, and the benefits are either ignored or at best simply recognized. To gain a better understanding of the benefits it is useful to discuss in greater detail the implications of the Austrian view of the functioning of the state.

The implicit theory of the state and its shortcomings

The liberal point of view implies the existence of a society that has adopted just one RULE (to be considered as a social contract). This rule states that all private property must be respected, including the rights and obligations agreed upon in voluntary contracts. Some anarchists automatically comply with this rule, because of its productiveness for all members. Liberals, however, consider governments as a necessary institution, a guarantee that the rule will be honoured. The result of this opinion is an administration of justice, with a police force and an army. Nearly all writers in the liberal-anarchists tradition recognize the necessity of some degree of coercion. In general, government action is justified in the case of pure collective goods, those which the private sector cannot produce because of the goods' collective character. Pure collective goods are collective goods that are wanted by everyone. Coercion is necessary to solve the problem of the 'free-rider'. Agreements that are wanted by everybody, or at least by a large majority of the population, can be embodied in a law, and a law can only be changed by unanimous or large majority decision. This theory must be interpreted as a normative theory.

A constitution formulated along Anglo-Saxon lines would not get a large majority. In the nineteenth century, though, suffrage was limited to a happy few and laws were mainly determined by liberal principles. Given such a political structure, the wages of the masses did not grow very quickly, in contrast to the incomes of the elite. The differences in wealth, as perceived by the majority of the population, became larger and larger, and most members of the working class were unable to make a real 'take-off'. The history of the labour movement in Western Europe shows what happens when inequality is

---

[1]F.A. Hayek, *New Studies in Philosophy, Politics, Economics and the History of Ideas,* London, 1978; especially chapter 9, 'Liberalism'.

large and growing. This situation led to the formation of egalitarian groups. Workers organized trade unions based on such biblical concepts as "Am I my brother's keeper" and the "Sermon on the Mount"[2]. The Marxist idea of class conflict also led to the formation of trade unions and political parties[3]. Through the formation of these groups the workers gained economic, social and political power, and were thus in a position to reformulate the conditions under which the liberal RULE was acceptable.

This formation of groups not only led to attempts at increasing wage and employment levels (which according to the Austrians is doomed to failure) but also implied a process of social integration, through which process members associate more closely with the group. The relevant aspects here are wage and income levels and distribution. In theoretical economic terms, group characteristics became embedded in the individual consumer's preferences. In sociology a group is defined as a set of individuals with a common set of values and norms. The main goal of those groups in Western society that opted for a welfare state was a more equal distribution of income, wealth, knowledge and decision-making power. The creation of greater equality, as opposed to the distribution resulting from a free market economy, must be considered as a collective good. Individual cost-benefit analyses and social cost-benefit analyses still have to be made before we can judge whether the creation of the welfare state has led to a better society. Such a society implies benefits for its adherents and costs for those who are socially privileged. Both cost-benefit analyses can of course be combined, because social costs and social benefits must always be perceived as such by individuals. The outcome of the political debate on the conditions under which the liberal RULE is valid is in fact a compromise, having the character of a zero-sum game if it is concerned with the social costs and benefits, or a non zero-sum game if it concerned with the individual costs and benefits. The social sciences can play an important role in calculating the cost-benefit ratio. By means of sophisticated analyses and reliable calculations of the costs and benefits of a large variety of policy measures, they can fulfil a very important function in the political decision-making process. Science, however, cannot resolve the political conflict between egalitarians and liberals by formulating an optimal compromise. To do so, the social costs and benefits need to be weighted, and a political philosophy is needed to determine the value of the weights.

This political conflict has been 'resolved' in the twentieth century by a representative, democratic political decision-making structure characterised by

---

[2]Source: Genesis 4, 9 and Matthew 5, 1-12. In the Netherlands the bible-inspired trade union was the protestant Patrimonium (1877).

[3]The first Marx-inspired union was the Social Democratic Union (1881).

universal suffrage. Under this structure every generation can formulate its own conditions for accepting the liberal RULE. If the population is denied the opportunity of regularly reformulating the conditions, the threat of non-democratic forces may arise. The 'Road to Serfdom' leads not only to the left, but also to the right; and neither direction leads to paradise, as history has taught us. The golden average of these two directions is determined by the culture of the society as a whole and in particular by the cultural characteristics relating to the ideal of equality. Democracy should imply above all else a respect for decisions taken by majorities. In extreme solutions, such as the Anglo-Saxon liberal and communist solutions, it is very difficult for the poor or those with entrepreneurial skills respectively to respect the democratic decision-making process.

A cost-benefit analysis of social policy

In his contribution Bellante discusses several policy measures that are specific to the welfare state. He believes that the measures have been rather unprofitable. Roughly speaking, I agree with him when he observes that the costs of these measures can be high in terms of loss of efficiency and, sometimes, employment. Some marginal notes can be made however. A universal, legally enforced minimum wage does not necessarily lead to unemployment. Unemployment can be avoided if other wage levels are flexible and equilibrium on the macro-labour market is guaranteed. The result of such a situation will be a more equal distribution of wage income and some loss of efficiency. Together with a universal, legally enforced minimum benefit payment for those without jobs, this will result in a guaranteed minimum level of material well-being for the entire population. The certainty of such a minimum level of material well-being can activate people, whereas uncertainty can paralyse them and can cause them to adopt passive attitudes. Moreover, such a minimum would form a sound basis for the education of children from the lowest income groups, so that they could become more productive members of society. Uniform measures such as unemployment insurance do lead to some loss of efficiency, but they are a part of an egalitarian culture. Analyses similar to those made by the Austrian school are necessary to calculate the price of such collective goods. Government interference in the issue of injuries sustained at work gives rise to high bureaucratic costs; but if the production of the good 'safety at work' is left to the free market process, production and consumption will have a slow beginning. The most important reason for this being the employees' lack of knowledge about the technical aspects of their work. The employer will be able to cut safety costs because of this ignorance. Some government assistance will be necessary to prevent the employees from making too many errors in their cost-benefit analysis of the work. In a free market economy without strong egalitarian groups, nobody will propose a uniform wage policy, an instrument which would probably have only negative effects. In a mixed economy, however, one in which unions have built up strong bargaining rights, it would be wise to implement a permanent wage policy. This does not necessarily imply actual intervention. The threat of intervention can be a strong argument for wage negotiators to act more moderately than is possible in the short run. The loss of efficiency will be larger if there is no permanent wage policy.

Austrian policy analyses tend to be useful price calculations. As long as the benefits are not mentioned, though, it is impossible to pass a balanced judgement about the desirability of social policy.

Conclusions

The Austrian school focuses its analyses on the free will of an individual: the individual himself is the best informed about his preferences and capabilities. The full right of each individual to make decisions about his own property therefore leads to an optimal use of scarce resources. An ideal society consists of individuals who cooperate with each other quite voluntarily and are only tied by voluntarily agreed contracts. The government's most important duty is to guarantee private property and compliance to the contracts. Economic history, however, shows a growing inequality in the material development of different groups. In Western Europe these inequalities have led to the formation of egalitarian groups, i.e. unions and political parties. In addition to achievement, solidarity became an important norm for rewarding labour input. Equality became a collective good, strived for by influential groups, but certainly not by all groups and individuals. This good can only become and remain a part of the culture of a society if the government, as the representative of the community, forcefully imposes rules upon all the members of that society. Since many people consider themselves not only as individuals, but also as members of a group (read society), they will accept some costs involved in maintaining the desired group characteristics.

The debate between the individualistic view, which leads to the adherence of the liberal RULE, and a more collectivist view, which leads to the adherence of quite another rule, must take place in politics. A solution via the market is by definition impossible, since it is concerned with the correction of market results. Politicians can take decisions with the aid of majority rule (democracy) or with minority rule (dictatorship, one-party system, limited suffrage, etc.). The market process is the most progressive discovery process for the production of private goods. In politics however, democracy is the most progressive discovery process for the production of collective goods. More people are involved in the decision-making process and they can provide politicians with a wider framework for assessing the costs and benefits of certain policies. A society that can avoid the polarization of prevailing ideologies has the greatest chance of stable development, a development which does justice to both aspects of human beings, the individual and the social.

JOOP HARTOG

Labor Market Policies from a Neoclassical Perspective: Implementing the Trinity

Neoclassical theory implies three goals for economic policy: enhance competitive market structures, correct for market failures and promote equity. Actual and potential labor market policies are evaluated from this perspective. The efficiency argument supports a number of government interventions: introduction and legal support of labor unions, provision of information on general labor market conditions, support of quality standards as a condition for market entry, corrective measures for market failures in job design and working conditions, provide insurance against earnings loss from unemployment, sickness or disability. The efficiency argument does not support general enforcement of collective agreements and leads to reservations on public employment service and on compulsory rules about working conditions.

To promote equity, neoclassical theory favors policies affecting the initial wealth (endowment) distribution. Subsidies on schooling and training, although proper instruments, seem to be applied perverseley, as the most able will benefit most. Considering the trade-off between equity and efficiency, evidence suggests that efficiency losses have reached substantial levels. Analytically the allocation of risk is a problematic subject.

The Trinity

I consider the neoclassical framework to consist of the nexus of markets made up with optimizing agents and the Paretian welfare theoretic evaluation of those markets. Standard results claim Pareto optimality in markets with perfect competition (except for external effects and public goods), dependence of the final welfare distribution on the initial distribution of wealth and the opportunity to establish a desired final welfare distribution through the market, provided one starts off from the proper wealth distribution. These standard results set the stage for the neoclassical guidelines on economic policy in general and labor market policy in particular:

1. let competition do its work: promote the smooth functioning of markets;
2. correct for market failures that arise in case of external effects and public goods;
3. strike a balance between the efficiency considerations of 1 and 2 and the distributional justice, i.e. between efficiency and equity. This balance has to be sought because the lump sum redistributions necessary according to the standard results above are barely feasible and hence usually insufficient to establish the desired welfare distribution.

It's this Trinity that determines the outline of the paper.[1] First, efficiency aspects will be treated and later, inroads will be allowed to the extent that they improve justice. Emphasis will be on structural effects and not on the details of particular policies. The standard neoclassical framework is used to analyze the question how and to what extent the government can improve the outcome of the labor market process. The emphasis on structural effects essentially leads to a comparison of institutional arrangements. It is hardly necessary to point out that it is impossible to give a complete treatment of the problem. Only some elements will be discussed. There is an overlap with parts of Hartog(1984) and Hartog and Ritzen (1986), of which the former discussed efficiency and the latter equity. It is only natural to bring them together here. Still, the treatment of topics involves a subjective selection, and there is no attempt to give equal weights to the elements of the Trinity.

To provide a link with actual developments, it's perhaps worth stressing at the outset that one may interpret policy developments in The Netherlands (and elsewhere as well) as showing a new swing of the pendulum: from a sustained, intensive emphasis on equity, a change has been made to greater emphasis on efficiency. For almost a decade perhaps, discussions have been going on about the increased rigidity of labor markets and the need to reduce it. It would seem that at last policies are indeed implemented to do so. The aim of this paper is essentially to survey existing knowledge rather than attempt an in-depth analysis of particular issues. Unfortunately, there are quite large omissions in the existing knowledge, and if anything, the paper suggests many lines of extended research.

---

[1] The paper builds heavily on standard results of Paretian welfare theory which can be found in any good advanced microeconomic textbook.

Efficiency: affecting the market structure

Although one might develop interesting theories about the endogenty of institutions and legal arrangements, such institutions will here be taken as given. Different institutional arrangements can be compared, and the comparison might be an indication of the different arrangements as policy targets. The basic approach here will be to take the auction market from the perfect competition construct as a starting point and then successively add complications.

Unions

Historically, labor unions have sprung up from the initiative of workers. Employers usually made attempts to suppress them, and government policies, historically and cross-nationally, can be observed to cover the spectrum of outlawing, permission and active support. Confronted with these differences, one may indeed ask for an analysis of optimal government policies. Should unions be supported or banned, should they be given exclusive bargaining rights, should the results of the bargaining process be imposed on those not represented in the bargaining room? Although there is a clear increase of the neoclassical research effort devoted to issues about labor unions, it is still far too early to draw definite conclusions. In this section, only a brief discussion of some effects on wages and employment will be given.

As a start, consider the situation of perfect competition, with atomistic market parties, and all the other necessary assumptions holding. The assumption of atomistic market parties involves small firms and individualistic labor supply. Hence, unions do not exist, possibly because they are simply outlawed. Under the usual conditions, the market would generate a Pareto-efficient equilibrium. Also, the emergence of labor demand under monopsonistic conditions would violate Pareto-efficiency, since the equilibrium wage rate would now deviate from the value of the marginal product. The introduction of labor unions in such an otherwise competitive environment (free mobility, no uncertainty, perfect information) cannot have much effect. In case of homogeneous labor, the union can never obtain any wage increases, as long as there is a perfectly elastic supply of non-unionized workers: firms will always evade the differential by hiring non-union workers. Only if the union manages to cover all workers could there be any effect. Full coverage on a voluntary basis is seldom observed, if ever. The union can only obtain a monopoly by legal support or some exclusivity based on contracts with a firm or an industry. The union's interest in such arrangements is obvious.

The impact of the union is shaped primarily by the counterfactual that is used for comparison. Compared to perfect competition, introducing a union with exclusive rights and compulsory membership would lead to efficiency loss as the result is no longer Pareto-optimal (Oswald, 1985). But in view of the historical developments and actual market structures, it is more natural to study the union as a countervailing power to monopsonistic demand structures. Assume the situation to be characterized by a dominant, large firm, facing an upward sloping labor supply curve, and a number of small, price-taking firms, following the wage set by the large firm.

Let the introduction of the union be based on freedom of contract: there is no law other than the one permitting the formation of labor unions. Consider the situation for the large firm. To derive an equilibrium, further assumptions are needed. Now, it is fully realized that there are many complications and the following is only a simple start. First, negotiations between the firm and the union will set a union wage rate (for union members only), leaving the firm the freedom to set employment of union members. In addition, the firm can hire non-union labor, at non-union wages, and does so by equating marginal value product and marginal wage cost along the non-union labor supply functions. Hence, the firm hires in two ways: union-members at the negotiated union wage rate and non-union members along an upward sloping supply curve.

Suppose, workers decide on joining a union solely on the basis of wages, considering the fact that they have to pay union dues. In that case, with freedom to join and leave the union, equilibrium *union wages* net of union dues should be equal to non-union wages, since otherwise the membership would adjust. Denote the union dues by ∂ In this simple world, they are equal to the cost (per member) of the union, which only serves to obtain better wages. In fact then, ∂ can be taken to represent the cost of wage negotiations, i.e. the transaction costs. So, freedom to join the union, with homogeneous labor, sets the wage differential $w_u - w_n$ equal to transaction cost t, in equilibrium; this is the first condition for equilibrium, based on individuals' decision regarding union membership. Note that this implies that the labor supply function is determined in terms of non-union wages w_n, equal to union wages w_u net of dues ∂, since this is in fact the wage that member and non-member both enyoy. Let the negotiations be such that a wage w_u is established for union members, but that the firm is free to decide on the volume of union labor hired, Ld_u Given the wage bargain, Ld_u will be found at the firm's VMP-curve; this occurs because at the union wage rate the firm can attract workers as long as the rate is not below the reservation wage given by the labor supply schedule $w_n(L)$. Given the volume of union labor, the firm will decide on the volume of non-union labor Ld_n by equating VMP and the marginal wage cost, derived from the labor supply curve. This is so because after exhausting union labor supply non-union members must be hired, along the wage schedule $w_n(L)$ and its implied marginal wage cost curve, $MWC(L_n)$. This provides a second condition for equilibrium, determining the total amount of labor hired. If it is the union's aim to obtain a job in the large firm for every union member, equilibrium is characterized as the situation in Figure 1. Given the wage rate w_n union labor demand (=union membership) equals Ld_u, and the firm hires additional labor Ld_n up to the intersection of the marginal wage cost curve and the VMP-curve, setting the appropriate wage rate w_n The double equilibrium condition is satisfied, as union dues ∂ equalize net union and non-union wages, while total supply at this net wage rate is just absorbed by the firm. Note the implication that the union faces a negative tradeoff between membership and wage rate, dictated by the negative slope of the VMP- curve and the desire to employ all members at the union wage.

Figure 1

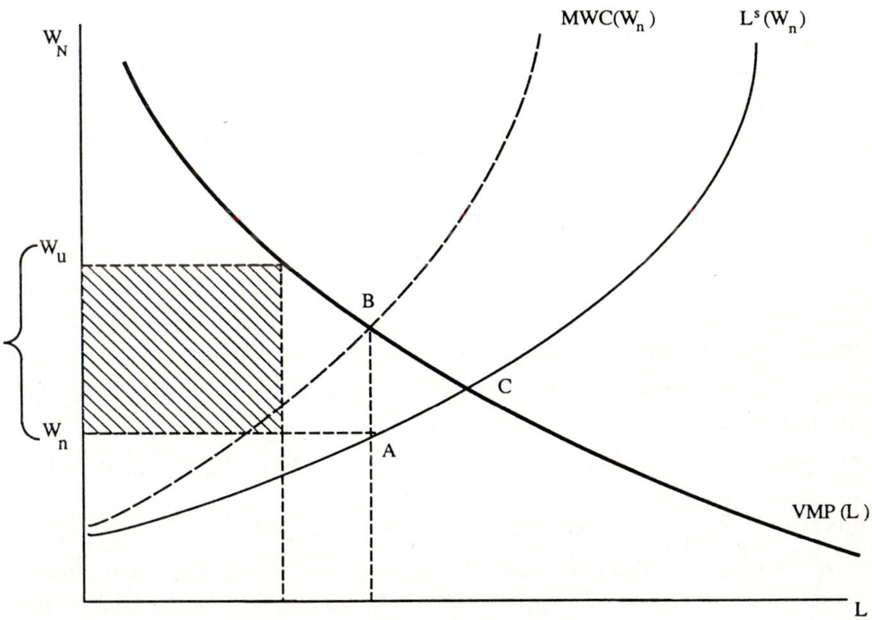

In comparing the result to unilateral wage determination by the firm, in the absence of a union, the location of $w_u$is critical. In the situation of Figure 1, unions have reached virtually nothing, since the equilibrium position (L^d, w_n) is unchanged. There is only some effect through transaction cost. Non-union members still receive w_n as in the no-union situation, and they still have somehow to negotiate this wage. Union members receive this non-union wage w_n as their union wage $w_u$minus union dues ∂, and do not have to negotiate for their wage. So, union members gain the transaction cost, as the union cost ∂ is paid out of the firm's surplus.

Now suppose, negotiations set a union wage in the range (w_n w_n + AB). Then, the firm will want to hire union labor (at constant marginal wage cost) up to the intersection of this wage rate and the VMP curve. From that volume of labor on, the marginal wage cost (of non-union members) is always above VMP and the firm will not hire any non-union labor. A wage intersecting $w_n(L)$ between A and C would lead to excess demand for union labor: the intersection of the wage with the VMP curve occurs at higher volume of labor. Similarly, a wage intersecting VMP between C and B would lead to excess supply. This suggests that an equilibrium may be established close to C, that is, at an employment volume where the gap between L_s and VMP just equals ∂ The size of this gap is dependent on the number of union members, as one may expect economies of scale here. With L^d large, the gap may be small. In such an equilibrium, all the firm's workers are union members, voluntarily. This case is a step forward compared to the unilateral no-union situation where the monopolistic firm would set an equilibrium at point B (VMP = MWC. The potential gains in the welfare triangle are fully captured (given inevitable transaction cost) and in fact the result is Pareto-optimal. Both wages and employment have increased relative to the unilateral situation.

It is important to compare this result to the literature. Oswald (1985) in a survey of trade union theory, distinguishes two main models in the literature. Model 1 is the monopoly model, in which a monopoly labor union, with exogenous membership can unilaterally fix the wage rate. Employment in the industry follows as all the (small) firms take the wage rate as given and hire labor according to their demand curve. The union then has to decide on the wage rate, and is assumed to maximize a utility function in the wage rate, volume of employment and value of non-employment. As with all monopolies, the result is not Pareto-efficient. Model 2 starts right-away from the assumption of efficient bargaining: parties will always settle at a point on the contract curve and will only bargain to determine which of these points is chosen. Hence the result is efficient by assumption.

The result outlined above is quite attractive. Introducing a union as a countervailing power to dominant firms leads to Pareto improvements and thus seems worthy of government support. The result is crucially dependent on the assumed behavior of workers and unions. Workers only judge unions by the wage gain, and equilibrium inevitably involves equal net wages. Unions aim for a job in the large firm, at the higher wage rate, for all their members and this deviates from the assumption of utility maximization referred to above. Unions are rather powerless if the membership decision is made solely on the basis of the wage differential, unless they could limit membership and obtain employment contracts with the firm. But that would lead to deviations from the equilibrium outcome near C in Figure 1 and involve efficiency losses. Government support for such deals seems unattractive.

The transaction cost of the union ∂ is essential in locating the new equilibrium: with large ∂ , the spread between w_u and w_n will be larger than BA, and no gain is made, with small ∂ the gains above are realized. Hence, this model predicts welfare gain from the introduction of the union as long as the cost of the union in obtaining wage settlements (transaction cost) is smaller than BA, that is, the difference between the supply wage and VMP at the intersection of VMP and marginal wage cost. Hence, competitive pressures on the union to keep these cost low are important for the nature of the result. But even efficiently run unions cannot prevent the dependence of the cost on the number of members: ∂ will fall with L. The absence of unions in some sectors may thus be explained from too small a basis to realize a gain.

It was assumed above that the sector also contains a number of small wage-taking firms. If the union cost ∂ is smaller than BA, the wage rate increases compared to the no-union case and hence, employment in these firms is reduced. In fact then, employment is transferred from these small firms to the large firm. This does not affect the welfare theoretic evaluation however: it's another manifestation of the welfare improvement through labor relocations to a more productive firm[2].

The next step is to analyze an institutional arrangement where the union wage is legally enforced on all workers and firms in the relevant branch of economic activity. Such *general enforcement* ('algemeen verbindend verklaring') is typical in The Netherlands, due to two laws. A law of 1927 enforces collective agreement on all workers in the firm signing the agreement. A law of 1937 authorizes the Minister of Social Affairs to enforce a collective agreement on all firms in the industry to which the bargaining parties belong.

[2] If the large firm is not a price taker in the product market, the shift may still be too small, as $P\partial Q/\partial L > \partial(PQ)/\partial L$.

General enforcement is applied as a matter of routine nowadays and its consequences are therefore worth studying.

General enforcement has mainly effect on the distribution of transaction cost. Since wages are alike for union and non-union members, the decisions on labor supply and union membership are separated. Labor supply responds to the collectively agreed ('union') wage and union membership becomes a consumption good. If the collectively agreed wage rate is a binding standard wage rate, the analysis of its effect is not different from the one given above. Unions will raise the wage above the unilateral level w_n and the firm will increase employment, since marginal wage cost is now equal to the wage rate. Equilibrium defined as zero excess demand is located at point C, where the full welfare gains are captured[3]. But now, the transaction cost (union dues) will be borne only by those who voluntarily subscribe, without any (visible) gain in wages. Within the present analysis, it is not clear if that has any efficiency cost. Even a small membership may be sufficient to support a union that can twist the firm's marginal wage cost into a flat curve, and lead to equilibrium in point C. In that case, the general enforcement has only enforced an unfair distribution of the transaction cost. But it is quite possible that unions may not be successfully organized, if the potential membership is too small because of this free ridership. This might be relevant for some sectors where unions are traditionally absent. A true test on this prediction would be to compare unionization in comparable sectors across countries with different institutional arrangements, in particular by comparing Holland to countries without general enforcement. This section suggests other empirical research as well. For example, the hypothesis on equilibrium labor union membership can be tested in countries where unions only negotiate for their members and where conditions vary across sectors of the economy. The equilibrium thesis can be expanded to state that in equilibrium, union dues will be equal to the sum of the wage gain and the imputed value of the other union services (insurance, legal support, etc.). However, since unions deal with more elements of labor relations than wages (working conditions, layoff rules, etc.) further development of the model would be needed.

Turning to the key question of government policies, it would seem that the Dutch rule of general enforcement without compulsory contribution to union

---

[3] The analysis leads to the same equilibrium point if the collective wage rate is a minimum rate. Marginal wage cost then jumps back to the old MWC-curve at the point where w intersects with the supply curve. The union would then needlessly forego gains if the wage is not set at point C.

funds is an inconsistent policy. General enforcement, even with compulsory union dues, is not supported by the present analysis. Whereas support for unions, as a countervailing power to monopsonistic firms, enhances efficiency, support for monopoly elements in the union position (exclusivity) is not warranted, and might even be banned on account of efficiency losses. But it should be pointed out that these conclusions are quite preliminary, as they are based on very simple analysis of union behavior, in a simple environment. Unions are not well understood, and the environment should be expanded to cover richer worlds (in particular worlds with uncertainty).

Information and labor market brokerage

A very fundamental assumption shaping the construct of a perfect market relates to information. To achieve efficiency, it is vital that market parties are well informed about the conditions under which supply and demand are available. Collecting information has a cost and it is easy to see that there are important economies of scale in generating and disseminating information about present and future, expected, conditions in specific labor markets of a rather general character. Average pay rates, the nature of jobs and their requirements, foreseeable shifts in demand and supply schedules: it is efficient if such information is produced by a specialized agency, devoting specialized resources rather than have it, haphazardly, produced by each individual in need of it. Moreover, such information, once produced, has the character of a public good. Hence, from the point of view of labor market efficiency, there is a raison d'être for some collective arrangement. If an agreement among labor market parties or their associations to establish such an institution is not forthcoming, there are good reasons for the government to step in and correct for this failure.

The efficiency argument is not very compelling for the establishment of government employment agencies. Why should the government deal with matching demand and supply in the labor market, and leave, e.g., the housing market to private brokerage? Centralizing supply and demand into one institution generates efficiency gains if the commodity is homogeneous and the institution also provides for the setting of the market price. This holds for the cases where actual auctions or exchanges are established, often with a ruling that forbids trade outside the exchange. But generally, labor is too heterogeneous to sell it in an auction. And then one might leave the brokerage to private firms.

Public employment service seems to be motivated mainly by two arguments: the distributional argument and the link with unemployment benefits.

Job search by individuals and firms' hiring activities often use informal networks, such as communication through friends and relatives, and there is evidence that disadvantaged groups in the labor market are poorly served by such networks (Addison & Siebert, 1979, p.180). In nineteenth century Holland, private labor market brokers ('placers') operated and it is alleged that this was to the disadvantage of workers, who often had to accept rather unfavorable conditions. The establishment of 'employment exchanges', first as a private initiative, later as a government activity, was a reaction to this situation (De Galan & Van Miltenburg, 1985, p. 178). It seems quite likely that the nineteenth century situation had much to do with the low level of development of the working class in those days and the effect of private brokerage would certainly be different in our time.

One might perhaps deduce the rule (still arguing only on efficiency grounds) that labor market brokerage (job placement service) might be left to private agencies and that the government may step in for those cases where such brokerage would no be forthcoming. It's hard to predict the absence of such brokerage for particular categories, even for the 'disadvantaged'. Efficiency considerations may indeed point to an optimum where information specific to individuals and to firms is produced by a combination of informal networks, private activities of individuals and firms and private labor market brokers. Perhaps some gaps may be left to be filled by the government, but they are hard to predict.

The Dutch institutional arrangement provides for much like a monopoly on labor market brokerage by a government employment agency: assisting in labor market search with the intention to make a profit is illegal without government permission since 1930 (De Galan & Van Miltenburg, 1985, p 105); permission is only given for a limited number of cases. Entitlement to unemployment benefits requires registration at the Employment Service. Since 1984, firms are obliged to register their vacancies with the Employment Service (De Galan & Van Miltenburg, 1985, p 207). There may be good reasons for these rulings in the domain of distributive justice, or in the advantage of reliable statistical information about the labor market. But it is not clear that these rulings serve efficiency. International evidence suggests that formal job search methods (such as through the Employment Service) lead to less satisfactory matches and to quicker separations than informal search (the network of friends and relatives). (Addison & Siebert, 1979, p 180). Evaluations of the functioning of the Dutch Employment Service also point to many deficiencies (De Galan & Van Miltenburg, 1985, section 5.4.1). The Dutch policy has been to strengthen the role of the Employment Service (obligatory vacancy registration), to improve the organizational structure of the service and to transfer the responsibility from the government to labor unions and employers' associations. On efficiency grounds, admission of private brokers would be another option worth considering.

Free entry and labor quality

The "blessings of a free market" can only be obtained if entry into promising sectors is free. Barriers to entry of qualified individuals into attractive market segments leads to distortion of the efficiency conditions and to monopoly gains for incumbents. The emphasis on free entry of qualified individuals is important here. Under imperfect information on qualities of individuals or their products, it is a risky decision to decide on buying or hiring. In many cases, labor services are 'experience goods' rather than 'inspection goods': only after experience, i.e. after the acquisition, the true qualities are revealed. Hence, consumers or firms may be disappointed and in some cases the cost may be quite high (such as with errors by unqualified medical specialists). In many cases, the problem is alleviated by career sequences: individuals are only trusted to the risky, far-reaching decisions at the top after they have proven themselves in related, preparatory positions. Internal labor markets can thus be understood as an efficient institution to deal with uncertainty about worker qualities.

In some cases, the equivalent of an internal labor market is not available, as a particular client only infrequently enters the market. This applies for example to the service of the professions.In these cases, often the government steps in by setting quality standards and outlawing activity by unqualified suppliers. Free entry is limited to protect the consumer from substandard quality provision. One might have instead trusted on the regulatory effect of reputation or on product (and service) liability upheld by the legal system. This may be too costly as quality should be upheld by the spread of information about suppliers, while poor qulities may persist in the meantime due to imperfect information. Then, enforced quality standards may be an efficient shortcut.

In the case of government enforcement, much depends on the details of the regulation. If qualified individuals have an interest in revealing and controlling quality levels, they may unite and create a labelling organization. However, once they have done this, the risk of monopolization (or cartellization) is large. The risk is increased if the government sanctions such labelling, and leaves the implementation to the organization. The best known example of such an inefficient structure, well documented, is medical practice (Kessel, 1958). The proper arrangement would be to have the government set, control and inspect the standards and to have otherwise free entry. Despite the wide recognition of the inefficiency in arrangements in favor of medical practice, it is remarkable that the arrangements are persistent and expanding, at least in The Netherlands. Physiotherapists, qualified by education, are denied freedom to start their own practice. Regulatory committees on general medical practice, deriving their authority from the City Council, are made up, indeed, of the locally established practitioners but do not include representatives from consumers or the general public.

Job design as market failure

Under conditions, perfect competition can establish Pareto-optimal allocation in the labor market. For a given set of jobs, characterized by job requirements and working conditions, and a given set of individuals, characterized by given productive capabilities and job preferences, free competition establishes an efficient allocation of heterogeneous individuals to heterogeneous jobs. Flexible wages are instrumental in this allocative process and in equilibrium reflect both productivity conditions and worker preferences.

The idyllic picture changes once it is recognized that jobs are not fixed entities, with characteristics exogenously determined. Commonly, there is a choice as to how particular jobs are created as combinations of activities to be performed and hence, on the levels of individual qualities that are best suited for such a job. Similarly, the environment in which the job has to be accomplished is open to variation: variables like noise, heat, toxic conditions, risks of sickness and death can be affected by deliberate economic choices. In fact then, job requirements (what sort of job will be designed) and working conditions are endogenous to the economic system. Hence one may inquire into the conditions for a Pareto-efficient outcome, and see how they can be realized.

If one writes down the conditions for Pareto-efficiency in job requirements and working conditions, one notes immediately that these conditions are analytically equivalent to those of pure public goods (Hartog, 1981). It is easy to provide the intuition for this result. The level of job requirements (the degree of difficulty or complexity of a particular job) that is set in a job applies to all workers in that job. Similarly, the working conditions chosen apply to all workers alike in a job and often in more than one job, as they pertain to the situation in the factory or the office.

The Invisible Hand fails in the case of public goods. A potential escape would be in organizing a perfect sorting of workers of identical preferences about job requirements and working conditions. In such a case, the efficient match between worker preferences and technical trade-offs can be made within each firm for its preference-wise homogeneous workforce. This would establish the equivalence of the Tiebout hypothesis on local public goods in the labor market. But such 'voting with the feet' may be expected to fail because of insufficient degrees of freedom: a firm for each set of preferences is certainly an unlikely outcome. Even less realistic would be the analytical solution of a Lindahl-equilibrium where wages are individualized, to reflect the individuals' valuation of the working conditions in their job.

If the market fails, then a different method to coordinate preferences and possibilities is needed. In Dutch labor relations, unions have a long tradition in centralized negotiations with employer associations. Emphasis on activities within the individual firm is only fairly recent, but certainly can use some support on efficiency grounds. The Law on Working Conditions, enacted in 1980 gives such support. It provides for compulsory consultations between management and workers about arrangements affecting health, safety and well-being of workers. It seems a better method than attempting to regulate working conditions by law, as in the case of many safety prescriptions, unless the minimum safety standard is clear, or firms are too small to be subject to the Law on Working Conditions. Central prescriptions by the government would necessarily be based on imperfect information and may be too general for the conditions of specific firms. Direct negtioations, under conditions, at the level of the firm, may lead to efficient bargaining outcomes.

Social Security

Social security, in the broad sense of guaranteeing decent living conditions to all members of society, has a large if not dominant branch related to the labor market. Both contributions and benefits are dependent on the labor market position of the individual. Social security therefore works in a number of ways such as to perpetuate an individual's relative income position in cases where this position would be threatened by causes exogenous to the individual (unemployment, disability). While social security is largely motivated by distributional arguments, there are also important efficiency considerations: correction for market failure is certainly a relevant interpretation.

It is well known that the Invisible Hand cannot deal adequately with uncertainty. Markets are not complete and contingent contracts are virtually absent. The Arrow-Debreu world is more informative about market failure than as a device to let a market system successfully cope with uncertainty. Within the labor market, the allocation of risk between workers and employers is an important issue. Usually, workers are assumed to be risk-averse and firms are assumed risk-neutral. In that case, the optimal arrangement is to let firms insure workers against risk. If however, the effects of exogenous risk mingle with information on individuals efforts, this moral hazard calls for risksharing between workers and firms.

Moral hazard may lead to market failure and thereby to a potential for efficiency enhancing government intervention. Unemployment insurance is a relevant case here. Private unemployment insurance, by profit-seeking firms, as far as I know, does not exist anywhere. Around the turn of the century, labor unions sometimes (not always) provided for unemployment compensation. The main motivation for the unions was to provide a floor in the wage level, i.e. to curb wage pressure from unemployment. Some unions in fact subsidized unemployed workers to search for a job in another region, through their 'travel fund' (De Jong, 1956, 95-97). The absence of private unemployment insurance can indeed be explained from the strong effect of the unemployed worker's effort to find a new job and hence, the need for costly monitoring of this effort. If the government creates an unemployment insurance (and makes it compulsory to prevent the problems of adverse selection; cf Rothschild & Stiglitz,1976, or Akerlof, 1970), it faces this problem of moral hazard. The benefit level should compromise between providing adequate insurance, calling for a high benefit relative to the former wage and the need to stimulate the unemployed's search effort, through a low relative benefit level. The financial incentive to search can to some extent be replaced by direct monitoring of search activity and this indeed favors a link between government provided employment service and unemployment insurance. Note that since relative benefit levels should provide a stimulus for job search, the stimulus may be stronger if the pay-off to search is higher. Relative benefit levels may therefore vary positively with the level of unemployment. Actual policies, however, tend to generate an inverse relationship.

The conclusion on the unemployment insurance can be generalized to insurance against earnings loss from other causes, such as sickness and disability. The problems of moral hazard and adverse selection prevent the market from providing optimal insurance packages. At best, one might expect low coverage and restriction to cases with easy eligibility criteria. But of course, the government cannot escape the fundamental problems of the optimum benefit level: the Dutch experience and surrounding discussions suggest that these are not easily solved.

In case of unemployment compensation there is the added effect on market wage flexibility. Structural shifts in the economy (as now occur due to international factors and to the information processing revolution) create unemployment and can only be countered with employment in other sectors. High and extended benefit levels prevent downward wage flexibility and limit individual transfers to different sectors, However, it is impossible, on efficiency grounds, to determine the optimal benefit level without the availability of large amounts of information on the economy.

A provisional summing up

In the neoclassical tradition, the distinction between the domains of efficiency and of equity is vital. This section has attempted a little survey on structural government policies evaluated from the efficiency criterion. The efficiency argument supports a number of government interventions: the introduction and legal support for labor unions, the provision of information on general labor market conditions, support of quality standards as a condition for market entry, corrective measures for market failure for job design and working conditions and providing for insurance against earnings losses from unemployment, sickness or disability. The efficiency argument does not support general enforcement of collective agreements and leads to reservations on public employment service and on generally enforced rules about working conditions. In the provision of social security, the government faces the difficult problem of setting optimal benefit levels and has to acknowledge the effect on wage flexibility. The question of optimum policy as a specific, quantitative question on the desired value of a parameter, is much harder to answer than the structural questions, which usually require no knowledge of parameter values.

Equity

Efficiency is established if the actual allocation lies within the opportunity set provided by true preferences and technological conditions and if no gainful substitutions are possible. Such an allocation depends on the initial endowments of individuals. If one allocation is preferred over another, one may make the market generate this outcome by properly redistributing wealth. If lump sum wealth transfers were possible, this would be the end of the economist's tale. Since they are not available in sufficient scope, the trade-off between equity and efficiency is born, to the delight of the economics profession. Individual preferences on social equity presumably can take any form and the economist could advise on measures to move towards any desired distribution. Here, however, it will be assumed that ceteris paribus, less inequality is preferred to more.

Affecting the distribution of earnings generating characteristics.

As stated in the introduction to this section, the neoclassical approach favors the combination of smooth markets and an adequate distribution of initial wealth in reaching out for desirable allocations. In the realm of labor market policies, this makes the distribution of individual earnings generating characteristics a policy target. 'Initial wealth' or endowment policies should improve the distribution of starting positions, market structure policies (as discussed in the second section) should realize the associated optimal allocation. Initial wealth in the labor market refers to skills, created in school, in training programs and in learning-by-doing. Hence, skill-augmenting policies are vital in the promotion of equity. The egalitarian preference above unequivocally would support a reduction of inequity in the distribution of initial wealth.

Schooling and training policies now find their motivation in two sets of arguments. The efficiency criterion promotes the optimal development of individual capabilities, as one specification of Pareto-efficiency. This leads to the advice to correct for capital market imperfection and improve conditions for individuals to invest in their skill development. Conceptually, it involves the aim to fully develop individuals' potential and it may lead to large inequalities. The equity criterion promotes the reduction in the dispersion of initial wealth. It leads to the suggestion to subsidize those of low marketable talent at the cost of those of high marketable talent. Actual policies may be evaluated against these two criteria and their implications.

Formal education is heavily subsidized in The Netherlands, with tuition perhaps never surpassing 10% of the average cost per student. Most government cost-of-living support is given as a grant, either in cash to the student or as a tax-credit to the parents. Even without detailed investigation, it seems safe to assume that in demand for formal education, capital market imperfections are adequately corrected: anyone capable of extended education and short of parental wealth, can obtain government support at interest rates not above the going market rate. In fact, it is quite likely that subsidies have gone beyond market corrections and involve substantial redistribution. It is an interesting topic for empirical research to determine whether this redistribution is in the proper direction. Is it the least advantaged, those with meager labor market endowments that benefit beyond efficiency correction, or is it the advantaged that are further advantaged? Such research would have to investigate lifetime subsidies, distinguished by ability levels. Available evidence suggests that abler individuals benefit more from extended education. Since those taking longer educations obtain more subsidies, it is not impossible that actual educational subsidy policies have a perverse effect. If so, a truly egalitarian 'initial wealth' policy would call for capital transfers to those who are unable to benefit from extended education.

Schooling of entrants is not limited to formal general education. Part of the government school system takes the form of vocational training for particular occupations. In other cases, the specific vocational training is obtained within a firm, or in a facility organized by an industry (jointly operated by workers' and employers' associations), sometimes in a joint effort with the government. In general, it is quite difficult to draw the line between general education and specific vocational training. There seems to be consensus that general education (serving more purposes than just labor market preparation) is a government task and that training for specific occupations is the responsibility of workers and employers. In abstracto, these are fairly clear principles, but reality is quite mixed. Training for particular occupations, from the point of view of firms utilizing this kind of labor, may contain large portions of general training, or general human capital: skills that are equally useful in all firms of an industry. In such cases, the incentives for firms to provide the training are limited and market failure may easily arise. If the required training facilities are not organized by the joint partners in an industry, the government may stimulate the establishment of such a facility. Such facilities should be closely linked to the actual practices of the trade. Recent experience in The Netherlands has demonstrated that institutions separated from such practice easily lead to emphasis on the wrong skills. Efficiency strongly favors a close institutional relation between training and work.

As to the financing of vocational training, the necessity for the government to correct for capital market imperfections is usually absent: firms have access to capital markets and can work out financial arrangements to find a solution for sharing of cost and benefits between workers and employers. Nevertheless, equity considerations may come in again. To improve the initial wealth distribution, governments may subsidize vocational training for the disadvantaged. This argument may gain strength if vocational training for the advantaged is also subsidized, as e.g. the academic training of engineers.

Finally there is the retraining of those whose skills have become obsolete. At present, retraining is mostly concentrated among the unemployed. However, with the high pace of technological change that is now common, efficient policies may anticipate such obsolescence and create institutions for recurrent education. The latter are not principally different from educations treated above. Retraining of unemployed is different, as unemployment beyond a few months often signals a disadvantaged labor market position (this may not be true in case of cyclical unemployment and too generous benefits). The efficiency argument favors support of the unemployed, as they will generally have poor capital market access. Unemployed in the low end of the wealth distribution may receive such support as a grant to counter their disadvantaged status. It is quite important though, to evaluate these policies within the complete set of policies dealing with unemployment benefit entitlements (see below).

Affecting the price of labor.

Since endowment policies are generally insufficient to achieve the desired distribution of welfare, prices have also become a policy instrument. Within the usual neoclassical framework this is a sin, but it is worth recalling that the condemnation of redistribution through prices depends crucially on the supposition that egalitarian goals are formulated in terms of individual welfare. As soon as distributive preferences are formulated in terms of specific commodities, affecting the price of the commodities or the commodity distribution itself becomes an efficient policy (cf. Tobin 1970). Concern for workplace safety standards is a case in point. If low paid workers are unable to buy better working conditions, the efficient policy is to improve their endowments, enabling them to buy the working conditions they desire. However, in most developed countries it is common practice to impose safety standards by legislation. The argument for doing so has been succinctly summarized by Frank Taussig, in 1915:

"It was not the miners who made the effort for compulsory use of the safety lamp, but the men of science and the social reformers. The rank and file of men are singularly indifferent to danger, or at least singularly slow in taking precautions against danger. Whether it be from bravado, or recklessness, or simple lack of intelligence, the fact is that measures for preventing accidents must commonly be enforced upon them. So it is as to unhealthy trades. Those engaged in them seldom protest but risk their health with apparent inability to visualize the inevitable future. The initiative in legislation on all these matters has come mainly from social reformers, men of science, physicians". (Taussig, 1915, pp. 289-290).

Clearly, there is an important issue whether only individual preferences should count or whether 'social reformers' should impose their preferences. It is also an interesting issue whether such imposition is a case of paternalism (deciding on what is best for someone else) or a case of altruism, as Taussig calls it. This will depend on the incidence of the cost of the improvements. If the workers wholly pay for their imposed working conditions, it is paternalism, if the cost wholly enters the product price, it is altruism to the extent that social reformers are the consumers of the product, mixed with paternalism on other consumers of this product. One might argue that in Taussig's days, when labor's position was quite weak, there was more reason for intervention than in our day, when labor's position is much stronger and workers are better informed. However, if anything, legislation is more extended in our day than in Taussig's.

Redistribution through prices has become an important policy: income (and wage) taxes are high and progressive. Certainly in The Netherlands, the marginal tax rate has reached substantial levels. Calculations for the United States, with lower marginal tax rates, suggest high excess burdens. For example, Ballard et al (1984) show a marginal excess burden from raising extra revenue from the income tax of 31 cents per additional dollar of revenue (Table 4, p 136, using their preferred elasticity values). Stuart (1984) in a much simpler model distinguishing only a taxed and an untaxed (informal and household) sector, estimates the marginal excess burden at over 20 cents of welfare loss per additional dollar of tax revenue. In a paper specifically aiming at measuring the equity efficiency trade-off, Browning and Johnson (1984) calculate that for each additional dollar gained by the lower quintiles of the income distribution, the joint loss for the three highest quintiles is $9.51. If they take into account the value of leisure, by calculating the equivalent variation, the cost to the top-3 quintiles reduces to $3.49 per dollar of income equivalent gain at the bottom, still a large amount.

In view of these high deadweight losses, one is led to think about alternatives, and investigate if it is feasible to design a tax structure that moves closer to the ideal of lump sum taxes. Suppose, instead of taxing earnings, one would tax earnings generating characteristics. In its extreme form, this idea has been promoted by Tinbergen as a tax on talent (measured through IQ scores, etc) and in a less extreme form as a tax that is geared to an earnings structure acknowledging worker qualities and job requirements (Tinbergen, 1975). It would be worthwhile to start thinking about an income tax that fixes annual tax liabilities on such characteristics as e.g. education, age and occupation, as a fixed sum independent of actual earnings. Surely, there would be many complications, but equally surely, there would be substantial gains in (short-run) efficiency. This is not the place to fully develop the idea, but it seems worthy of additional analysis.

The most direct price policy is the imposition of a minimum wage. Analytically, there is no need for an extended discussion, as undergraduate textbooks sufficiently point out the employment loss that will follow the imposition of a minimum wage rate above market equilibrium. Neither employment effects nor wage effects are restricted to the initially subminimum category, as substitution effects may transfer part of the impact to other labor markets.

Affecting the allocation of risk

The standard Invisible Hand Theorems are commonly applied to allocation in a static world without uncertainty. The Arrow-Debreu construction of contingent markets is not taken as a realistic case on which to found one's confidence in the qualities of a market system. The static case does have an implication for market flexibility, though. An allocation can only be efficient relative to the given circumstances in terms of endowments, preferences, and production technologies. Hence, if these exogenous variables change, the allocation should change, thereby bestowing the effects of such changes on individuals. Changes in preferences or technologies can dramatically change the relative scarcity of endowments. It will generally not be efficient to protect individuals from systematic, long-run changes in relative scarcities, although there may be compelling reasons on equity grounds.

Stochastic variations in an otherwise stable environment lend themselves to insurance however. Socially diversifiable risks from stochastic components in product demand, production technologies etc may be shifted from risk-averse agents to risk-neutral or at least less risk-averse agents. This is the basis for common insurances, but it is also postulated to be relevant for the relations between labor market parties. This is investigated in implicit contract theory (see the survey by Rosen, 1985). The simplest case arises if there is 'common knowledge'. The result of efforts in the firm has random components due to demand uncertainty and shocks to technology and other input supplies, beyond the control of the contracting parties. All relevant information is available to all parties. Then, to the extent that workers and firms have different taste for risk, the labor contract can provide for a trade of such risks. The contract, implicitly, specifies the wage and the amount of labor utilized dependent on the realization of the stochastic component. It is in fact a state-contingent contract.

The analytical approach of contract theory is different from usual analyses within the neoclassical framework: implications are sought from the basic postulate that the implicit contract is Pareto-optimal. It is assumed that the relations between employees and firms can be treated as if they follow from maximizing worker utility subject to the firm's profit constraint. There is virtually no discussion of market conditions, but the implicit assumption is that competition will ensure such a result. The contract specifies wages and employment for all states of nature and interesting conclusions on this dependence are summarized in Rosen's survey. For example, if worker preferences are strongly separable in consumption and leisure, the optimal contract has a fixed wage rate, independent of the stochastic variations. If the income effect on demand for labor is zero, the contract fully assures ex post utility, with compensating movements in consumption (real wage) and working time (which increases in more favorable states of nature). Rosen rightly emphasizes that 'implicit contract markets do not imply real wage rigidity for uninsurable risks' (p. 1154). Shocks that equally affect the entire economy or permanent real shifts in relative scarcities will not (and should not) be insured, but in practice it will not be easy to recognize an outcome as the particular draw from a given urn and the installation of a new urn, i.e. real changes in relative scarcities. Hence, it would seem that in a dynamic world the contracts that yield Pareto-optimal allocation of risk in a stationary environment create rigidities to the extent that the diagnosis of changing fortunes is erroneous.

The situation is complicated in case of asymmetric information rather than 'common knowledge'. Rosen extensively treats the case where only the firm is informed on the realization of the stochastic variable (e.g. in product demand), while the worker is ignorant. Since much information about the firm's position is easily dissipated, it would seem that asymmetry on the other side is much more likely: the firm cannot immediately decompose output fluctuations into the effect of worker effort and uncontrollable random events. This creates the moral hazard problem, which calls for monitoring the workers and for coinsurance. Even though optimal allocation of risk would completely insure the worker against these random events, moral hazard calls for a contract that has the worker bear at least part of the risk, to stimulate efforts.

The allocation of risk, and the nature of the labor contract is a vital political issue, but the analytical framework to handle the problem is by no means clear. For example, the discussion on the relative flexibility of labor markets in Europe and the U.S. (the 'Eurosclerosis'; see Ellman, 1985), turns to a large extent on the effects of different incidence of risk on the dynamic performance of the economy. In Holland, reward systems in overwhelming majority pay for time worked, without relation to performance (it has the lowest incidence of payment by performance evaluation in Europe). Is this a case for government intervention? And if so, how? As stated, the analytical framework is not well developed in this area. The government does affect the market allocation of risk, at least in The Netherlands, through its labor legislation, an important element here is the legislation on lay-offs. Lay-offs require the consent of the Public Employment Service. The termination period can amount up to 6 months, and be increased by another month in case of collective lay-offs (measures for more flexible lay-offs are in preparation). There are no obvious efficiency grounds for a test on dismissal by the Public Employment Service. The termination period may be valuable in conjunction with an unemployment system where contributions of the firm are not related to the firm's record of dismissals: it will prevent firms from utilizing the unemployment benefit subsidies in adjusting to short-run demand fluctuations. It is not clear however, how long the notification period should be to prevent this, and it may be that experience-rated unemployment contributions are more efficient. In all, it seems likely that distributive motives are more important than efficiency motives in developing legilation that shelters the worker form shocks on the product market.

The allocation of risk is most substantially affected by the system of social security. Social security essentially protects individuals' earnings position as obtained in the labor market. Earnings losses due to unemployment, disability and sickness are made up by collective insurances. In deciding on the benefit levels the moral hazard problem encountered above returns: optimal allocation of risk through full insurance is countered by the need to limit the 'damage' with financial incentives. Fostered by the prosperity of the 'sixties' (and the neglect of adverse behavioral responses), a lenient and generous social security system has been created. Eligibility rules and benefit levels seem to have been inspired more by equity considerations than by efficiency. Stated otherwise: equity has been bought at an efficiency cost that is now considered too high by many and substantial trimming of the social security system is well under way (see Haveman, 1985 for an evaluation). Insight in the trade-off between efficiency and equity that is relevant in those situations is still very sketchy, however.

Concluding remarks

This paper has attempted to outline a survey of labor market policies within the framework of the neoclassical Trinity: stimulate competitive forces, correct for market failure and improve the distribution. Quite in line with the main emphasis of welfare economics, analysis is easiest in a deterministic static world. This analysis mainly needs detailed empirical work to get useful insight in the trade-off between equity and efficiency.

It appears that in the dynamic, uncertain world, analysis is not so easy. The emerging literature on contract theory is very promising, but has not yet reached the stage where clear policy implications can be derived. Here, much more analytical work is needed. Just as in the deterministic case, one would like to compress the problem to a choice between efficiency and equity, preferably expressed in some clear numbers. After all, in the neoclassical perspective it is not meaningful to judge policies as a 'success or a failure' (except for isolated evaluation of target effectiveness of a particular policy): the best one can do is to calculate the efficiency 'price-tag' of egalitarian policies.

References

Addison, J.T. and W. Stanley Siebert (1979), *The market for labor: an analytical treatment*, Goodyear, Santa Monica, California.

Akerlof, G.A. (1970), The market for 'lemons': quality, uncertainty and the market mechanism, *Quarterly Journal of Economics* 84, 488-500

Ballard, C.L., J.B. Shoven and J.W. Whalley (1984), General equilibrium computations of marginal welfare costs of taxes in the United States, *American Economic Review*. 75(1). 128-138

Browning, E.K. and W.R. Johnson (1984), The trade-off between equality and efficiency. *Journal of Political Economy*. 92(2), 175-203

Ellman, M.J. (1985), Eurosclerosis?, Research Memorandum 8506, University of Amsterdam, Department of Economics.

De Galan, C en van Miltenburg (1985) *Economie van de arbeid*. Alphen: Samsom.

Hartog, J, (1981), Capabilities, allocation and wages, rapport no 10, Arbeidsmarkt en Beloningsstruktuur, Den Haag: NPAO.

Hartog, J. (1984), On the efficiency of labor markets, *De Economist*, 132(3), 279-299

Hartog, J, and J.M.M. Ritzen (1986), Theoretical issues in size income distribution policy, *International Economic Association* volume on Incomes policy, to be published.

Haveman, R.H.(1985), *Does the welfare state increase welfare*? Leiden: Stenfert Kroese.

Jong, Fr. de (1956), *Om de plaats van de arbeid*, Amsterdam: Arbeiders pers.

Kessel, R. (1958), Price discrimination in medicine, *Journal of Law and Economics*, October 1958.
Oswald, A.J. (1985) The economic theory of trade unions: an introductory survey, *Scandinavian Journal of Economics*, 87(2), 160-193.
Rosen, S. (1985), Implicit contracts, *Journal of Economic Literature*, XXIII (3), 1144 - 1175.
Rothschild, M. and J. Stiglitz(1976), Equilibrium in competitive insurance markets: and essay on the economics of imperfect information. *Quarterly Journal of Economics*. 90. 629-649.
Stuart, C.(1984). Welfare costs per dollar of additional tax revenue in the United States. *American Economic Review* 74(3), 352-362
Taussig, F.W. (1915) *Principles of economics*, New York: Macmillan.
Tinbergen, J. (1975). *Income distribution: analysis and policies*, Amsterdam: Elsevier
Tobin, J. (1970), On limiting the domain of inequality, *Journal of Law and Economics*, XIII(2), 263-77.

Comment by Victoria Chick (University College London)

Professor Hartog's paper gives an admirably clear and full account of the obstacles to acceptance of unqualified neoclassical results concerning the labour market as a guide to 'economic policy in general and labour market policy in particular', while remaining, on the whole, within the neoclassical tradition, where departures from neoclassical assumptions are seen as imperfections. Thus, the purity of an atomistic market is sullied by union power, its flexibility is compromised by the restraining influences of legislation, and these departures from grace are taken to be the cause of difficulties unless proven otherwise.

My comments on Professor Hartog's paper are based on another tradition. Confirming the worst fears of those who see economics as a form of theology, I shall contrast his neoclassical Trinity with the approach of Keynesian fundamentalism. Keynesian fundamentalists, like the Greeks, allow a god for each significant occasion, with suitable personal characteristics. Keynesian religion is post-Kronos, after the invention of time, and it claims to share the Olympian, macroeconomic, perspective of the gods. It also understands unequal power, though in contrast to Marxists that understanding has tended to remain implicit.

First I want to deal with some implications of time. Its influence is felt immediately, for a perspective including time challenges the starting point of neoclassical labour market analysis: the auction market. The auction market begins every day *de novo*, with everyone up for employment. There is no continuity in work. Of course, there used to be markets like that, but they are rare now. This latter empirical fact is one element in Keynesian criticism of the use of this piece of analysis.

In the context of the present paper one can perhaps ask whether comparisons of labour market behaviour with and without its various 'imperfections' conducted using such a starting point are legitimate or whether they are potentially misleading. For example, continuity of employment, equity in the job, is fundamental to the existence of unions.

The other assumption of neoclassical analysis, that both demanders and suppliers of labour are 'zero-weight', also flies in the face of facts: one knows that unions began as a counterweight to the power of firms. However many of them there are, firms are never 'zero-weight'. Firms have power because they possess capital. Possessing capital, by definition they have continuity, and that continuity establishes the expected marginal value product as a reservation price in the auction market.

Labour, by contrast, only has a reservation price if it has alternative employment. When neoclassical theory was being developed, one could, I suppose, imagine the urban labour force returning to the land if the industrial wage fell below an acceptable level - as they still do, for example, in some developing countries. But in the Western economies now the only major alternatives to wage labour are housewifery or the dole. The current fashion for suggesting that self-employment is a serious alternative to wage labour is unrealistic for all but those able to muster sufficient capital, and when those do, they become firms in their own right, even if they employ no-one. Minimum wage legislation can be seen as a way of providing a reservation price which is seen as 'fair', when the reservation price indicated by alternative employment possibilities is perceived as 'too low', and exploitable by capital. Unions not only represent the continuity that the starting point of the analysis denies, but in providing strike pay to their members they alter, in the same way as unemployment benefits, the reservation wage and thus the labour supply curve. Therefore it is difficult to contrast the effects of unions with the results of the neoclassical starting point.

Indeed, Professor Hartog does not, when it comes to the point, make this contrast. His analysis presupposed a large firm which is unionized and small firms which are not. His welfare improvement does not come from the the transfer of quasi-rents from firms to workers obtained by the introduction of countervailing power (which anyway is only an unambiguous welfare gain as long as the quasi-rents of firms, or their distribution to their shareholders, are of no direct or indirect consequence), but from the transfer of employment to the more efficient large firm. This firm's greater efficiently is evidenced by its ability to pay higher wages. So we must infer that if the union did not compete them away, there *would* have been quasi-rents, contrary to the neoclassical model. Keneysian analysis would be quite happy with that. Keynesian acceptance of quasi-rents in this context illustrates again the significance of time: we say it takes longer to eliminate quasi-rents than to change wages or levels of employment, and reckon each point of the demand for labour curve to indicate a different level of quasi-rents. Furthermore we can accept both quasi-rents and a divergence of the marginal cost of hiring from the labour supply curve for small as well as large firms. (See Chick 1983, pp. 159-163.) The divergence arises from continuity of the labour force: when wages change the new wage is paid to those already in employment as well as to those newly taken on.

Another area in which the neoclassical model as a starting point may be more of a hindrance than a help is on the question of the distribution of income-earning endowments and the related questions of taxation, subsidy and legislation to counter the effects of discrimination by colour, class or sex. Neoclassical theory predicts that in pressing for a rise in their wages, members of these underclasses will 'price themselves out of the market'. But it has been shown (e.g. Zabalza and Tzannatos 1985) that experience with sex discrimination legislation in the US and UK has not revealed this effect; rather, there was a rise in both the relative wages of women compared to men and women's relative employment. This result could be attributed to an 'increased cost of indulging a taste for discrimination', à la Becker (1957), or the results of a forced 'opportunity' to discover that ascribed differences are greater than real ones. But interestingly, Zabalza and Tzannatos emphasize the costs of adjusting the workforce to the new wage structure - hiring and firing costs and the loss of morale - as reasons why no significant loss of employment of women was observed. Continuity of employment confounds neoclassical predictions.

It is a pity that amongst his excellent discussion of endowments and taxation Professor Hartog did not discuss the possibility that taxation can be used to increase pay differentials between groups with ascribed differences as well as decrease them (see Apps 1981). A tax on the capacity to generate earnings would be grossly inequitable in a society which systematically, both overtly and by psychological pressure, discourages members of its underclasses from using such capacities as they manage to acquire and rewards them relatively badly when they do make use of their capacities.

Now I come to the second major difference between a Keynesian starting point and a neoclassical one: the macroeconomic perspective. From that perspective the separation of 'labour market policy in particular' from 'economic policy in general' is seen as difficult if not impossible: the Principle of Effective Demand precludes it. It is, similarly, impossible to separate the analysis. For example, if unions or minimum wage legislation increase average wages, they do not necessarily do so at the expense of profits (if quasi-rents are allowed) and/or employment: aggregate demand may respond positively to the change. The potential interplay between aggregate demand and the labour market is perhaps most obvious in Professor Hartog's discussion of risk allocation. Keynesian thinking readily accepts implicit contract theory, as far as it goes, but the sharp contrast between random and systematic variations in demand are not enough. Keynes's analysis deals with the reactions of firms to perceived future changes in demand which are neither purely unpredictable nor permanent: i.e., cyclical variations, changes large enough and expected to persist long enough to require a response. On this, implicit contract theory unfortunately has little to say.

References

Chick, V. 1983, *Macroeconomics After Keynes*, Philip Allan, Deddington, Oxford.

Zabalza, A. and Z. Tzannatos 1985, The Effect of Britain's Anti-Discriminatory Legislation on Relative Pay and Employment, *Economic Journal* 95, September, pp. 679-699.

Becker, G.S. 1957, *The Economics of Discrimination*, University of Chicago Press, Chicago.

Apps, P. 1981, *A Theory of Inequality and Taxation*, Cambridge University Press, Cambridge.

Macroeconomic Stabilisation

PASCAL SALIN

Macro-Stabilization Policies and the Market Process

The paper begins with a discussion of the meaning of stabilization and equilibrium. It is stressed that these concepts cannot be defined but from an individualistic point of view. In fact, equilibrium prevails when individuals obtain what they wish, given the constraints they meet, among which those which depend on the existence of other people. A social equilibrium implies that all individuals in the society are in equilibrium or, in other words, that they are satisfied. Moreover, equilibrium cannot be considered as a static concept, but it is continuously changing in ways an external observer cannot know precisely.

In turn, the concept of "stabilization" is related to the efforts made by individuals to reach their prefered position at any time. However, this "individual stabilization policy" is, by itself, the object of choices between, for instance, the cost of information and its return in terms of individual equilibrium. As information cannot be perfect, each individual chooses what he considers as the "optimal variability" of the variables which are important to him. Therefore, "macroeconomic stabilization" cannot be defined without referring to individual choices and the argument against macroeconomic stabilization is parallel to the one against central planning, which has been emphasized by the Austrian tradition. By destroying the signals which help people to make their own stabilization decisions and favor the coordination of decisions between individuals, macroeconomic "stabilization" policy is, in fact, destabilizing. The ideas of the Austrian school about the role of the market as a coordination process also constitute an answer to the argument according to which "macro-stabilization" would be a "public good".

The analysis of these basic concepts makes possible a study of the business cycle according to the Austrian school. Austrians are more concerned by processes than by aggregate quantities. Thus, it is essential to make a distinction between a system of "commodity credit" and a system of "circulation credit". In the second case, banks can distribute credits which do not correspond to the true desire of people to save, i.e. to choose between the present and the future.

The desire of governments and businessmen to "stimulate" the economy induces an excessive creation of money and credit together with a decrease in the real interest rate. But this period of expansion cannot last for ever and there is necessarily a turning point where over-investment is eliminated and real interest rates better reflect the true scarcity of savings. Thus, the business cycle is the consequence of the illusions created by the government, under the pretext of a stabilization policy. This process is aggravated in our time by the more or less complete nationalization of the banking systems.

The present paper ends with some applications of the previous views on macroeconomic policy. It emphasizes the monetary and financial nature of modern economic crises. In fact, the events of the seventies and the eighties give a good illustration of the Austrian theory of the business cycle. The Austrian approach would be helpful in evaluating and criticizing all macroeconomic policies. The example of exchange rate policies is given in the present paper.

Foreword[1]

In traditional textbooks on macroeconomics and economic policy, it is usually assumed that the State has three main roles: allocation of resources, redistribution of wealth and macroeconomic stabilization. In recent years, economic theory, as well as practical experiences, have made it clearer and clearer that the allocative role was better played by the market. Ideas have also changed as regards the redistributive role: the very concept of social justice is disputed[2], and transfers appear mainly as instruments used by politicians on the "political market"[3] to get or maintain their personal positions. But less people, even among those who consider the market to be the best solution to the problem of "social cooperation", would accept the idea that

---

[1] I want to thank François Guillaumat for very valuable remarks on a previous version of the present paper.

[2] See Friedrich Hayek, *Law, Legislation and Liberty*, volume 2, *The Mirage of Social Justice*, London, Routledge & Keagan Paul, 1976.

[3] The term "political market" has been popularized by the public choice school (James Buchanan and Gordon Tullock). However, one must be cautious in using it, since the political market has important differences with what is usually called a market:on the "political market" politicians exchange goods which do not belong to them, for instance public privileges and so-called "public services", against votes.

macro-stabilization is not a specific responsibility of the State. It seems that macro-stabilization has some of the characteristics of a "public good", and can thus best be produced by the State. The present paper tries to explain why such a view is wrong.

In the first section of the paper we discuss the meaning of stabilization and we stress that one cannot speak of "macro-stabilization" without a clear understanding of this term on the micro-level. All individuals are continuously implementing activities to reach their desired positions, i.e. individual equilibrium. But such choices are necessarily made in a framework of uncertainty and the individual has to choose the optimal amount of information he desires in comparison to other possible goods. The problem of stabilization is mainly one of information. The Austrian economists have made it clear that, in a world of uncertainty, the market is the best way to coordinate human activities. The latter has important implications for the allocation problem as well as for the stabilization problem.

Section 2 is devoted to the analysis of the business cycle. It is stressed that modern business cycles are of a monetary and financial nature. As the production of money is mainly made against credit and as the monetary authorities have control over the production of money, it is evident that they are responsible for the business cycle. In a world where savings are made lower by interventionist policies, governments believe that they can stimulate investment and growth through illusions, namely by financing investment without corresponding savings. As illusions cannot last for ever, the economic crisis will necessarily occur some time or other.

In the last section, some examples are given to illustrate this theory. It seems that the Austrian theory of business cycles shows us a very efficient way in which to explain historical events and understand better the fallacies of current policies.

1. The meaning of stabilization

Before proceeding to specific analyses of the economic system we begin with general views and an effort at specifying definitions.

Individual and global equilibrium

The notion of "equilibrium" is both unavoidable and dangerous. The only proper way to define it is an individualistic one: an individual is in equilibrium when he is satisfied, which means that he sees no reason for further activities given his perception of the constraints he meets (among which the constraints of resources, environment, and information may be the most important ones). Equilibrium therefore refers to the logic of individual choices and preferences.

Macroeconomic equilibrium exists when all the individuals of a society are satisfied in the above sense. This implies that all of them meet constraints, some of which stem from the interplay of each individual's decisions: in an exchange process the wants of each supplier-demander are constrained by the wants of the other one.

If not properly understood, the very concept of equilibrium is dangerous, however, for two reasons:

- Firstly there is a possible confusion between the economic sense of the word, as defined above, and the accounting sense (which reflects the unavoidable fact that any transaction has two sides of equal value, purchase and sale). As an example, let us take the words "balance of payments equilibrium". As an accounting identity it is a tautology, which, however, is useful to remember. From an "economic" point of view the words are meaningless: a balance of payments cannot be satisfied... Unfortunately, people are accustomed to use expressions such as "the external equilibrium of a country" instead of discussing the "possible satisfactions and choices - on one or several *markets*- of the individuals living in one given country". Many errors in the field of economics may come from this habit of referring *a priori* to some global aggregate and forgetting the *human beings* who decide and act. Some sort of collective will is then attributed to societies and groups of men to which aims and "instruments" are attributed. This merely reflects the prejudices of the macro-economist, the politician and the journalist.
- Secondly, individual equilibrium is often conceived more or less according to the Walrasian tradition, namely as a static concept. After some iterations, "perfect" information prevails and people are in a situation of steady -or *stable*- equilibrium. In analysis, the assumption of a static world (the "evenly rotating economy" of Ludwig von Mises) may be useful as a point of reference. But it cannot give a description of the way a human society really works, nor can it be described in any way as an ideal state. Individual equilibrium is a continuously moving equilibrium and acting individuals are continuously changing their preferred positions. The distinctive characteristic of men is that they live in time.

Men are rational, which means that they adapt their acts to their own specific aims, given the constraints they face. But their aims are continuously changing, as well as their constraints, due to their own activities or those of others. As we know, some of the contraints are information constraints. Individuals "buy" better information, but they never choose to get "perfect" information, which is not even conceivable. According to his own preferences at a given time, each individual chooses his specific desired bundle of information and other goods. The information he thus gets changes his plans and preferences. An outside observer cannot know these ever changing preferences and choices: individual equilibrium cannot be defined *a priori* and independently from the man who thinks and acts. This is due to the fact that it is impossible for an outside observer to get relevant information.

Evidently, a situation of global (or macroeconomic) equilibrium, i.e. a situation where all members of a society are in equilibrium, is still more difficult to define.

Individual stabilization

Since individual equilibrium - and, therefore, "macro equilibrium"- is a moving equilibrium (i.e. equilibrium does not mean fixity) how can we define terms such as "stable equilibrium", "stabilization" or "macroeconomic stabilization policy" ? In traditional macroeconomics, stabilization is conceived as the minimization of the gaps between the actual and the desired values of certain so-called macroeconomic variables. But what is the cost of this process of minimization ? Who can define the desired values of the variables? We cannot answer such questions without referring to the decisions of individuals and, before attributing any possible meaning to the concept of "macro-stabilization", we first have to clarify the meaning of individual stabilization.

Relying on the Austrian tradition, we have already dismissed the Walrasian view of a "stable equilibrium" defined as a static equilibrium. We now suggest the following definition of stability: an individual is in a situation of "stable equilibrium" when he is not forcibly prevented from choosing, *at any point in time*, his preferred bundle of information and other goods (present and future). At any moment, he will meet constraints - expected or unexpected ones - and he has to choose between acting within the framework of these constraints or trying to change them (by buying information, changing his production processes, etc...). This means that each individual is continuously implementing his own - and ever-changing - "*stabilization policy*", which cannot be viewed separately from his production process. This means that, on the macro level, stabilization cannot be separated from the process by which wealth is created and "distributed".

Let us just imagine for a while that information can be perfect and can be obtained freely (which, as we know, is impossible). In such a case the stabilization policy of an individual could be defined as the suppression of all gaps between his desired position and his actual one. This objective could be obtained, by assumption, at no cost, since information is free.

As information cannot be "perfect" and is always costly, an individual takes decisions which may subsequently appear to be mistaken. He may therefore try to improve the quality of his decisions, for instance by decreasing the degree of risk or the variability of certain variables which he considers to be of importance to him. He cannot, however, desire to abolish risk and uncertainty completely, and he rather chooses what seems to him the "optimal expected variability" of the relevant variables.

Stabilization cannot therefore be defined in absolute terms, but only in relative terms, as the result of choices between different actions. Optimal stabilization is thus obtained when the marginal utility of the expected diminution of the gap between desired and actual positions is equal to the marginal subjective cost of the necessary actions (purchase of information, changes in activities, etc..). Once more, from this point of view, optimal variability and, therefore, optimal stabilization cannot be defined by an external observer, except in the completely impossible case where the observer knows the changing preferences and informations of the deciding individual at all times.

There are different techniques to modify the degree of risk to which an individual is exposed. He can, for instance, change his activities via some technical progress (substituting a more foreseeable industrial production for an agricultural production dependent upon highly variable weather conditions); or, he can buy insurance, should such be possible. Both techniques imply costs, as does any other possible technique. It is only an illusion to believe that they can be costless, as it is implicitly assumed by the defenders of so-called "stabilization policies" who substitute their own choices for those of the individuals concerned.

The market as a coordination process

The view according to which the market is a coordination process is characteristic of the Austrian tradition. Mises, Hayek or Kirzner, in particular, have convincingly shown that the price mechanism is the best way to coordinate human activities. We, however, shall not develop that point, since it is addressed by Israel Kirzner in the present volume.

We have just explained how each individual "stabilizes" his own activities. Someone unfamiliar with Austrian analysis might think that the efforts of all individuals in a society towards stabilization might lead to disorder. We have in fact seen that individual efforts at stabilization were mainly a problem of choosing the best information at any given time. The price system is the less costly way to provide individuals with relevant information on the behaviour of the other members of a society.

In other words, the argument against any macroeconomic stabilization policy by some public authority is exactly the same as the one against central planning. Government intervention, for instance for so-called economic stabilization, interferes with the price system. It is then more difficult for individuals to adjust to changing conditions, since these conditions are made even more unpredictable. Through intervention, government officials destroy the very information individuals need to make relevant decisions: individuals can no longer inform others about their choices and equilibrium - i.e. "stabilized" - positions. As an example, we shall later see that economic crises are mainly due to distortions in the structure of prices by government intervention and the creation of wrong information.

In very general terms, macro-stabilization policy consists in a claim made by government officials to alleged identification of places in the economic system where, for instance, buyers would make "wrong" choices and potential suppliers are badly informed. Two objections, however, can be raised to any state intervention:

- On a free market it is in fact impossible to identify places where the demand-supply is over-estimated or under-estimated, since, in the context of ever-changing individual changes, people seek to avoid the losses linked with the changes in supply-demand.
- Even if this identification were possible, one could dispute, from an ethical point of view, the right of the government to modify supply-demand: public macroeconomic stabilization necessarily entails a violation of property rights.

The decentralized decision-making process of the market is made possible by contracts. Contracts allow social coordination over time: they give the contracting parties more reliable information on their future environment. The more stable the contract is, the higher individual stabilization is. Macroeconomic stabilization thus results from an infinity of microeconomic contracts. It cannot be defined by discretionary decisions of the state, since discretion means unpredictability. When state intervention actually does exist, the more predictable the policies are, the more stable the economic system is, but this is only a second-best solution ; for instance, it is better to have a monetary rule rather than discretionary changes in the quantity of money, when control over the supply of money has been monopolized by the state, but a market solution is to be preferred.

It is precisely to "stabilize" their environment that individuals sign contracts. When accepting a contract, an individual commits himself to behave according to a pattern decided in advance for some specific activity. In doing so, he certainly accepts some risk, but also he buys some information on the behaviour of the other contracting party. In other words, each individual has more information than anyone else on his own possible decisions and behaviour. When concluding a contract, he accepts some risk, since he decides on future behaviour without having a perfect knowledge of his future environment. The cost of this increased degree of risk is, however, amply compensated by a decrease in the risk involved by uncertainties on the future behaviour of others. In some sense, a contract is an exchange of risks.

Some contracts are specifically insurance contracts, but not everything can be insured; or, rather, people do not choose insurance for everything, the cost being considered as excessive in comparison with the subjective utility of the risk coverage.

It may be so that all members of one given group of men (a "society") suffer from the same risk, for instance crop fluctuations in an agricultural society, or a volcano eruption. Their environment is "unstable", but this does not mean that there is a "need" for stabilization: given the cost of the risk coverage, the individuals *decide* not to buy an insurance, nor to change their environment. Macro-stabilization, on the other hand, implies that an authority draws resources from individuals by force (more or less directly, via taxation, price controls or regulations) in order to develop such activities as individuals have chosen not to embark upon. In that sense macroeconomic stabilization always involves a spoliation.

From a more general point of view, the history of human activities might be interpreted as the *unintended result* of decisions made by individuals to *stabilize* their environment. This fact may be overlooked by people who are accustomed to consider macro-stabilization as necessarily designed by the state. In fact, the progress of humanity mainly came from efforts by individual innovators to free themselves or others from the "whims of nature", i.e. to ensure macro-stabilization. We will later see how modern governments, interfering with the free working of the market, have become the main source of instability, in spite of their claims to "stabilizing the economy".

Is there a "public good" argument for state macroeconomic stabilization ?

From the previous individualistic approach it appears that there is no room for a "macroeconomic stabilization policy" and that macroeconomic stabilization occurs when all individuals are free to act as they wish. We have to consider, however, one of the most important and most critical arguments for government intervention, the existence of "public goods". Could public macroeconomic stabilization be considered as a public good? Should it actually be possible for the government to pursue a stabilization policy, it would then seem that such a policy would share the usual characteristics of a public good: it is impossible to exclude someone from the benefits of macro-stabilization and the consumption of stabilization services by one person would not decrease the potential consumption by others[4]..

If this view on macro-stabilization were ever acceptable, it would not imply that the government would have to execute it by using coercive means. For instance, people can voluntarily enter into a non-profit organization to oblige themselves mutually: they consider their activities to be more efficient if each member feels morally obliged to contribute to the common aim. There is a private production of a "public good".

But there is a more general reason for not accepting such a line of reasoning. Our previous arguments, following the general conceptions of the Austrian school, aimed at demonstrating that the free interplay of wills leads to the most efficient system of social coordination. And how to define social coordination if not as a *public good* ? In other words, we have already shown that the public good "social cooperation" or "macro-stabilization" could best be reached via *private production*. Thus, we cannot find any justification for government macroeconomic stabilization by having recourse to some sort of public good argument. If ever it can be shown that public goods exist -which is disputable- social stabilization might imply that the state produces them if the private sector does not: the discussion on macroeconomic stabilization brings us back to the delimitation of the public and the private sphere. The fact that macroeconomic stabilization might be a public good is however not a sufficient argument *per se* to justify a discretionary macroeconomic policy.

---

4 We mentioned here the traditional characteristics of what is defined in part of the literature as a "public good". However, we do know that the very concept of a "public good" can be challenged, since the public good argument in favor of government intervention always implies some kind of "externality" problems, which may be difficult to solve only in the case of immaterial services. Moreover, even in such cases, there is no reason to believe that the public sector is the most capable of producing the services. It may be preferable to speak of "collective services" (private or public) instead of public goods.

We have already seen that macroeconomic stabilization problems are mainly information problems, but information is not a public good and it is always costly. Information is best provided by those who have an interest in providing it (for themselves or for others in a process of exchange). The government is badly equipped to produce information. It only transfers resources coercively from people who created them and intended to use them (to get information and other goods) to bureaucrats who look for information which is linked to their own objectives (for whose benefit ?).

The only relevant question is the following: are government officials likely to be better speculators than capitalists ? The answer is certainly a negative one since government officials do not manage their own resources and should they ever cause losses (for others), they would not be eliminated, contrary to what would happen on private markets.

If there are uncertainties on a private market there is scope for private speculation and the efficient speculator benefits from his forecasts. It may also happen that someone else, too, benefits from the stabilizing activity of the speculator, without having to pay for it. In such a case one could be tempted to say that stabilization creates "externalities", so that it would be "socially optimal" to nationalize stabilization activities. In other words, the "social return" of stabilization would be higher than the "individual return" so that a private production of stabilization would be sub-optimal. This traditional view of government intervention must be dismissed: the fact that someone benefits from the activities of other people, without having to pay for it, is a logical feature of an efficiently working system of social cooperation. The best system of social cooperation emerges from the free interplay of individual wills. The fact that, in a process of exchange, we benefit from the free activity of our partners, does not imply that trade has to be monopolized by the government, under the pretext that it produces "externalities". This perfectly applies to the specific case of producing stabilization services.

When the government makes a plea in favour of stabilization policies, citizens are victims of an illusion, since they can see the effects of the policy, but they cannot evaluate lost information and the highest cost incurred by all individuals to get information on the new environment, especially when public decisions are unpredictable. As was underlined by Frédéric Bastiat, government officials tend to give visible benefits at a cost which is not visible. We are thus left with the following conclusion: there is no justification for macroeconomic policy. The following pages give illustrations of this principle.

2. The business cycle

The belief in a government's capacity to stabilize the economy is linked to the assumption that a market economy is fundamentally unstable, so that there is a need for outside stabilization. It ought to be self-evident that such an assumption is wrong for one simple reason. A long time ago, for instance in medieval society (or in present societies which are still poorly diversified), the fluctuations in economic activity mainly came from "real exogenous shocks". All members of society suffered from these shocks and the possibility to be protected against them, for instance through insurance, was restricted (one can think, for instance, of periods of starvation due to climatic fluctuations). In diversified modern economics such shocks are without importance.

But new causes of instability have appeared: business cycles and crises during the XIXth and XXth centuries were of a monetary and financial nature, as is evidenced by the fluctuations in the relevant variables (interest rates, quantity of money, etc...). The evolution of monetary systems during these periods has been characterized by progressive nationalization and government control. Modern governments have the ultimate decision power as regards money creation. They are, therefore, responsible for monetary instability. As money is not directly controlled and produced along market principles, it is obvious that the market system cannot be considered as fundamentally unstable. And it seems illogical to expect stabilization from the very people who create instability..

The Austrian theory of business cycles

In this section we shall only recall the main lines of the Austrian theory, as it appears in the books by Ludwig von Mises and Friedrich Hayek. It may however be recalled that they are heirs of a tradition going back as far as Richard Cantillon in the XVIIIth century, through Jean-Baptiste Say and Charles Coquelin in the XIXth century in France, and free banking economists in Great Britain. The Austrian economists give a detailed and persuasive explanation of the "destabilizing" influence of monetary policies in modern monetary systems. As is well underlined by Roger Garrison (1978), they concentrate on processes and not on aggregate quantities and so-called functional relations between them. Contrary to Keynes (or the monetarists), they do not give a theory of real income determination -the very concept of "real aggregate income" being considered as meaningless- but a theory of coordination. In that sense Austrian micro-economics and macroeconomics coincide to a large extent.

The Austrian theory, like the monetarist theory, concentrates on the effect of increases in the money supply on the "general level of prices" (if ever such a notion has any meaning). It is however mainly concerned with changes in relative prices of goods due to monetary expansion, and, particularly, with relative prices between capital goods and consumption goods or, according to the Austrian terminology, between goods of higher and lower value. The interest rate is thus a mere reflection of the changes in relative prices, since it is determined by all markets and not only by the market for loanable funds. Besides, the Austrian theory emphasizes the real effects of monetary expansion (which cannot be considered as neutral).

The Austrian theory shows a greater interest in the processes through which money enters the economy than in the total variation of the quantity of money. Taking this interest as a starting point, a clear distinction is drawn between two different ways in which banks grant credits:

- In a system of "commodity credit" (Mises' words), credits are backed by the equity capital of banks and by the funds that are placed at the banks' disposal by their customers. Banks are thus mere financial intermediaries. They transfer real savings, according to time preferences of individuals, and the financial system is based on the existence and transfer of individual property rights on savings and capital. No business cycle can appear in such a system, in which money creation is constrained by the existence of a commodity money (gold, for instance), or, possibly, by currency competition. In a 100 % reserve gold system, for instance, long-run swings in the price level can exist according to the relative rates of growth of the quantity of money (gold) and the real quantity of commodities produced. There are however no sudden and unpredictable upturns, which may indicate no "instability".
- In a system of "circulation credit", credits are backed by the creation of fiduciary media (notes and deposits). Money can be introduced into the economy through the granting of credits. Under some specific institutional arrangements -which necessarily imply government intervention- a rapid expansion of the money supply can take place and inflation occurs. By discounting a 3-month bill, banks "exchange a future good for a present good which they produce out of nothing" (Mises (1978), p. 120).

In the first case the actual (market) rate of interest is close to the natural rate, i.e. the rate which allows for equilibrium between voluntary savings and the demand for savings by firms for investment purposes. Except under the unlikely assumption when a large set of innovations would cause a sudden and large change in the rate of return on capital (at least in the short term), the natural rate of interest is probably mainly stable. The natural interest rate is in fact determined by the supply and the demand for savings. The demand depends on factors such as technical changes, which cannot change very suddenly and cannot constitute short-term shocks. On the other hand, there is no reason for sudden changes in the preferences of individuals between the present and the future, which would explain changes in the supply of savings.

If "circulation credits" are granted, under non-competitive conditions, there can be a growing discrepancy between the real rate of interest and the natural rate of interest. An excessive creation of credit - and, correlatively, of money - decreases the real rate of interest (although the nominal rate may increase). Cheap credit induces the firms to decide on "over-investments", i.e. investments the rentability of which does not correspond to the actual scarcity of savings, i.e. to the time preferences of the participants in the market. As Friedrich Hayek puts it, the production process is lenghtened, firms choosing more capitalistic techniques of production. As no one is really willing to forgo consumption to finance these additional investments, the latter are financed via "forced savings", i.e. inflation tax.

Monetary authorities push towards the creation of credits and what is (wrongly) called "cheap money", since the cost of financing is hidden by indirect government violence (compulsory government intervention in the financial and monetary processes). They believe, or businessmen believe, that a low real interest rate indicates a greater availability of present resources and, therefore, stimulates economic activity. Everyone -businessman or politician alike- has the feeling that any specific activity is made easier by low interest rates, but he does not see the over-all (macroeconomic) consequences. Only the "market" is able to "see" these consequences by gathering and conveying relevant information on scarcity of present relative to future goods. The interest of politicians, on the other hand, is to generate illusions so that businessmen and -may be- the general public believe that they can stimulate economic activity. In a controlled system of "circulation credit", moreover, no one can know the natural rate of interest, which can only be given by a free market (i.e. free banking) interest rate. It is obviously impossible to "stabilize" the interest rate or any other price or macro variable if one cannot even know the figure that should be attained through stabilization.

Every day monetary authorities pretend to stabilize interest rates, exchange rates or income without knowing to which level they should stabilize and without having even a personal interest in knowing it. Politicians decide upon economic policies according to macroeconomic aggregates which are meaningless: they aim for instance, at maximizing the "total amount of investment" through violent means, for instance by control of the banking sector, to achieve a low real interest rate, instead of accepting the *optimal* level of investment which would prevail on a free market. As stressed by Ludwig von Mises, the true cause of the business cycle is ideological: people believe that real interest rates can be lowered not by an accumulation of capital from voluntary savings, but by an artificial creation of credit.

One may ask why banks react positively to the endeavours of the monetary authorities to decrease the real rate of interest in the first phase of the business cycle. The expansion of credit increases the risk for banks: the illusion of financing investments without corresponding desired savings cannot last for ever, and, therefore, they could forecast the future rise of the real rate of interest and the difficulties of the borrowers in reimbursing their debt, since they have implemented investments with a lower expected rate of return than the future market rate of interest will actually be.

Banks accept the continuous financing of investments via credits (and money creation) because the world is more and more characterized by a collectivized monetary and financial system, in which personal responsibility and individual property rights are continuously narrowing. The nationalization of banks, when it occurs, is only the ultimate symbol of that collectivism. The most important feature is in fact the role of the central bank as a "lender of last resort": it is more and more accepted that it is the responsibility of the monetary authorities to prevent bankfailures, which would cause "indue" losses to their customers and create the possibility of a series of bank failures. Intervention by the central bank to support the banks is thus regarded as a means of "stabilizing" the financial system by people who do not understand that, in any activity, failure is an essential feature of market systems which induces people to make responsible decisions, i.e. to answer market signals appropriately and, therefore, to *stabilize the economy*. The banks are also more inclined to grant credit out of money creation when regulations allow them to pay a low interest on deposits. Regulations always increase the gap between borrowing and lending rates, but, more specifically, in many countries, payments on deposits are limited or prohibited, which artificially raises the profitability of credit expansion. In such cases, the profitability of money creation is high. The banks however would hesitate to expand money and credit creation indefinitely, if they feared an increasing degree of risk. This brake works less efficiently if, for instance, the managers of the banks have the feeling that the risk of failure is low, due to the role of the central bank as a "lender of last resort".

Ludwig von Mises and Friedrich Hayek explain that the newly created money and credit are first attributed to producers, which induces them to "bid labour and non-specific capital away from the later stages of production and into the earlier stages and begin construction of whatever specific capital is needed to take advantage of the (apparent) profitability of these long-term projects" (Roger Garrison, p.32). As time goes by, the newly created money progressively flows from the new investors to the other economic agents (workers, for instance). Individuals in society, however, are not ready to accept more savings, since their time preferences can not possibly be affected by the process of money and credit creation. After some time, part of the new investment appears not to be profitable any more and the real interest rate goes back to its former higher level or, even, to a (temporarily) higher level than the natural rate. The producers have to abandon the more capitalistic structure of production and go back to the initial structure corresponding to the time preferences of people, i.e. to their willingness to abandon present consumption for future consumption. The economic crisis sets in.

Alternative monetary systems

From the above discussion it follows that the stabilization of an economy depends on the possibility to check any over-issue of "circulation credit". The monetary rule, à la Friedman, is one possible answer. Two main objections, however, can be raised to the latter.

- Firstly, when constrained in the rate of growth of one given monetary aggregate, banks are inclined to invent new monetary instruments and to develop another monetary aggregate which is not a priori limited. On a market where full competition is not allowed to exist, this leads to over-issue and the subsequent business cycle.
- Secondly, and more importantly, to try and impose an a priori maximum rate of growth for the money supply is of a constructivist nature: the latter is no less a pretence of knowing - more than anyone would be able to - than attempts at central planning of the supply of money (the so-called managed money) are: one cannot be certain that the corresponding rate of growth in "circulation credit" will be optimal in the sense that the natural interest rate will prevail. Although preferable to a discretionary monetary policy, because the latter is liable to inflationary pressures from politicians, a monetary rule is inspired by the same sort of prejudice, namely the idea that external observers are able to decide what ought to be the "true" value of a market variable.

A gold-based monetary system (or any system based on a commodity money) puts a check on the possibility of expanding the quantity of money. Long-run swings of overall inflation or deflation do exist, due to changes in the relative scarcity of the money base relative to other commodities. There is, however, no room for the creation of an excessive quantity of "circulation credit", at least if the rules of the system are correctly played. Historical experience, however, shows that monetary authorities often freed themselves from the rule of contract, which - as we have already mentioned - is the foundation of a market system. When there is a "national" currency linked to gold, and a central bank, the latter implicitly promises to exchange, at a given, fixed, price, its national money-substitutes for gold without limits. The temptation to pursue an "active" monetary policy, via the creation of credits and fiduciary media, still remains, for instance as a possible way for governments to overcome financial difficulties.

Such an expansion of money is incompatible with the basic rule of a system in which national money is supposed to be convertible against gold at a fixed price. It clearly demonstrates, however, that "monetary authorities", when embarking on such an expansion, have decided on *destabilizing* policies. Devaluation is one possible, and rather frequent, result of such an incoherent policy. We want, however, to stress that devaluation means that the central bank unilaterally breaks the implicit (or, sometimes, explicit) contract it had concluded with the users of money. In the private sector, such a dishonest decision is naturally punished by the Courts, but the statesmen pretend to be "above the laws" and to have the right to take discretionary and unpredictable decisions. Such behaviour certainly has a destabilizing effect for reasons we have previously underlined.

A third solution to the problem of putting limits to the creation of money is currency competition or free banking, which, from our point of view, is the best solution. We, however, shall not elaborate on this point, since it is developed by Roland Vaubel in another chapter of the present book.

Let us only say that there are reasons to believe that free banking would produce both a lower inflation rate and less instability, so that stabilization policies or "counter-cyclical" policies would clearly appear to be useless. A bank in a competitive situation has to produce "good" money. Among other things, it has to create confidence, namely confidence in its capacity to guarantee the convertibility of its liabilities. One way in which this aim can be reached is to have a ratio between equity capital and other liabilities which is in favour of the former.

The bank, in a competitive setting, is mainly a financial intermediary and, possibly, a producer of money (via "circulation credit"). Historical examples seem to confirm this view. The brake thus put on the propensity of banks to create "circulation credit" and money is lightened whenever the state imposes regulations, which necessarily decrease competition (for instance the monopoly right of a central bank to issue bank notes, legal tender provisions, etc.). From a system of individual responsibility of bankers and savers, one shifts to a collectivized system, where the coordination of activity is less and less determined by individual choices. The instability of the system increases. It is therefore somewhat paradoxical or even indecent to hear statesmen argue in favour of their capability to stabilize a system, which, in fact, is only destabilized through their interventions.

3. Applications of the theory

We do not intend to give an exhaustive set of applications in the limited framework of the present chapter, but we only intend to choose some illustrations of the previous principles.

Historical examples

Let us begin with some examples drawn from the XIXth century (which we took from a study by Philippe Nataf, "The Business Cycle Theories of Mid-19th Century France"). The French crisis of 1805 had been correctly identified by Dupont de Nemours as a consequence of a previous over-issue of notes by the Banque de France, which in 1803 had obtained from Napoléon Bonaparte (one of its main share-holders...) the privilege of issuing notes. It is noticeable that this crisis was the second one in the history of France after the crash of the bank of Law in 1720 (which had over-issued notes). This is an illustration of the fact that business cycles have a monetary origin and that they result from the privileges given to banks. In a competitive situation (which had existed in France between 1797 and 1803), credit is the counterpart of equity capital of banks (or borrowed funds); credit is abundant and stable (as is the structure of the balance-sheet of banks).

It is also important to see that, during the monetary crises of 1837 and 1857, the depression was strongest in those regions where banks were heavily regulated (for instance in the state of New York), but that it was mild or nil in states and countries where the monetary system was freer (for instance Scotland or Massachusetts and Rhode Island, which were close to New York, but did not import its instability).

In the XXth century the 1929-31 crisis is well known. It has been studied in detail by economists such as Milton Friedman, Benjamin Anderson or

Murray Rothbard. From their research it appears that this crisis can be explained along the lines previously developed: over-expansion of "circulation credit", followed by a dramatic decrease in the quantity of money. Expectations being difficult to form in such an uncertain environment, this situation led to all sorts of real consequences:the high level of unemployment for instance can be explained by the fact that wages decreased considerably less than prices did. Contrary to what is usually said, President Hoover did not adopt a "laissez-faire" policy. In fact, he worsened the crisis by imposing price and wage floors, adopting protectionist measures, decreasing work time, subsidizing exports, increasing the number of civil servants, etc...

The recent so-called "debt crisis" is another interesting example. This crisis is a mere consequence of generalized state interventionism, both in developed and under-developed countries, and both in monetary systems and other fields, particularly in the field of taxation. The excessive taxation of savings creates a scarcity of voluntary individual savings (particularly in the form of shares, i.e. direct property rights). To finance their growth, firms ask banks for funds. The banks can grant loans because they belong to systems which are more or less collectivized and in which individual responsibility has been greatly diminished. Meanwhile, a large part of the credits during the seventies was borrowed by states or public firms which did not care much about the profitability of their investments. There has been over-investment at a time when real interest rates were very low (or even negative). The low rate of return on wrong investments makes it difficult to pay and reimburse interest. There is no other solution for such problems than to go back to a system of individualized property rights and laissez-faire. As regards the present "debt problem", this means that governments which have borrowed too much ought to privatize their activities. From a more general point of view, it means a restoration of personal savings and a complete deregulation of the monetary and financial systems[5].

Specific policies

One might take innumerable examples of specific policies which are frequently adopted and which are destabilizing due to interference by governments with the price system (income and price policies, interest rate policy, exchange rate policy, etc.). Let us take only one example relative to exchange rate stabilization in a system of floating rates. It is generally thought that exchange rate fluctuations are "excessive" and that monetary authorities have

[5] We develop the analysis of the debt crisis in Salin (1986).

to intervene in order to stabilize them, if possible via coordinated interventions of several central banks. The question we would like to ask is the following: who is best suited to "stabilize" the exchange rate: private speculators or the central bank ? To say that exchange rate fluctuations are excessive and that there is a need for stabilization implies that one has some idea of the "normal" or "equilibrium" exchange rate.

There is, however, no reason to assume that the central bank, in comparison with any other institution, has a better understanding of the working of the hyper-complex world economic system from which the equilibrium exchange rate can be deduced. There is no more reason to believe that it is better informed than the market, except in the case of one specific variable: its future monetary policy, which has a major influence on the exchange rate. Two solutions can be given to this problem of differences in information:

(1) The first solution consists in concluding that, the central bank being better informed than the market, it has to stabilize the exchange rate: dirty floating is then prefered to pure floating.

(2) The second solution consists in demanding that the central bank gives the market the specific information it has on its future monetary policy, the participants on the market having to determine the consequences as regards the determination of the exchange rate. Precisely, the Friedman monetary rule, which has already been quoted, enables the market to get such information. In such a case, it could be considered that the private speculators and the central bank, having the same understanding of the system and the same information, it is equivalent to choose pure floating or dirty floating (the market solution or the interventionist solution). In fact, there is one powerful reason for choosing the second solution *and* pure floating: private speculators have every incentive to use their knowledge and their information in a stabilizing way, whereas the attention of central bank officials has other concerns, since they do not use their own wealth to intervene on the market. In fact, the central bank may even have incentives to produce illusions deliberately, as it has been previously explained about the business cycle and the production of illusions.

In this field of exchange rates one could take another example: it is usual to say that the European Monetary System has worked well, since exchange rates have been mainly stable (in fact, it would be more correct to speak of fixity and not of stability), except for some parity changes. In fact, equilibrium exchange rates are determined at any time by all the variables of the over-all economic system (among which monetary variables play a fundamental role). By preventing, for more or less long periods of time, the exchange rate from changing according to market conditions, the authorities probably increase the variability of some other variables (for instance, interest rates or the availability of credit, etc.). But, because of an insufficient information on the working of this macro-system, one usually does not understand the connection between the increased variability in some variable and the exchange rate policy. Once more, Frédéric Bastiat was right: there is what can be seen and what cannot be seen.

4. Conclusion: the true meaning of macro-stabilization policies

We have already stressed that the subject of macro-stabilization led us to the problem of the desired frontier between the private sphere and the public sphere. Let us accept the Hayekian idea according to which the working of a free society implies the definition of "general rules of conduct" which can partly be defined and sanctioned by an institution called "the state". Individual stabilization and, therefore, macro-stabilization, according to what we have explained previously, are made easier if these rules are stable and predictable. Therefore, the contribution of the state to macro-stabilization ought to be stabilization of the rules, the definition of which is its specific responsibility.

References

The present list of references is not exhaustive. It is intended to give some of the main contributions to the subject and those we particularly used.

Coquelin, Charles, "Les crises commerciales et la liberté des banques", *Revue des deux mondes*, 1848.

Garrison, Roger W., *Austrian Macroeconomics: A Diagrammatical Exposition,* Menlo Park, Institute for Humane Studies, 1978.

Hayek, Friedrich, *Monetary Nationalism and International Stability*, London, Longmans, Green and Co, 1937.

Hayek, Friedrich, *Prices and Production,* London, 1931.

Hayek, Friedrich, *Law, Legislation, and Liberty*, London, Routledge & Kegan Paul, 1973, 1976 and 1979.

Hayek, Friedrich, *Monetary Theory and the Trade Cycle*, London, Jonathan Cape, 1933.

Mises, Ludwig von-, *The Theory of Money and Credit,* London, Jonathan Cape, 1934.
Mises, Ludwig von-, *On the Manipulation of Money and Credit*, New York, Free Market books, 1978 (papers from 1923, 1928, 1931, 1933, edited by Percy L. Greaves).
Mises, Ludwig von-, *Human Action*, Yale University Press, 1949.
Nataf, Philippe, "Competitive Banking and the Cycle", unpublished paper, 1984.
Nataf, Philippe, "The Business Cycle Theories of Mid-19th Century France", unpublished paper, 1984.
Rothbard, Murray, *America's Great Depression,* Kansas City, Sheed and Ward, 1963.
Rothbard, Murray, and Garrett, Garet, *The Great Depression and New Deal Monetary Policy*, San Francisco, Cato Institute, 198O.
Salin, P., "Collapse Through Collectivisation", *Economic Affairs*, October/November 1986.
Sennholz, Hans F., *The Truth about the Great Depression*, Lansing, Mich., Constitutional Alliance.

Comment by J.C. Siebrand (Erasmus University)

For practical reasons my defense of stabilization policy will be divided into two parts. In the first part I will discuss non-Neo-Austrian criticism of stabilization policy, which has some points in common with the Neo-Austrian view, and explain my attitude towards stabilization policy in general. In the second part I will consider the typical Neo-Austrian points of view, as worded by Professor Salin in its contribution to his volume.

Non-Neo-Austrian criticism of stabilization policy

The relevant arguments of the non-Neo-Austrians can be summarized as follows.

1. There is no intrinsic need for stabilization policies. Provided that governments and central banks are restrained properly in their behaviour, private sector developments tend towards stability. Errors in anticipation may occur and cause cyclical variations, but these errors will not be systematic. Rational reactions to anticipation errors will automatically correct those errors and thereby stabilize development. Predictable policies will not have an effect on developments in the private sector as they are already a part of the anticipations; unpredictable policies will only lead to counter-productive disturbances.
2. Even if private sector developments were not intrinsically stable, stabilization policies would still fail. Official forecasts tend to be defective, and policy instruments lack adequate flexibility. For these reasons alone, fine tuning is not a realistic option. In addition, the instruments that governments can use tend to generate perverse indications of scarcity and their use would therefore hamper essential long-term adjustments.
3. The recognition of these arguments has serious consequences. Stabilization policies should be implemented only to make the behaviour of governments and central banks predictable and stable. This requirement could be met if policies were restricted to discrete decision rules, such as a balanced budget and a fixed rate of growth in money supply. In addition, policies should attempt to remove obstructions to market flexibility. More ambitious policies would be counter-productive.

Although these arguments appear to reinforce each other, they are in fact rather heterogeneous. Some are based on assumptions about the proper description of the economic system in general, others on the quality of information that various agents have and the speed with which it is acquired, still others on institutional factors. Quite different types of reasoning are therefore needed to evaluate them.

The most basic argument, the inherent stability of the private sector, appears to be a belief rather than an empirically-based stance. Consequently, there is not much point in arguing against it. We lack a dynamic theoretical model that embraces the rich diversity of the markets and the production techniques that can be observed in the real world. It is therefore impossible to ascertain whether the private sector in intrinsically stable and tends towards stability. It does not appear rational to give belief a dominant place in actual decision-making.

If it is not certain that the private sector will tend towards stability when it is left to its own devices, the opponents of stabilization policy may still argue that minimizing official intervention would lead to the least unstable growth path. The arguments behind the more rigid position, mentioned above, may also be relevant to this position. Important issues in this respect appear to be whether private anticipations are unbiased, whether the observation of anticipation errors will lead to learning processes that are self correcting, and whether unbiased anticipation errors imply that there is no systematic deviation from a path that would be consistent with correct anticipations. The issue of the quality of private anticipations cannot be resolved without further empirical research. There is no satisfactory evidence that shows that all relevant anticipation errors have a random character. This stance therefore appears to be aprioristic. The existence of learning processes is less debatable, since such processes appear to be basic elements in human adjustment to external conditions. It is far from certain, though, that processing information obtained form an ever-changing environment will lead to a decline in the number of anticipation errors. In general, there will be a lag in the supply of information and it is obvious that the government, which is usually equipped with specialized agencies, will be better informed than the average economic agent. At all events, governments too can "learn".

The link between unbiased anticipation and an absence of systematic deviation form the full-information path should be rejected on theoretical grounds. Disequilibrium analysis demonstrated unequivocally that in the absence of fully flexible prices, incorrect, but possibly unbiased anticipations of trade possibilities will cause a downward bias in the quantities traded. Similar arguments apply in other cases: overinvestment does not generate extra output, underinvestment reduces output. In economics, chances missed are often chances lost. There also appears to be abundant empirical evidence that not all prices are always completely flexible. There is therefore a real case to try and reduce the effects of potentially distorting anticipations.

To summarize these issues, stabilization carried out with instruments that are sufficiently flexible to compensate for misled private action could improve the economic welfare, at least in theory. This brings us to the criticism of stabilization policy at the more mundane level of actual practice. Doubts about the quality of official anticipations and the flexibility of potential instruments cannot be easily waived aside. There are many examples of government actions based on incorrect perceptions of actual developments, which ex-post proved to be destabilizing in terms of activity levels. Although counter examples can also be provided, the instances in which stabilization policies proved to be either ineffective or counter-productive are numerous enough to cast doubt on the viability of short-term stabilization. In practice, not all attempts at such fine-tuning policies have been abandoned, but economic policy in almost every industrial country reveals a shift towards a medium or long-term orientation. This shift may reflect the fear that attempts to stabilize short-run development would be destabilizing in a longer-term perspective. This fear is related to the potentially perverse indications of scarcity associated with the implementation of short-term stabilization instruments, mentioned as another basic criticism of stabilization policies. Although a proper evaluation of these arguments would require more empirical research than has so far been carried out, it would not be wise to neglect them. On the contrary, the longer-term implications should be given greater weight when considering the implementation of instruments to stabilize the economy. This will certainly reduce the scope of the instruments in short-term stabilization. It will, however, not necessarily imply that the optimal use of instruments in any situation is to stick to the constant values implied by a decision rule that abstracts from actual conditions. Since the average situation seldom occurs, the average reaction is seldom adequate. The quality of the official diagnosis of a situation is crucial in this respect. In other words, governments should be able to ascertain the direction in which actual developments should be corrected. There appears to be a fundamental difference between the assessment of short-term development and long-term development. Developments beyond for example three months up to say two years ahead are often very difficult to forecast, partly because they are based on rather unstable demand conditions and, particularly in the past ten or twenty years, partly because of uncertainties concerning the government policies in some major countries. Less volatile supply conditions are much more important for medium-term development, and the relevant supply conditions are not as difficult to assess. The lower uncertainty is a valid argument for giving more weight to these supply conditions. Accordingly, practical obstacles to fine tuning should not result in an absence of medium-term stabilization, but a shift towards it. That is not to say that short-term stabilization should receive no consideration at all, but rather that uncertain events should not receive inappropriate attention. In order to meet these requirements the analytical framework for the design of these policies should cover both short and long-term developments and the mechanisms behind them. Within the possibilities of the available techniques, all theoretical and empirical insights that have some bearing on the policies under considerations should be taken into account. It is not rational to rely on aprioristic argument.

This being said, it is only fair to recognize that in many cases economists hold widely diverging views on almost all matters that are relevant to the design of economic policy, e.g. the diagnosis of the actual situation, the likely development of external events, the adequate description of the working of the economic system, the size of the operational horizon, the priorities within this horizon, the proper conditioning of the future beyond this horizon in terms of (intermediate) targets within the planning period. Some of these issues may be resolved with empirical analysis, but certainly not all of them. Some differences are based on different visions about the most realistic description of the economy and a dispute between different simplifications of the economic system cannot be settled easily. In practice the variety of opinions may be so wide that it is virtually impossible to take all views into account. To resolve the problem of which economic policies should be implemented, however, it will generally be possible to recognize major views and attribute probabilities to their validity. In a formal decision procedure these values amount to weights given to different views. In this way the attribution of values can support risk-averse decision-making. Since, at least in principle, contrasting views can be dealt with in rational decision-making, it does not seem wise to fall back on one or two simplistic notions in the design of economic policy.

From a theoretical point of view, stabilization policy, when feasible, should be based on a balanced set of ambitions and deal with as many items as are considered important. In practice, policy makers can take much more into account than is usually assumed, provided they are properly assisted. In recent years substantial progress has been made with the application of optimal control theory and game theory to resolve problems of economic policy. Techniques have been developed to deal with short and long-term considerations simultaneously, with the existence of competing models, with certain types of uncertainty, and with game situations, such as the existence of different national authorities or policy-making by different countries. The framework for introducing a wide range of considerations is technically available, although it may not be possible for the time being to deal with all the complications simultaneously. Nevertheless, a framework is emerging that integrates several views and that is a remarkable improvement on the unfruitful confrontation of different partial views.

It is not unlikely that the combination of a wide range of considerations will generate arguments against certain types of stabilization policies. The confrontation of conflicting long and short-term targets probably reduces the scope for interventions. Similar arguments apply to the combination of conflicting views and other types of uncertainty. Warnings against ill-advised stabilization policies may therefore be in order. But there is a wide gap between bringing more realism into stabilization policy and substituting this policy with a few simplistic behavioural rules for policy makers. Whether we like it or not, the behaviour of governments and central banks is important for many different reasons. Not only is the government's budget deficit relevant, but also the size of government revenues and expenditure, the way in which the revenues are collected, the direction of expenditure, the existence of obligatory saving and insurance schemes, all have an impact on the private sector. The behaviour of central banks affects not only certain elements of the money supply, but also other assets and liabilities held by other banks, both at home and abroad, and the private sector in general; it affects interest rates, exchange rates and other financial conditions. The application of fixed rules to just a few of these items will tend to cause major deviations in the others. This creates an argument for enlarging the scope of the rules so that they cover a large number of items. These rules would, as a result, become far less simple, because the items will generally be strongly interrelated, and even if all the relevant items were to be covered the practical problem of closing the gap between the existing configuration and a target configuration would require the deviations from the fixed rules to be specified. We need an analytical framework to make the relevant decisions. Once this need has been recognized and an analytical framework has been established, the problem arises of determining how the "ideal" decision rules can be best adjusted to the actual situation. This problem is equivalent in formal terms to the problem of how economic policy can be best adjusted to a heterogeneous set of considerations conditioned by relatively high costs attributed to changes in policies.

So far the argument against one or two simple decision rules has been mainly abstract. There are however additional practical considerations. The adoption of monetary targets has made other items more volatile. Uncertainty about interest rates, fixed investment and production has often replaced the uncertainty about money stocks. At the practical level it is obviously not effective to stabilize only one or two items. A realistic policy should operate in terms of the major determinants of the behaviour of firms, households and financial institutions. The tension between short and long-term targets is of fundamental importance in this respect. It is relatively easy to stimulate short-term demand, but as a rule a price has to be paid in terms of worsening business conditions: the implied changes in profits, taxes and interest rates usually undermine the longer-term expansion of supply. In the long run sound business is a prerequisite for the maintenance of private income and the collective sector. In the past most emphasis has been placed on sales perspectives rather than on supply conditions. If we were able to stabilize business income at a level that on the one hand would permit a sufficient expansion of supply, and on the other would leave enough room for parallel growth in private demand, much would be gained. Part of this objective may require an improvement in the functioning of the labour and capital markets; stabilization policies directed at income distribution may also be required. It would be wrong however to concentrate on the problems of the recent past in our attempts to stabilize the future. Stabilization policy essentially requires an holistic approach, one which provides room for all the important indicators of activity, allocation and distribution. In my opinion that is the most important lesson to be learnt from the past.

The Neo-Austrian criticism of stabilization policy

To begin my comment on Professor Salin's contribution I must confess I do not recognize the world in which we live in the picture he sketches. His world is very abstract. He appears to think of atomistic economic agents, incessantly trying to improve their grip on the future by up-dating their information and by contracting with other agents in order to reduce their uncertainty. These individuals operate in markets that would work efficiently if big, bad governments stopped interfering and frustrating both the market mechanism and the possibilities of making rational anticipations about the future. The free operation of market forces would, in Professor Salin's view, yield more than just the most efficient and least unstable allocation; the free operation of market forces also appears to be a moral issue, since intervention interferes with property rights and therefore reduces private responsibility.

This description of the working of the economic system conflicts with many elements found in the economic literature. The doubts about the working of the market system, external influences and other factors that lie behind the arguments for an equitable allocation of public provisions can serve as examples. I will elaborate on some of these issues below, but to put my argument into a proper perspective I should express my admiration for Professor Salin's lucid exposition and indicate that I do not disagree with all of his position. I agree with his general stance that in many instances the dangers for allocation were and are unduly neglected in government intervention and this has caused serious damage to our economies in the past. I also admit that non-scarcity-conform policies tend to destabilize our economies particularly in the medium or long-term perspective. That is why I am in favour of holistic stabilization policies, which deal with allocation problems as well as short-term disequilibrium. I am also aware of the fact that government actions other than stabilization policy can destabilize our economies. If conflicting targets are present, compromises will have to be made. In my view the market system should be supplemented with a political system that generates the weights to be given to different priorities. I share the view that we run great risks if we fully replace the market system with a system of political decisions, but I would equally fear to live in a system that is governed solely by buying power and selling power. There are such huge differences in capabilities, resource endowments, production techniques and market structures that we cannot be confident of the concentration of power resulting from an economic Wild West yielding an acceptable distribution of income opportunities, let alone income or wealth. With respect to the equity argument we can observe that our societies do not tend to accept the distribution of incomes that would result from a free play of market forces. We do not want to see beggars, particularly not in the streets where we live. We are even willing to pay so that we do not have to, but private philanthropy creates a free-rider problem, which in turn creates a case for intervention directed at the redistribution of incomed. Such equity-induced interventions generally reduce efficiency, but the price is acceptable in principle given the ensuing gains in distribution. We should of course be aware of the potentially damaging effects of the redistribution of income. Individuals may neglect the opportunities they have to organize private insurance against a fall in their income, but a society that does not want to see poverty must either accept it or organize obligatory insurance schemes. For these reasons social security and social insurance schemes can be considered as public goods. The existence of such schemes is likely to generate perverse indications of scarcity in certain periods. The flexibility of labour supply will suffer from the availability of non-labour income. This inflexibility can partly reduce the time in which people have to adjust to true labour scarcity, e.g. by temporarily subsidizing labour costs, with potential benefits for all parties concerned.

I will illustrate my point with an example. Even if many agents realize that wages are too high and profits too low to expand employment and absorb rather wage-insensitive labour supply, wages still need not be flexible. The government can then consider speeding up adjustment by subsidizing labour costs at the expense of household income. Whenever collective action is required to break a deadlock, stabilization policy can be considered as a public good. Whether the actual implementation of stabilization policy is performed by the public or the private sector is, in my opinion, not essential. I do not see however where or how Professor Salin has demonstrated that the optimal producers of this public good would be private parties as he claims in his analysis. Professor Salin's argument that the state is badly designed to produce information conflicts sharply with the authority that public forecasting offices have with private business. Business planners use the information from national planning offices and official agencies such as the OECD and the IMF intensively.

Professor Salin attributes business cycles solely to monetary and financial causes. In the economic literature however quite a number of different cycles and many more possible explanations are suggested. These include financial causes, but also the dynamics of capital formation and obsolescence, the dynamics of income generation, income distribution, expenditure and saving, the interaction between different sectors of production, the dynamics of technological innovation and the diffusion of technology, the interaction between welfare and desires, international interaction, demographic and psychological factors, and political and institutional dynamics. We are simply not able to establish an all-embracing framework that enables us to indentify one or two factors as the only ones having empirical relevance. Professor Salin's examples cannot prove his case. Even if the financial explanation of business cycles were realistic, it should be obvious that modern governments could not neutralize the relevant impulses since their control over the financial markets is far from complete. Professor Salin should be worried by the fact that long waves have been attributed to gold discoveries. There is no reason to believe that financial systems that are not controlled by the government or are not nationalized would be less volatile in modern economies.

I agree with Professor Salin that is is dangerous to neglect relative prices but unlike him I am convinced that it is equally dangerous to neglect "the general level of prices", for this would obscure the transmission between the real and the financial sector and international interaction too. I see no grounds whatsoever for Professor Salin's conjecture that commodity money or currency competition would increase stability. Commodity markets, where price competition is often fierce, are notorious for their unstable prices, as the examples of gold, tin, oil and coffee abundantly illustrate. Since the prices of commodities are unstable, in terms of each other and in terms of goods produced, and the sales value of produced goods is much higher than that of commodities, commodities are the least suitable to act as a monetary base. I cannot understand that anyone would really want to base our money on a commodity such as gold, the value of which crucially depends on the political situation in such countries as South Africa and the Soviet Union.

I agree that a stabilization of real interest rates may be helpful in stabilizing investment activity, although I believe that we would have to think in terms of decades rather than in years. In my opinion, though, such a stabilization cannot be hoped for if market forces are completely left alone.

Since I am convinced that a commodity-based monetary system would be very unstable, I reject the idea of basing the credit system on such a volatile foundation. Like Professor Salin I will not discuss currency competition or free banking in depth. If it is impossible to keep the maffia out of other sectors, there is no justification for the belief that criminals would not perversely exploit previously built-up confidence. I believe that is is technically impossible to reduce the role of all the banks in the world to that of pure intermediaries. There is no institution that has the power to enforce such a situation. If the latter is true and if "real" expansion requires some monetary expansion, there would always be a need for some control over credit expansion. Full liberalization of the monetary and financial systems is not a realistic option. Due to economies of scale, banking is big business. Within a very short time of liberalization, new collective organizations would be established, performing functions comparable to those of the central banks, the IMF, BIS, etc., formally if allowed, informally if forbidden.

I do not find Professor Salin's remarks on exchange rate policies convincing either. Any economist could see that the recent high value of the US dollar was unmaintainable. Nevertheless, it took concerted official action to bring the value of the dollar more into line with its true scarcity. Central banks are better informed, their staffs outclass the average operators on the exchange markets, and those big, private operators who have the most information also have incentives to crate illusions in order to benefit from speculation. Why should we prefer the Kaufmanns to the Volckers? I agree that the more or less stable exchange rates within the EMS will have caused extra fluctuations in some other variables, and that we do not necessarily evaluate the latter properly. On the other hand, though, there are also hidden advantages in terms of trade relations not being broken up by unreliable prices. My guess would be that on average gains are higher than losses.

With respect to Professor Salin's conclusions I have made it clear that in my view the adherence to one or two simplistic decision rules would be a very poor policy. I also believe, however, in the possibility, for both governments and central banks, of giving the private sector a reliable idea about their views on the working of the economic system, their expectations about external events and their priorities when coping with complex situations.

This idea would enable the private sector, or at least its experts, to predict official intervention.

In summary, I consider Professor Salin's stance to be an ideological one. He says that the market should be our only norm. Here I fundamentally disagree. There is no reason to believe that the market forces, left alone, would generate ideal allocation, distribution and stability. On the contrary, there is a great deal of evidence that challenges this claim. Theoretical models of atomistic competition have only limited relevance because economies of scale lead to concentration, future markets are scarce and the vulnerability of agents to risks decreases with their size. In addition, different initial capabilities and external effects create a case for correction. Private correction is unfeasible because of prisoners' dilemmas, free-rider situations, a very unequal distribution of power, its smaller scale and inferior information. Democratic elections provide a base for political intervention. Will such intervention destabilize the economy? Possibly, but not necessarily. Indeed, stabilization policies should reduce risks, facilitate adjustment and help the market system to act properly. Whether they will do so depends on the stance of governments and central banks. If these bodies correctly assess the extent of their power, they may simultaneously correct allocation and distribution, and provide the right signals for private adjustment, both to short and long-term conditions. If they overestimate their power or are overambitious they are bound to generate false impressions of scarcity, which will have destabilizing effects. Stabilization policy requires a well-balanced and holistic approach. The essential points in such a policy can be and should be made known beforehand. This would make them largely predictable, reduce uncertainty and so stabilize our economies. Some poor experiences in the recent past are no more a reason for completely discarding the ambition of stabilization policy than the economic crisis in the thirties was for giving up the market economy.

In conclusion, I think that Professor Salin has presented a clear exposition of some very fundamental ideas, ones which deserve the attention of all would-be interventionists, but I also believe that those ideas should not be brought into practice in the form he suggests, because then the cure would be worse than the disease.

S.K. KUIPERS

Stabilization Policy: A Non-Market Clearing View

In this paper some a priori arguments have been given and some empirical evidence has been presented which support the Keynesian view that capitalist market economies are characterised by macroeconomic disequilibria which can be long-lived. It has been argued that the new-classical view of commodity and labour markets is not only at variance with the actual institutional characteristics of these markets, but moreover leaves important facts unexplained. This led to the conclusion that capitalist market economies need to be stabilized.

The Lucas critique of the use of macroeconometric models for policy evaluation has been rejected with the argument that stabilization policy consists mainly of quantitative policy measures which do not change the stochastic environment in which individuals have to take their decisions. So the Keynesian claim, that market economies can be stabilised, can be maintained.

The monetarist warning for the side-effects of discretionary stabilization is more serious than their attacks on the two other fronts, as experiences in the last two decades indicate that discretionary stabilization policy may impair the efficient allocation of resources. In order to prevent long-run efficiency losses from exceeding welfare gains of stabilization policy, governments should guard against the improper use of stabilization policy instruments.

1. Introduction

During the first three decades after the Second World War most academic economists and policy-makers held the view that a capitalist market economy - to quote Modigliani[1] - "needs be stabilized, can be stabilized and therefore should be stabilized." This can be considered partly a reaction to the traumatic

[1] F. Modigliani, "The Monetarist Controversy or, Should We Forsake Stabilization Policies?," *American Economic Review*, 67 (1977), pp. 1-19. Reprinted in P.G. Korliras and R.S. Thorn (eds.), *Modern Macroeconomics*, New York, *etc.*, 1979, pp. 114-133. Reference is made to the reprint, esp. p.114.

experience of the depression of the 1930's and partly an acceptance of the tenets of Keynesian economics. In Keynesian economics the ultimate causes of the instability of capitalist market economies are twofold:

(1) commodity prices and nominal wages are not perfectly flexible, in particular not in the downward direction;

(2) because of liquidity preference of households and firms the interest rate does not coordinate savings and investments.

Under these circumstances an autonomous fall in an expenditure component does not decrease commodity prices and money wages sufficiently to maintain output at the full-employment level, while because of liquidity preference this task can not be performed by the interest rate either. In the extreme situation of completely downward rigid money wages this fall results in a stable unemployment equilibrium. To restore full employment expansionary fiscal and monetary policies are inevitable. Since in the Keynesian view the interest elasticity of expenditure is low compared with that of money demand, the former policy is considered more effective than the latter. After the Second World War the Keynesian insights led to the use of fiscal and monetary policy as a means of deliberate counter-cyclical demand management.

As early as the late 1940's Friedman challenged the policy conclusion as drawn from Keynesian macroeconomic theory.[2] In his opinion economists are much too ignorant about the lags in the reactions of economic subjects and about the fundamental causes of business fluctuations to justify the discretionary use of fiscal and monetary policy to counteract cyclical fluctuations.[3] Although at that time he did not deny the existence of price rigidities, he proposed fixed rules instead of discretionary actions.[4]

It was not before the 1960's, however, that the real debate between the mo-

---

[2] M. Friedman, "A Monetary and Fiscal Framework for Economic Stability," *American Economic Review*, 38 (1948), pp. 245-264. Reprinted in M. Friedman, *Essays in Positive Economics*, Chicago and London, 1953, pp. 133-156. Reference is made to the reprint.

[3] Friedman (1948), *op.cit.*, p. 144.

[4] These rules included:

" 1. A reform of the monetary on banking system to eliminate both the private creation or destruction of money and discretionary control of the quantity of money by central-bank authority.

2. A policy of determining the volume of government expenditures on goods and services - defined to exclude transfer expenditures of all kinds - entirely on the basis of the community's desire, need, and willingness to pay for public services.

3. A predetermined program of transfer expenditures, consisting of a statement of the conditions and terms under which relief and assistance and other transfer payments will be granted.

4. A progressive tax system which places primary reliance on the personal income tax." Friedman (1948), *op.cit.*, pp. 135-137.

netarists and the Keynesians started. The issues at stake were:
(1) the stability of the demand for money function and the interest elasticity of money demand;
(2) the relative instability of the velocity of money and the investment multiplier;
(3) the stability of the Phillips curve.

From a theoretical point of view issues (1) and (2) have been titled a non-debate as both the Keynesians and the monetarists base their arguments on the same analytical structure, *i.e.* the IS/LM-model.[5] The matters in dispute are empirical in nature. Issue (3) is more fundamental, and it is on this issue that the controversy between Keynesians and monetarists concerning the need for stabilization policy centered since the late 1960's. In Keynesian theory the Phillips curve represents the missing equation that makes it possible to explain the simultaneous appearance of inflation and unemployment. It is a stable adjustment equation according to which inflation is the result of tensions in the commodity and labour market where these tensions are indicated by the unemployment rate. The existence of a trade-off between inflation and unemployment means that the policy-makers can choose between stabilizing the economy on a high or on a low employment level. In the former case they have to accept a high steady inflation rate, in the latter case they can realise a low rate of inflation.

In his 1967 Presidential Address to the American Economic Association Friedman attacked the Keynesian interpretation of the Phillips curve in two points.[6] First, he denied the stability of this curve, as in his opinion the curve would move as inflationary expectations were adjusted to realised inflation. Secondly, he rejected the adjustment-equation interpretation. In his opinion the relation between inflation and unemployment should be interpreted as a supply curve of labour: labour supply will exceed its long-run value as long as the rate of inflation is underestimated and will be below its long-run value if the reverse is the case. In the long run, a trade-off between inflation and unemployment does not exist; unemployment is at its natural level, *i.e.* the level which exists if all markets are cleared and expectations come out. In the short run, the unemployment rate can deviate from the natural rate, not because of non-market clearing - unlike in his 1948 article, prices are now assumed to be completely flexible - but because of expecta-

---

[5] B.M. Friedman, "The Theoretical Non-Debate about Monetarism," *Kredit und Kapital*, 9 (1976), pp. 347-367. See also J. Snippe, *Macroeconomic Adjustment Processes: A Sequential Analytical Approach*, Doctoral Dissertation ,Groningen, 1984, p. 4.

[6] M. Friedman, "The Role of Monetary Policy," *American Economic Review*, 58 (1968), pp. 1-17.

tions adapting only slowly to realisations. Demand management can therefore temporarily change the unemployment rate. Expansionary monetary and fiscal policy aimed at lowering the unemployment rate will in the long run only result in a higher inflation rate and crowding-out of private expenditure, respectively. Although short-run stabilization is possible in principle, it is rejected on the same grounds as in his 1948 paper: the lags between policy measures and the reactions of the private sector are long and of a variable length.

The controversy on the stability and the character of the Phillips curve elucidates the fundamental difference of opinion between the Keynesians and the monetarists. Whereas the Keynesians have their doubts about the stability of the private sector, the monetarists consider it essentially stable. These fundamentally different ideas on the working of market economies appear even more clearly in the variants during the 1970's of the two mainstreams in macroeconomics, *i.e.* the non-market clearing approach to macroeconomics and the new-classical theory. Both approaches to macroeconomics postulate maximising behaviour of households and firms. They differ with respect to the assumptions on market clearing and expectations formation. In new-classical theory all markets are perfect in the sense that they are cleared by price adaptations at every moment of time, while expectations are formed rationally. In the non-market clearing approach, or disequilibrium theory as it is sometimes called, it is denied that commodity and labour markets can be considered auction markets. Although prices are not completely rigid, neither are they so flexible that no non-price rationing occurs. Moreover, individuals are not assumed to have enough information so that, apart from random disturbances, they can forecast the future perfectly.

The implications of the new-classical theory for the need of stabilization are even more straightforward than Friedman's variant of monetarism: as in the former theory deviations from long-run equilibrium are only due to random shocks, stabilization policy lacks any justification, not only in the long run but also in the short run. In disequilibrium theory deviations from long-run equilibrium are at least partly caused by coordination failures. Since these deviations, when occurring at the macro level, need not be automatically corrected, there is a fundamental need for stabilizing the economy.

It is already useful at this stage to confess to being an adherent of the non-market clearing approach to macroeconomics. This article will therefore be written in defense of stabilization policy. In Section 2 the theoretical framework of the non-market clearing approach will be outlined and some empirical evidence will be presented. The new-classical critique of discretionary stabilization policy will be discussed in Section 3. Finally, in Section 4 some conclusions will be drawn.

2. The non-market clearing approach to macroeconomics

2.1 Theoretical framework

General equilibrium theory is characterised by price-rationed markets and perfect foresight. In order to show how general equilibrium might be established, Walras introduced the auctioneer.[7] Via a process of calling out prices, of determining the degree to which markets are cleared at these prices and of revising the prices as long as not all markets are cleared (the tâtonnement process), the vector of equilibrium prices is ultimately fixed. Actual trade is postponed until all markets are cleared. There is no trade at non-equilibrium prices, or in the terminology of Hicks, there is no false trading.[8]

In the non-market clearing approach to macroeconomics both of the basic assumptions of general equilibrium theory, namely the assumption of perfect foresight and the assumption of markets being auction markets, are questioned. According to this approach price adjustments as well as the adjustments of expectations to realisations take time. To see the implications of the latter, assume first that prices are perfectly flexible, so that markets are always cleared by price rationing. If expectations do not come true, then there are only temporary equilibria,[9] but there is no intertemporal equilibrium. The temporary equilibria change from period to period as long as the subjects adjust their expectations. Whether the sequence of temporary equilibria ultimately tends to the Walrasian equilibrium is not at all certain. It has been mentioned that Friedman expects this indeed to be the case. Iwai has made clear, however, that this proposition is based on a very restrictive assumption with respect to the expectations of the different individuals.[10] According to Iwai one has to distinguish between situations in which individuals base their decisions on wrong expectations but where the expectation errors of some individuals are compensated by the errors of other individuals, and situations where such a compensation does not occur. Only in the former case is there reason to assume that Friedman's proposition is true, as then, in contrast with the latter case, there will be no initial disturbance of market equilibrium. Assume, for instance, as Iwai does, that firms are price setters and households are price takers. Firms with too optimistic expectations will adjust their prices downward in the next period, while firms with too pessimistic expectations will raise their prices. In a situation where positive and negative

---

[7] L. Walras, *Elements of Pure Economics*, London, 1954 (Jaffé edition).

[8] J.R. Hicks, *Value and Capital*, Second Edition, Oxford, 1946, p. 129.

[9] Hicks (1946), *op.cit.*, pp. 122 ff.

[10] K. Iwai, *Disequilibrium Dynamics, A Theoretical Analysis of Inflation and Unemployment*, New Haven and London, 1981.

expectation errors cancel, there is no reason that during the process of price adjustment market equilibrium will be disturbed. If positive and negative expectation errors do not cancel, however, than not only will individual price expectations be adjusted but also market prices. In case of generally too pessimistic expectations market prices will rise. Under these circumstances the individual firm with too pessimistic expectations can not realise what it wants to realise, namely a relative price increase in order to get rid of the excess demand for its products. This makes him raise his price in the second round, with the consequence, because the majority of pessimistic firms will do the same, of a further increase of the market price. Unless this process of price increase evokes expenditure restricting forces, there is no reason why this inflationary process will come to an end. Although in a monetary economy these forces indeed exist, for instance restrictive monetary conditions, destabilizing forces also exist, for instance the increased attractiveness of making debts or increasing spending as the result of an expected acceleration of inflation.

Mutatis mutandis, the same argument holds in case of generally too optimistic expectations. Under these conditions a cumulative deflationary process is not excluded.

The above makes it possible to conclude that even in the case that prices are perfectly flexible, capitalist market economies are not necessarily stable. Errors in expectations may give rise to cumulative inflationary and deflationary processes. The Friedman proposition of stability depends essentially on the assumption that too optimistic and too pessimistic expectations cancel, so that market equilibrium is not disturbed. Or in other words, it depends on the assumption that Say's Law holds.

The adherents of the non-market clearing approach point out that not only does the adjustment of expectations take time, but also the adjustment of prices in most commodity and labour markets. Only on auction markets, such as the markets for raw materials, foreign exchange, and the stock exchanges, can the assumption of price-rationed markets be maintained. On the customer markets, for example the market for produced goods and the labour market, this is not possible. Since in these markets the participants have to adjust the prices themselves, a fast price adjustment which immediately clears the market will be an exception, whereas a slow price adjustment will be the rule. As a consequence, exchange occurs at non-equilibrium prices. In particular, if the disequilibria on the various markets are the same in nature, *i.e.* if they are macroeconomic in nature, the consequences may be quite serious, as will become clear in what follows.

If in case of market disequilibria price adjustments are not infinitely fast, the markets in question will not only be cleared by price rationing but also by non-price rationing. The consequence is that market participants on the long side of the market can not realise their expectations. This forces them to reconsider their intentions with respect to other markets (Clower's dual-decision hypothesis[11]). Hereby the equilibrium on other markets will also be disturbed, which in turn will reinforce the initial disequilibrium tendency. In these circumstances effective demand and effective supply do not depend only on relative prices and the initial stocks, as do the notional quantities in general equilibrium theory. Instead, as has already been shown in the 1950's and the 1960's by Patinkin with respect to labour demand, and Clower with respect to consumer demand[12] they also depend on the rationed quantities in the other markets.

As Malinvaud has shown, non-price rationing within a macroeconomic framework (one commodity market and one labour market) may give rise to three disequilibrium regimes[13]:

(1) Keynesian unemployment: households are rationed on the labour market and firms on the commodity market;

(2) inflation[14]: households are rationed on the commodity market and firms on the labour market;

(3) classical unemployment: households are rationed on both the commodity market and the labour market.

This result may give rise to two remarks. First, it has been proven that the disequilibria considered by Keynes, namely Keynesian unemployment and inflation, are compatible with maximising behaviour of households and firms. Keynesian theory can not therefore be discounted as a set of *ad hoc* statements, as is sometimes done by new-classical economists.[15] Secondly, Key-

---

11 R.W. Clower, "The Keynesian Counterrevolution: A Theoretical Appraisal," in: F.H. Hahn and F.P.R. Brechling (eds.), *The Theory of Interest Rates*, London, 1965, pp. 103-125.

12 D. Patinkin, *Money, Interest and Prices*, Second Edition, New York, *etc.*, 1965, Chapter 12. Clower (1965), *op.cit.*

13 E. Malinvaud, *The Theory of Unemployment Reconsidered*, Oxford, 1977. A fourth regime, in which firms are rationed on both the commodity market and the labour is not more than a borderline case between inflation and Keynesian unemployment if stockpiling is taken into consideration. For the latter see J. Muelbauer and R. Portes, "Macroeconomic Models with Quantity Rationing," *Economic Journal*, 76 (1978), pp. 788-821.

14 In his 1977 book in which commodity prices and norminal wages are completely rigid, Malinvaud speaks about repressed inflation.

15 For instance, Bomhoff's criticism of the Central Planning Bureau models of the Dutch economy, as being non-rational, or inconsistent, can be interpreted as such. E.J. Bomhoff, "Models or Markets: Two Approaches to Employment Policy," in: A. Maddison and B.S. Wilpstra (eds.), *Unemployment, The European Perspective*, London and Canberra, 1982, pp. 125-147, esp. p. 133; "Monetarisme en investeringen," in: A.

nesian theory mostly restricts itself wrongly to two regimes of disequilibrium, namely Keynesian unemployment and inflation, thus suggesting that unemployment can only be caused by deficient effective demand. The above indicates, however, that unemployment can also be caused by too low commodity prices and too high money wages and, hence, by too high a real wage rate.[16]

An important question is whether a market economy, characterised by quantity rationing and spill-over effects due to too low adjustment velocities, will ultimately tend in the direction of Walrasian equilibrium under the influence of price adjustments. There is no *a priori* reason that this might occur. The main argument is that under these circumstances individual decisions do not depend so much on price signals as on quantity signals. For instance, a situation of actual underspending, in which productive capacity is underutilised and part of the labour supply is unemployed, will not necessarily disappear if real wages decrease under the influence of the disequilibria in the commodity and labour market. If effective demand does not change, firms have no incentive to increase production. The reverse might even be the case. If relative price changes make the quantity restriction more severe, disequilibrium may still increase.

The conclusion might therefore be that market disequilibria, especially if they are macroeconomic in nature, need not be short-run phenomena if a process of quantity rationing has begun. By this the non-market clearing approach, as developed by Patinkin, Clower, Leijonhufvud, Barro and Grossman, Malinvaud and others has given a micro-foundation to Keynes' main proposition that a capitalist market economy may show disequilibria which are not necessarily short-lived.[17] The reason is not only that individuals react to price signals *and* quantity signals, but also that in a disequilibrium situation relative prices do not reflect long-run relative scarcity. If individuals' long-run decisions, for instance saving and investment decisions, are guided

---

van der Zwan (ed.), *Nederland in zaken, Investeren, winst en werkgelegenheid*, Utrecht-Antwerp, 1985, pp. 97-116, esp. p. 104.

16 Solow and Stiglitz had already arrived at this conclusion in 1968. See R.M. Solow and J.E. Stiglitz, "Output, Employment and Wages in the Short Run," *Quarterly Journal of Economics*, 82 (1968), pp. 537-560.

17 Patinkin (1965), *op.cit.*; Clower (1965), *op.cit.*; A. Leijonhufvud, *On Keynesian Economics and the Economics of Keynes*, London, *etc.*, 1968; R.J. Barro and H.I. Grossman, *Money, Employment and Inflation*, Cambridge, 1976; Malinvaud (1977), *op.cit.* E. Malinvaud, *Profitability and Unemployment*, Cambridge, 1980. Model simulations also point in this direction. See, for instance, Malinvaud (1980) *op.cit.*; K. Groenveld, *Onevenwichtige markten: een sequentie-analytische benadering*, Doctoral Dissertation, Groningen, 1982; Snippe (1985), *op.cit.*

by relative prices, the danger is not just hypothetical that they react to false signals, with the consequence that long-run disequilibria are not precluded.[18]

2.2 Some Empirical Evidence

In Section 2.1 it has been concluded on *a priori* grounds that macroeconomic disequilibria are not necessarily short-lived. In this section some empirical evidence will be presented which supports this view. It concerns time series of capacity labour demand, labour supply (minus frictional unemployment) and the capacity utilisation rate in the private sector of the Dutch economy in the periods 1921 - 1939 and 1959 - 1984. Capacity labour demand is defined as the demand for labour at full utilization of productive capacity. The rate of capacity utilization is defined as actual output divided by capacity output, where capacity output is the output at full capacity utilization. Productive capacity corresponds with a utilization rate that equals one.

Capacity labour demand and productive capacity as referred to in Table 2.2.1 and Figure 2.2.1 are calculated by means of a clay-clay vintage model of the private sector of the Dutch economy as estimated over the periods 1921 - 1939 and 1959 - 1976.[19] These series as referred to in Table 2.2.2 and Figure 2.2.2 are calculated by means of a putty-clay vintage model of the private sector of the Dutch economy, as estimated over the period 1950 - 1980.[20]

Figure 2.2.1 shows that both the interwar and the postwar period are characterised by alternating periods of labour shortage and capital shortage:

1921 - 1930	labour shortage
1930 - 1939	capital shortage
1959 - 1970	labour shortage
1970 - 1976	capital shortage

With respect to the interwar period, the Dutch economy passed from a situation of labour shortage to one of capital shortage in 1931. This result is

[18] This has already been pointed out in an early stage by Witteveen. H.J. Witteveen, *Structuur en conjunctuur*, Haarlem, 1956, pp. 75 ff.More recently it has been pointed out by Malinvaud (1980), *op. cit*; S.K. Kuipers, *Over structurele en conjuncturele ontwikkelingen binnen de Nederlandse economie sinds de eerste Wereldoorlog*, Openbare les, Amsterdam, 1977, p. 26 and C.J. van Eyk, "Het werkgelegenheidsplan," *Economisch-Statistische Berichten*, 67 (1982), pp. 395-399.

[19] S.K. Kuipers, J. Muysken and J. van Sinderen, "The Vintage Approach to Output and Employment Growth in the Netherlands, 1921-1976," *Weltwirtschaftliches Archiv*, 115 (1979), pp. 485-507.

[20] S.K. Kuipers and G.H. Kuper, "Een bouwjaaranalyse van de groeivertraging in Nederland sedert het begin der jaren zeventig," in: A. van der Zwan (ed.), *Nederland in zaken, Investeren, winst en werkgelegenheid*, Utrecht-Antwerp, 1985, pp. 53-80. The estimation in this article is a re-estimation of the putty-clay model in S.K. Kuipers and A.H. van Zon, "Output and Employment Growth in the Netherlands in the Postwar Period: A Putty-Clay Approach," *De Economist*, 130 (1982), pp. 38-70.

Table 2.2.1 - Capacity utilization rate according to the clay-clay vintage model of the Dutch private sector, 1921-1939 and 1959-1976

Year	1921-1939	Year	1959-1976
1921	0.903	1959	0.948
1922	0.903	1960	0.968
1923	0.910	1961	0.950
1924	0.938	1962	0.933
1925	0.945	1963	0.915
1926	0.983	1964	0.954
1927	0.989	1965	0.961
1928	1.000	1966	0.941
1929	1.000	1967	0.952
1930	0.945	1968	0.961
1931	0.865	1969	0.972
1932	0.853	1970	1.000
1933	0.852	1971	0.991
1934	0.867	1972	0.996
1935	0.901	1973	1.009
1936	0.938	1974	1.007
1937	1.011	1975	0.978
1938	0.989	1976	0.998
1939	0.983	-	-

Source: Kuipers, Muysken and Van Sinderen (1979), *op. cit.*, p. 498.

Table 2.2.2 - Capacity utilization rate according to the putty-clay vintage model of the Dutch private sector, 1965-1984

Year	1965-1974	Year	1975-1984
1965	0.988	1975	0.992
1966	0.952	1976	1.030
1967	0.940	1977	1.010
1968	0.942	1978	0.990
1969	0.956	1979	0.961
1970	0.981	1980	0.922
1971	0.985	1981	0.881
1972	0.985	1982	0.847
1973	1.000	1983	0.855
1974	1.011	1984	0.843

Source: Kuipers and Kuper (1985), *op. cit.*, pp. 68 - 69.

Figure 2.2.1 - Capacity Labour Demand, Actual Employment and Labour Supply, 1921-1939 and 1959-1976

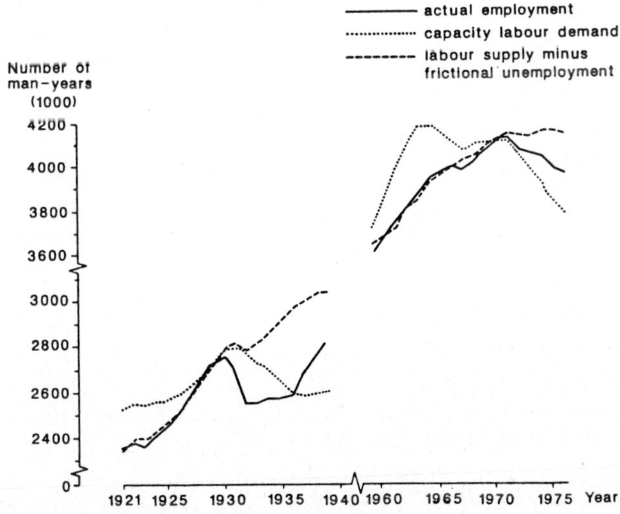

Source: Kuipers, Muysken and Van Sinderen (1979), *op. cit.*, p. 501.

in conflict with Clark's conclusion that the 1920's were still characterised by capital shortage and the 1930's by capital abundance,[21] and with Matthews' opinion that the interwar period was one of capital abundance.[22] Contrary to the last opinion, Witteveen suggests that the whole interwar period suffered from capital shortage.[23] With regard to the post war period it appears that between 1959 and 1969 the Dutch economy is characterised by labour shortage; this situation turns to one of capital shortage in the late sixties. The latter result corresponds with that obtained by means of a putty-clay model, as is shown by Figure 2.2.2.

Figure 2.2.2 - Capacity Labour Demand and Labour Supply, 1965 - 1984

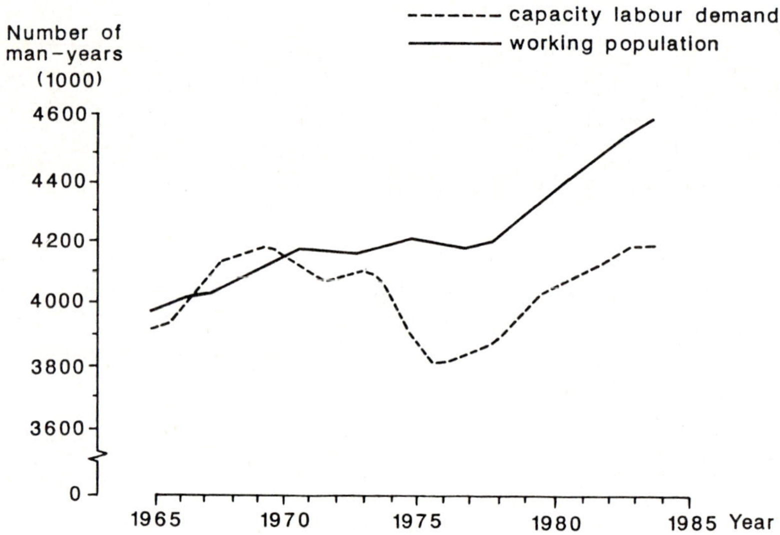

Source: Kuipers and Kuper (1985), *op. cit.*, p. 70

---

[21] C. Clark, *The Economics of 1960*, London, 1942, p. 95.

[22] R.C.O. Matthews, "Why has Britain had Full Employment since the War?," *Economic Journal*, 78 (1968), pp. 555-569, esp. pp. 564-566.

[23] Witteveen (1956), *op.cit.*, p. 90 and H.J. Witteveen, *Het vraagstuk der kapitaalschaarste in Nederland, meer in het bijzonder de schaarste aan risicodragend kapitaal*, Vereniging voor de Staathuishoudkunde, The Hague, 1950, p. 159.

This figure also shows that capital shortage continues until the mid 1980's. Other studies also conclude a situation of labour shortage in the 1960's and capital shortage in the 1970's, for instance Den Hartog's and Tjan's pioneering study.[24] The period of labour shortage in the 1960's is preceded by a period of extreme capital shortage in the 1940's and the early 1950's, which is mainly due to war damage.[25]

Tables 2.2.1 and 2.2.2 show that in contrast with the interwar period changes in the degree of capacity utilization are minor during the first three decades after the Second World War. The fall in the capacity utilization rate since the late 1970's shows, however, a striking correspondence with that in the 1930's. In the 1920's the low degree of capacity utilization is mainly structural in nature, in the sense that it is due to labour shortage. In this respect, these years differ strongly from the 1930's which, in the structural sense, show an abundance of labour but where the degree of capacity utilization is extremely low due to deficient effective demand. In the 1960's productive capacity is also underutilized. The reason for this is the same as for the underutilization in the 1920's: a shortage of labour.[26] When this shortage diminishes, capacity utilization increases. The rate of capacity utilization is rather high in the 1970's. At the end of this decade capacity utilization is deteriorating considerably. In the early 1980's it reaches a level as low as that in the 1930's. Just as in the 1930's, this low level of capacity utilization is due to effective demand deficiency.

Although the above might tempt one to conclude that the transition from a situation of labour shortage in the 1960's to that of capital shortage in the 1970's and the early 1980's resembles closely the transition from labour shortage to capital shortage in the interwar period, it must be noted that the fundamental cause of this transition is quite different in the two periods.[27] In the interwar period the life span of oldest equipment was entirely determined by technical depreciation (the life span is always equal to its maximum technical value). In the 1960's, the 1970's and the early 1980's it is determined by economic factors and shows a falling tendency until the late 1970's. This fall is essentially due to the very high growth rate of real wages (about six percent a year compared with a growth rate of average labour productivity of

[24] H. den Hartog and H.S. Tjan, "Investments, Wages, Prices and Demand for Labour, A Clay-Clay Vintage Model for the Netherlands," *De Economist*, 124 (1976), pp. 32-55.

[25] Kuipers (1977), *op.cit.*

[26] This conclusion does not follow directly from Figure 2.2.2 as this figure indicates capital shortage before 1967. It is also compatible with this figure, however, if one takes account of the considerable extent of labour hourding that has likely happened in these years. See Kuipers and Van Zon (1982), *op.cit.*

[27] Kuipers, *et al.* (1979), *op.cit.*, pp. 500-501.

about four percent a year). These factors account for the essential difference in the causes of the fall of capacity labour demand in the 1930's and the 1970's. Whereas in the 1930's capacity labour demand falls due to an extremely low level of gross investments (induced by the strong fall in the capacity utilization rate), in the 1970's the main cause of the fall in capacity labour demand is the very high rate of obsolescence: the result of the too strong real wage increase. This explains why in the 1970's, in contrast with the 1930's, capacity utilization remains high. Not until demand management became severely restrictive at the end of the 1970's did the utilization rate begin to decrease to values comparable with those in the 1930's.

The above indicates that macroeconomic disequilibria may be long-lived. Since 1960 the following regimes as defined by Malinvaud can be distinguished:
(1) 1960 - 1970 (increasing prices and labour shortage): inflation;
(2) 1970 - 1979 (increasing prices, capital shortage, high degree of capacity utilization): classical unemployment;
(3) 1979 - 1984 (decelerating price increases, capital shortage and strongly falling rates of capacity utilization): Keynesian unemployment, superimposed on classical unemployment.

The appearance of these medium-term disequilibria means that either medium-term stabilization policy was absent, or, in case it was present, it was of the wrong kind or not vigorous enough. From Figure 3.1 in the next section it can be seen that in the Netherlands during the period 1960 - 1984 stabilization policy has been of the wrong kind repeatedly. This is true for fiscal and incomes policy in particular: a broadly speaking too expansionary stance of fiscal policy in the 1960's and 1970's and an unsufficiently restrictive stance of incomes policy in the 1970's.

3. The monetarist critique of discretionary stabilization policy

The analysis of Section 2 leads to the conclusion that a capitalist market economy needs to be stabilized. As Keynesians are mostly optimistic with respect to the effectiveness of stabilization policies, they rather easily conclude that governments should stabilize the economy. In Section 1 it has already been mentioned that monetarists do not share this conclusion. Their attack is directed at all three stages of the argument: (1) a capitalist market economy does not need to be stabilized, (2) it can not be stabilized, and (3) it should not be stabilized.

With respect to the need for stabilization of the economy the most clear-cut view is developed by the new-classical economists. Although they share the view of the adherents of the non-market clearing approach that most commodity markets and the labour markets are not auction markets, so that the market participants themselves have to set prices and find the market-clearing price, they do not think that there is any reason why the market participants would not succeed. They state that market disequilibria are unprofitable for the participants on both sides of the market. This will make them adjust prices rapidly in order to maintain market equilibrium.[28] However, not only is it likely that markets are always cleared by price adjustments, it is also likely that expectations do not deviate systematically from realizations. The argument for the latter proposition is the hypothesis of rational expectations, as formulated initially by Muth[29] and applied in the field of macroeconomics by Lucas, Sargent, Wallace and others.[30] This hypothesis is based on the idea that those subjects who collect the best information about their environment will make the biggest profit. This does not only mean that there is an incentive to be as well-informed as is possible, but also that the only market participants who will survive competition are those who have forecast the actual developments perfectly - except for random disturbances. In this way it is justified to assume that there will be no systematic discrepancies between forecasts and realizations. This does not mean that deviations between forecasts and realizations will not arise. Moreover, these deviations are not necessarily small. Serious random shocks may cause large deviations. The lack of systematic deviations between expectations and realisations only means that on pain of perishing in the competitive struggle, the subjects have to adjust rapidly to changing circumstances.

The assumption of price-rationed markets can be criticised in several ways. (1) It is at variance with the institutional features in most western countries. This is especially true with respect to the labour markets. In most western countries competition in the labour market has decreased considerably in the course of this century. Not only through the strengthening of the trade union movement, but also by government regulations with respect to wage formation and the dismissal of workers. Collective labour agreement acts, acts

---

[28] See, for instance, R.J. Barro, "Second Thoughts on Keynesian Economics," *American Economic Review*, *Papers and Proceedings*, 69 (1979), pp. 54-59. See also P. Korteweg, *Beheersing van de overheidsuitgaven*, Prof. Mr. B.M. Teldersstichting, Geschrift nr. 41, 1981, pp. 5-14, esp. pp. 12 and 13.

[29] J.F. Muth, "Rational Expectations and the Theory of Price Movements," *Econometrica*, 29 (1961), pp. 315-335.

[30] See, for instance, Th.J. Sargent and N. Wallace, "Rational Expectations and the Theory of Economic Policy," *Journal of Monetary Economics*, 2 (1976), pp. 169-183 and R.E. Lucas, "Understanding Business Cycles," in: K. Brunner and A.H. Meltzer (eds.), *Stabilization of the Domestic and International Economy*, Carnegie-Rochester Conference Series, Amsterdam, 1977, pp. 7-29.

which declare collective labour agreements to be binding, and acts which enable governments to declare collective labour agreements to be unbinding have decreased wage competition to a very low level and make it impossible to conceive of labour markets as flex-price markets.

The main objective of regulating competition in the labour market was to protect workers against exploitation and thus to achieve a juster distribution of income. In this view wages are not only considered an instrument of market clearing, but also an instrument of achieving a fair society. In many western countries, particularly in Western Europe, trade unions stress the latter role of wages. One of the consequences of this is their preference for equiproportional wage increases irrespective of the scarcity conditions on the different labour markets. This may be one of the causes of the well-known phenomenon of the rigid wage structure. This is another argument for the claim that it is not possible to conceive of labour markets as continuously price-rationed markets.

A last argument supporting this claim is that trade unions in many countries, at least in the Netherlands, but as far as I know also in other Western European countries such as Great Britain and Sweden, not only strive for a fair distribution of income, but also for employees' participation in management. As entrepreneurs will resist the latter claims more strongly than wage claims, a wage level may be eventually agreed which deviates considerably from that which corresponds with labour market equilibrium.

Although to a less extent, the above argument also holds with respect to the commodity markets. By means of price and competition policy governments intervene in these markets, which makes it difficult to conclude that the working of these markets corresponds with that assumed in new-classical economics. Government intervention is not the only cause of the non-correspondence however. Oligopolistic price-setting behaviour and cartel agreements in times of serious excess supplies also account for this.

(2) Empirical evidence is also at variance with the new-classical assumption of continuous market clearing.

(a) In Section 2.2 evidence on the Dutch economy has been presented which suggests that market economies may be characterised by lasting periods of capital shortage, labour shortage and underutilization of capital. This evidence corresponds with that presented by Bruno and Sachs, which indicates that real wage rates exceeded marginal labour productivity considerably in the 1970's and the early 1980's in most western countries.[31]

(b) If the new-classical assumption of continuous market clearing would hold true, then the strong rise in unemployment in Western European countries

---

[31] M. Bruno and J. Sachs, *Economics of Worldwide Stagflation*, Oxford, 1985,Ch.9.

since the early 1970's would either imply an increase of the same size in frictional unemployment and unemployment due to discrepancies in the labour market, or a considerable fall in labour supply due, for instance, to improvements in the social security system. Empirical evidence for the Netherlands obtained by means of UV-analysis suggests that, although unemployment due to market imperfections has risen sharply, from about 77,000 persons in 1967 to about 138,000 persons in 1981, actual unemployment rose from about 90,000 persons in 1967 to 396,000 persons in 1981, implying a fall in the ratio of unemployment due to market imperfections and actual unemployment from 0.86 in 1967 to 0.35 in 1981.[32] As the influence of social security benefits on the duration of unemployment seems rather small,[33] one has to conclude that the rise in the unemployment rate in the 1970's and the early 1980's has been much stronger than is compatible with a price-clearing labour market. Only 20% of the rise in unemployment between 1967 and 1981 can be explained by the rise in unemployment due to market imperfection.[34]

(c) Lastly, incompatibility between actual developments and the new-classical market-clearing assumption can be concluded by examining the variability of real wages, which is necessary for market clearing, and actual variability. According to Malinvaud, who presents evidence for the French economy, observed variability of real wages is much too low for the market-clearing assumption to hold true.[35]

The above indicates that there is ample reason to argue that the monetarist proposition, namely that a capitalist market economy does not need be stabilized, can not be maintained. This conclusion is still reinforced if expectations are not formed rationally and may be a destabilizing factor of their own, a possibility which, as discussed in Section 2.1, can not be excluded. Moreover, it is well-known from monetary growth theory that if, in an inflationary situation, expected price increases are adjusted very quickly to the actual

---

32 D.J. van den Berg, "Specification and Estimation of the Unemployment-Vacancy Curve in the Period 1956-1979," *De Economist*, 130 (1982), pp. 397 - 419, esp. p. 412.

33 Nickell's estimate of the elasticity of the duration of unemployment with respect to the ratio of unemployment benefits and wages lies in the interval 0.6 - 1.0. S.J. Nickell, "The Effect of Unemployment and Related Benefits on the Duration of Unemployment," *Economic Journal*, 89 (1979), pp. 34-49.

34 Malinvaud's "guestimate" for France is of the same size. E. Malinvaud, *Mass Unemployment*, Oxford, 1984, p. 27.

35 Malinvaud (1984) *op.cit.*, pp. 27-30.

price increases, then the inflationary process proves to be an unstable process.[36, 37]

To conclude that a capitalist market economy needs stabilization does not necessarily mean that it can be stabilized by government regulation. As appeared in Section 1, Friedman in his article on the monetary and fiscal framework does not exclude price rigidities, and therefore the principal need of stabilization. Nevertheless, he rejects discretionary stabilization policies for the reason that governments are much too ignorant with respect to the working of the economies, a standpoint that was repeated in his Presidential Address to the American Economic Association (1967). Instead of discretionary policies he proposed fixed rules.

It is essential to note that when monetarists are speaking about stabilization policy they have in mind stabilizing the Kitchin or the Juglar business cycle. Friedman's counterargument of long lags and lags of variable length essentially refers to these kinds of short-run disequilibria. By implicitly assuming that a capitalist market economy is stable, medium-and long-run disequilibria, as discussed in Section 2.2, are not considered. Stabilization policy in monetarist treatises is policy that aims to reduce the amplitude of the Kitchen or the Juglar. Thus, monetarists' interpretation of stabilization policy is more restrictive than that of Keynesians, who argue that capitalist market economies may not only show short-run but also medium- and long-run disequilibria. So, in the Keynesian view, governments should not only combat short run but also medium- and long-run disequilibria.

The use of macroeconometric models for policy evaluation can be considered the Keynesian answer to Friedman's ignorance argument. It is to this practice that the Lucas critique was directed.[38] The essence of this critique is that shifts in policy may change the behavioural relationships of the models and will hence make these models useless for policy evaluation. Only by re-

---

36 This was already found in 1956 by Cagan. P. Cagan, "The Monetary Dynamics of Hyperinflation," in: M. Friedman (ed.), *Studies in the Quantity Theory of Money*, Chicago, 1956, pp. 23-117, esp. pp. 64-73.

37 The adherents of the rational expectations hypothesis are also confronted with this unstability property in their inflation models. Instead of rejecting the rational expectations hypothesis, they postulate an even stronger hypothesis: subjects are not only assumed to be able to forecast the present period's rate of inflation properly, but they are even thought to be able to calculate the equilibrium rate of inflation. See, for instance, T.J. Sargent and M. Wallace, "The Stability of Models of Money and Growth with Perfect Foresight," *Econometrica*, 41 (1973), pp. 1043-1048. For a comment see D.A. Peel and J.S. Metcalfe, "Divergent Expectations and the Dynamic Stability of Some Simple Macro Economic Models," *Economic Journal*, 89 (1979) pp. 789-798.

38 R.E. Lucas, "Econometric Policy Evaluation: A Critique," in: K. Brunner and A.H. Meltzer (eds.), *The Phillips Curve and Labour Markets*, Vol. 1, Carnegie-Rochester Conference Series on Public Policy, Amsterdam, 1976, pp. 19-46.

lying on the existence of fixed rules can the consequences of policy be assessed sufficiently reliably. This restricts the class of policies to that of fixed rules.[39]

The Lucas critique is less clear-cut and its consequences for economic policy are less evident as it might seem at first sight. With respect to the critique itself it seems useful to remember Tinbergen's distinction between quantitative policy, qualitative policy and reforms.[40] The first kind of policy measures refers to changes in the values of existing policy instruments, and are therefore of a routine character to a large extent. Hence, they will not change the stochastic environment in which the individuals have to make their decisions.[41] These measures will not therefore change the structure of the model, implying that the model estimated by means of past data can be used to evaluate different policy scenario's. Qualitative policy and reforms imply changes in the social organization, for instance a change in the number of taxes and the introduction of a social security scheme, respectively.[42] Hence, policy measures of these kinds are not of a routine character, and will therefore change the stochastic environment. If attempts are made to assess their consequences by means of models estimated with past data, the Lucas critique holds. Most macroeconomic policy measures which aim to stabilize the economy do not belong to these latter classes of policy, however. The Lucas critique can not therefore be considered to be of much consequence for stabilization policy. This conclusion does not change the fact that existing macroeconometric models may be subject to all kinds of errors, for instance specification errors. As far as this is the case these models are indeed unfit for policy evaluation. But this does not mean that macroeconometric models are essentially unfit to do this job.

Even if one shares Lucas' opinion that present-day macroeconometric models are unfit to evaluate discretionary macroeconomic policy measures, it does not follow straightforwardly that, on the contrary, one might be able to assess the consequences of fixed rules, since for this assessment one also needs a well-specified model of the economy. One can not get rid of the impression that the monetarists' preference for fixed rules is based more on some primitive and superficial notions of the working of the economy than on a thorough empirical analysis of the working of the economy under a fixed-rule

---

[39] R.E. Lucas, "Rules, Discretion, and the Role of the Economic Advisor," in: S. Fischer, *Rational Expectations and Economic Policy*, Chicago and London, 1980, pp. 199-210, esp. p. 205.

[40] J. Tinbergen, *Economic Policy: Principles and Design*, Amsterdam, 1966.

[41] See for the same argument C.A. Sims, "Macroeconomics and Reality," *Econometrica*, 48 (1980), pp. 1-48.

[42] Tinbergen (1966), *op.cit.*, p. 7.

regime[43]. Finally, a preference for rules above discretion does not logically rule out discretionary stabilization policies, as these policies themselves can be considered to be a fixed rule, namely the rule specifying the countering of macroeconomic disequilibria by means of well-defined and appropriate macroeconomic policies, a conclusion which does not seem to be denied by Lucas[44].

The third front on which the monetarists attack the Keynesian pro-stabilization policy position is their third proposition that a market economy should not be stabilized. The main argument is that stabilization policy may impair long-run efficiency and therefore long-run growth[45]. This attack seems to be the most serious of the three as the experiences of the last two decades have taught.

(1) The aims of short-run stabilization may be in conflict with those of medium-run stabilization. As medium-run disequilibria are generally more fundamental than short-run disequilibria, this makes counter-cyclical policy (*i.e.* short-run stabilization) impossible. In these cases stabilization policy will prove to be pro-cyclical. From Figure 3.1 on the cyclical nature of stabilization policy in the Netherlands in the postwar period it appears that fiscal policy, monetary policy and incomes policy have been pro-cyclical in quite a number of years. In many of these years this can be explained by the fact that the Dutch government allowed concerns about medium-term stability to prevail above those of short-run stability:

(a) in 1954 - 56 fiscal policy was pro-cyclical because it was thought necessary to increase investment allowances in order to stimulate investments and so reduce the medium-term disequilibrium of capital shortage;

(b) in 1961- 62 fiscal and monetary policy were restrictive in order to combat the medium-term disequilibrium of tied labour markets, excess demand and accelerating inflation;

(c) in the early 1980's fiscal policy, monetary policy and incomes policy were restrictive in most years in order to combat the medium-term disequilibrium of inflation and capital shortage.

These examples lead to the conclusion that if medium-run stability prevails above short-run stability - as it should - the scope for counter-cyclical policy in the sense of short-run stabilization is small in times of serious medium-term disturbances of macroeconomic equilibrium.

(2) The possibility of the discretionary use of instruments of stabilization policy may clear the road for the improper use of these instruments. Political

---

43 For the same kind of criticism, see also Malinvaud (1984), *op.cit.*, p. 79.

44 Lucas (1980), *op.cit.*, p. 206.

45 See, for instance, Friedman (1948), *op.cit.*

decision-making and the influence of pressure groups may lead to a use of these instruments that is either in conflict with the aims of stabilization policy itself or with the fundamental conditions for the efficient allocation of resources within a capitalist market economy. The uncontrollability of government expenditures and the strong increase in the share of tax and non-tax receipts and social security contributions in national income in the 1970's, the extremely high marginal tax rates and the growth of the underground economy give a clear indication of the dangers of the discretionary use of instruments of fiscal and incomes policy.
(3) Centrally regulated incomes and prices policies may lead to rigidities in the labour and commodity markets, and in this way create a wage and price structure which is at variance with the reigning scarcity conditions. As such these policies may significantly impair the flexibility of the economy.

Figure 3.1 - The cyclical nature of stabilization policy in the Netherlands in the postwar period.

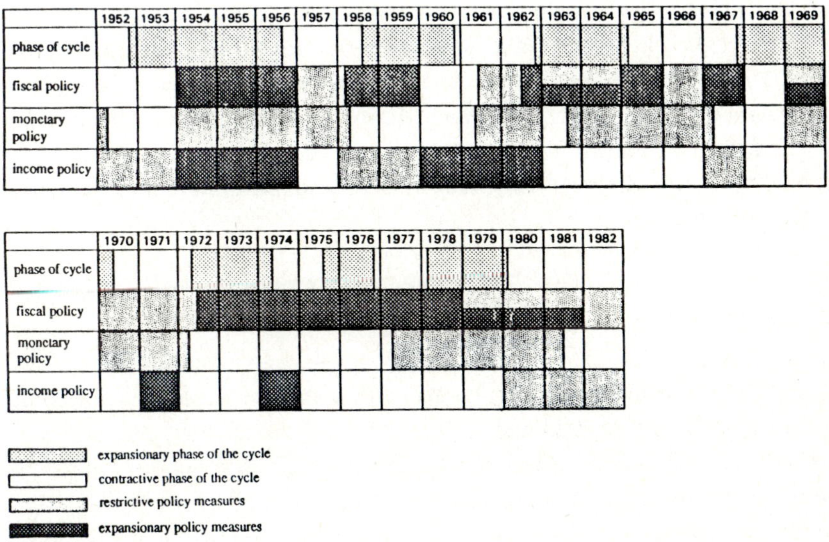

The above does not imply that discretionary stabilization policies should be relinquished in favour of fixed rules. The costs in terms of loss of welfare, in particular due to medium-run disequilibria would be too high. It does imply that stabilization policy should essentially aim at preventing and combating medium-term disequilibria with the consequence that short-run stabilization may often be out of range. It also implies that high demands must be made upon government behaviour:

(a) the proper use of the instruments of stabilization policies by preventing the use of these instruments for distributional aims;

(b) avoiding that stabilization leads to the distortion of the market mechanism.

The latter demand may considerably restrict the use of incomes and prices policies as instruments of stabilization policy. In particular, if these instruments are used to reach medium-term stabilization goals, the danger is certainly not just hypothetical that stabilization leads to rigidities in the wage and price structure, thus impairing the flexibility and by this the growth perspectives of the economy. The extent to which these policy instruments can be used will depend on the one hand on the seriousness of the macroeconomic disequilibria and on the other hand on whether one succeeds in creating an institutional structure which makes it possible to prevent the allocational distortions to a considerable extent. In the author's opinion the guided wage policy which existed in the Netherlands during the 1950's can be considered a good example of an institution which makes it possible to reach the macroeconomic stability aim without giving rise to a substantial distortion of microeconomic efficiency.

4. Conclusion

In this paper some *a priori* arguments have been given and some empirical evidence has been presented which support the Keynesian view that capitalist market economies are characterised by macroeconomic disequilibria which can be long-lived. It has been argued that the new-classical view of commodity and labour markets is not only at variance with the actual institutional characteristics of these markets, but moreover leaves important facts unexplained, such as the small variance in real wages, the strong increase in unemployment and the considerable degree of underutilization of capital during long periods of time. This led to the conclusion that capitalist market economies need to be stabilized.

The Lucas critique of the use of macroeconometric models for policy evaluation has been rejected with the argument that stabilization policy consists mainly of quantitative policy measures which do not change the stochastic environment in which individuals have to take their decisions, and will not therefore change the structure of the model. On the other hand the monetarist proposal of fixed rules is criticized as its consequences have not been assessed by means of a thorough empirical analysis of the economy. Although macroeconometric models are less than perfect, their contribution to policy evaluation justifies the Keynesian claim that market economies can be stabilized.

The monetarist warning for the side-effects of discretionary stabilization is more serious than their attacks on the two other fronts. Experiences in the last two decades seem to indicate that they are right with their warning that discretionary stabilization policy may impair the efficient allocation of resources. In this paper, however, this has not led to the conclusion that discretionary stabilization policy should be relinquished in favour of fixed rules since the costs in terms welfare loss, in particular due to medium-term disequilibria, will be quite high. This conclusion is not however without reservations. In order to prevent long-run inefficiency losses from exceeding the welfare gains of stabilization policy, governments should guard against the improper use of stabilization policy instruments, in particular against the use of these instruments for distributional aims.

Comment by J. Weitenberg (University of Groningen, NCW)

Simon Kuipers has presented a very stimulating analysis of the continuing theoretical debate between the adherents of Keynes and those scholars in economics which have been labelled monetarists. Recently, the latter school of economic thought has also been called the neo-classical or Neo-Austrian School. The great merit of Kuipers' contribution lies in its lucid and clear sketch of the differences between these two main streams of economic thought. These differences boil down to quite distinctive views on the market clearing function of prices.

The neo classicists hold a fundamental belief in the clearing function of prices and actually deny that there can be a long-term disequilibrium in either the goodsmarket or the labour market. They therefore conclude that government should abstain from market intervention, since this would result in a loss of economic welfare. Governments should implement only so-called fixed rules in their policies, so that the risks of false expectations are minimized. The Keynesian school places far less trust in the clearing function of prices. On many markets there is no perfect flexibility of prices, and especially not in a downward direction. In addition, there is no perfect foresight, and only a few markets function as an auction market. Since price adjustments need time and expectations do not always adapt rationally, other mechanisms, for instance unanticipated changes in stocks, fluctuations in deliverytimes and queuing, assume the market-clearing function. Due to these factors the ex-post equilibrium is not stable and this may give rise to such fundamental imbalances in the economy as structural shortages of labour or capital and uncontrolled inflation or deflation.

It is quite clear that Simon Kuipers belongs to the neo-Keynesian school of thought. It is also clear that he is in favour of the proposition that markets should function on the basis of relative scarcities. He therefore does not oppose the clearing function of prices. On the contrary, like a real supply-sider he advocates price flexibility and prefers markets that closely approximate to the ideal of the auction market. We cannot ignore the fact, however, that economic life differs so much from the theoretical paradigm presented by the neo-classicists. I believe that this has been Kuipers' rationale for adhering to the neo-Keynesian approach rather than the monetarist or neo-classical approach.

If the Keynesian view of non-market clearing is supported by empirical evidence , then the key question is whether that evidence is so convincing that the neo-classical approach has to be rejected. Kuipers has drawn his conclusion from a clay-clay vintage analysis of the Dutch economy during the interwar period and the period following 1945. For both periods he concludes that long phases of labour shortage were followed by long phases of capital shortage. Moreover, during the postwar period the transition from labour to capital shortage - the late sixties and a large part of the seventies - was accompanied by high and accelerating rates of inflation. During both periods there were phases of capital shortage, that were also characterized by low rates of capacity utilization, although there were different causal factors.

Not too much significance can be attached to the empirical results from the interwar period. It is well known that the statistics from that period are rather poor. This is true not only for data on the capital stock and the changes in that stock as a result of investments and scrapping, but also for the data on labour supply, employment and unemployment, which are far from complete. I do not blame Kuipers for the poor quality of his statistics (I know that he has used the best available), but the results of his analysis for the interwar period should be treated very carefully.

Data of a far higher quality were used to reach the results for the postwar period. Furthermore, Kuipers' results for that period are quite similar to those of other studies, e.g. those of Den Hartog and Tjan. I think he is completely correct in concluding from his study that the sixties were marked by a structural labour shortage, whereas the dominant feature of the mid-seventies was a structural capital shortage. We cannot draw the unreserved conclusion from these results, however, that the developments in the Dutch economy support the Keynesian view and that we should therefore reject the neo-classical approach.

To make myself clear, I disagree with Kuipers' proposition that most economic policy measures in the Netherlands belonged to the quantitative measures as defined by Tinbergen. Many of them did, but many important ones should be classified as qualitative policy and reform measures. In this context I refer to the following measures:

- the introduction and extension of the social security system;
- the various wage- and price policy measures during the seventies;
- the establishment of a minimum wage rate solely for distribution considerations;
- the more restrictive applications of the hiring and firing legislation;
- the introduction of various income-tied subsidies and contributions;

- and the marginal tax rates which have become very high for a large proportion of the wage earners.

All these measures have fundamentally changed the behaviour and reaction patterns of individuals and enterprises. Or to put it differently: government intervention and regulation has moved the economy away from the ideal type of market (the auction) and has been the source of increasing rigidities and inflexibility. Since this is the present situation, as a second best solution even more government interventions and policies are needed to tackle and adjust the structural imbalances that have been largely caused by the aforementioned reforms and qualitative measures. Should we not interpret Lucas' critique in this way and should policy evaluations based on econometric models as a result be considered useless?

To prevent misunderstandings, I agree with Simon Kuipers that the functioning of our economy is far from being the ideal situation of individuals with perfect foresight and markets that are cleared by a fast adjustment of prices. The basic conditions and assumptions of the neo classical approach are thus not fulfilled. I am not certain though that Kuipers shares the opinion that markets can only function better after fundamental institutional reforms have been carried out.

Speaking about reforming the institutional framework of our economy, I would prefer the following changes:

1. lowering or maybe even withdrawing the minimum wage regulations and creating the possibility of wage earners receiving supplementary benefits to guarantee a decent standard of living;
2. people in the working age groups should be entitled to a higher disposable income if they are employed than if they are completely dependent upon benefits;
3. the various income-tied subsidies and contributions should be abolished or at least the group of potential beneficiaries should be substantially reduced, in order to limit the number of modest income earners who are facing prohibitively high marginal effective tax rates;
4. the income tax system should be reformed and simplified and tax rates should be lowered. This measure could be financed by cuts in the budget and/or by raising indirect taxes;
5. similar reform of the tax on profits and subsidies for investment seems to be necessary, although a small economy must be aware of its limitations so that it can match its facilities to those of foreign countries;
6. finally, regulations on hiring and firing in the labour market and on licensing new business settlements should have a more global character.

I am aware that these reforms cannot be called modest, but if we want a more efficient economy, one that will raise our level of economic welfare, we will inevitably have to restructure and reshape the institutions we have. This is not a specifically Dutch problem. In its Economic Outlook of December 1985, the OECD observed that many economies have recently started the process of adapting their institutions so that they will be more market-orientated .

The Monetary System

ROLAND VAUBEL

Currency competition: Free Entry Versus Governmental Legal Monopoly

Barriers to entry in the production of money lead to a higher price of holding money and to a lower real quantity of money because they raise the inflation rate. Currency competition among central banks is restricted because the benefits of currency competition accrue to money holders and users, while the cost (the greater difficulty of determining the optimal rate of monetary expansion) has to be borne by the central bankers. The five main arguments that are traditionally advanced to justify barriers to entry from private suppliers are analysed and found wanting. In particular, it is shown that money is not a public good.

Whether political agreement on a common money is a public good or a public bad depends on whether money is a natural monopoly good. However, the only operational test of whether money is a natural monopoly good and whether the government is the most efficient provider of it is to permit free entry. A survey of recent historical research on private competitive note issue confirms that the production of money does not converge to a single supplier if entry is possible.

1. Barriers to currency competition

Currency competition for the established national central banks can come from foreign central banks or from private money suppliers (at home or abroad). At present, currency competition from both sources is severely restricted in many countries.

Currency competition from *foreign central banks* can be restricted in several ways:

- the currency issued by the national central bank can be prescribed as a private unit of account[1];

---

[1] For instance, the national currency is prescribed for the denomination of company capital in W.Germany, France, United Kingdom and for all obligations

- contracts in foreign currencies can be prohibited by law or discouraged through discriminatory contract enforcement in the courts[2];
- governments can restrict or discourage the holding of foreign currencies by residents (or the holding of the domestic currency by foreigners) and thereby interfere with the choice of means of payments;
- governments can refuse to accept any other currency than the one issued by their central bank.

Currency competition from *private money suppliers* is not admitted in any industrial country, but there have been many instances of such competition in monetary history (see Vaubel, 1978a, pp. 387-400). To the extent that money may be issued by private enterprises at all, it must usually be denominated in the currency issued by the central bank. Moreover, with minor exceptions, private enterprises are not permitted to issue currency (notes and coins). Their supply of deposits is subject to reserve requirements and many other regulations.

The existence of these barriers to entry raises three questions:

- What welfare-theoretic grounds are there to justify restrictions of currency competition from foreign central banks?
- If there is a case for free currency competition from foreign central banks, why doesn't this case extend to private banks as well?
- If private banks should be free to supply currencies of their own, why should the government (its central bank) supply money, or a monetary unit of account, at all?

These questions are the topics of the following three sections which represent a synthesis of Vaubel (1976, 1977, 1978a, b, 1980, 1982a, b, 1983, 1984). Section 5 adds some considerations about the probable characteristics of the private currencies that might emerge. At the editors' request, the paper concludes with a survey of recent historical research on private competitive note issue.

2. The case for free currency competition among central banks

The standard argument against barriers to entry is that they narrow the consumer's freedom of choice and that they raise the price, and reduce the supply and the quality, of the product in question. Prima facie, an increase in "price"

---

land register (W.Germany, France) or which have to be notarized (Belgium, France).

[2] In the United Kingdom, for example, the courts do not award foreign currency claims if the contract has been concluded between residents or in a "third" currency.

and decrease of supply may seem to be desirable in the case of money. Do not a smaller supply and a higher "price" of money imply less inflation? No, because the argument confuses the price of acquiring money (the inverse of the price level) with the price (opportunity cost) of holding money[3] and overlooks the fact that the holding demand for money is a demand for real balances. Since money is an asset to be held, demand for it depends on the price of holding it. The yield foregone by holding a money that bears no interest or is subject to non-interest bearing reserve requirements, is larger, the higher the expected inflation rate. An inflation-prone central bank loses real money demand to less inflation-prone foreign central banks[4].

In this way, it loses both revenue and its power to affect the national economy through monetary policy. Thus, the removal of barriers to entry encourages less inflationary monetary policies. In real terms, the standard case against barriers to entry applies to the product money as well: the removal of barriers raises the *real* quantity of money and reduces the relative price of *holding* it.

If the standard case for competition applies, it implies not only removal of barriers to entry, but also prevention of collusion among the public producers of money. Collusion is the international coordination of monetary policies[5]. In the extreme case, it takes the form of fixed exchange rates, an international holding-price cartel among money producers[6].

Competition among central banks reduces inflation in at least three ways:

1. "*Exit*"[7]: the world demand for money shifts from the currencies that are expected to depreciate and to be risky, to currencies that are expected to appreciate and to be more stable.
2. "*Voice*"[7]: even if exit does not help, public opinion in the more inflation-ridden countries is impressed by the example of the less inflation-ridden

---

[3] Harry Johnson (1969) has pointed out the same confusion in the work of Pesek and Saving (1967).

[4] In the absence of a forced or legal disequilibrium exchange rate, the less inflationary money prevails, ultimately, not only as a store of value but also as a means of payment. "Gresham's Law" operates only under very specific conditions created by government interventions (Vaubel, 1978a, pp. 82-89.

[5] For a critical analysis of the welfare-theoretic arguments in favour of monetary policy coordination see Vaubel (1985). Vaubel (1978 b) shows that, in 1969-77, the average rate of European monetary expansion has always been negatively correlated with the dispersion of national rates of monetary expansion in the seven main countries.

[6] For a more detailed exposition see Vaubel (1978 a, pp. 33 f.). De Grauwe (1985) shows that, in 1979-84 the (full) members of the European Monetary System reduced their inflation less than the other major OECD countries on a weighted average.

[7] This is the terminology of Albert Hirschman (1970).

countries. It makes the government (the central bank) responsible for its inferior performance. In politics, too, competition works as a mechanism of discovery and imitation.
3. *Acceleration effect*: even in the absence of exit and voice, an inflationary monetary impulse in one country affects the price level faster than a simultaneous monetary expansion of equal size that is common to all, or several, countries. This is because the uncoordinated national monetary impulse affects the exchange rate, and to that extent the price level, almost immediately. By rendering the causal connection between money supply and price level more transparent, international currency competition reduces the likelihood of inflationary monetary policies.

In spite of these beneficial effects, free entry and, more generally, international currency competition are not usually advocated by national central banks, not even by the competitive ones. The Bundesbank, for example, launched a campaign in 1979 to convince the German public and foreign monetary authorities that everything had to be done to prevent the mark from taking over a larger part of the dollar's position as an international currency, especially as an official reserve currency[8].

Typically, central bankers object to international currency competition on the grounds that
- it renders national monetary management more difficult and risky, and that
- it destabilizes exchange rates and the whole international monetary system.

It is true that a spatial money monopolist enjoys a quieter life than a competitive producer, who must take into account not only the changes in total money demand, but also changes in its composition. If the demand for money shifts among currencies, a simple x percent rule for monetary expansion is not likely to be adequate. The forward premium and a world portfolio growth variable will have to be included in the money demand function[9] .Each central bank has to allow for the money supply decisions of other central banks.

Is international currency competition undesirable from an international point of view? It disciplines those who try to supply their product at too high a price. For instance, if international shifts in the demand for money have been responsible for the dollar's and sterling's weakness in the seventies and

---

[8] Deutsche Bundesbank, "The Deutsche Mark as an International Investment Currency", Monthly Report, November 1979, p. 33. For a detailed critique see Vaubel (1982 a). In a later article under the same title, the Bundesbank called foreign holdings of DM assets "neither too large nor too small" (Monthly Report, January 1983, p. 13 of the German edition).

[9] For a theoretical and econometric implementation see Vaubel (1980).

for the weakness of the French Franc in the early eighties, they have played a crucial role in bringing about a correction. International shifts in the demand for money are not the cause of monetary instability but its consequence and symptom. They are part of the corrective feedback mechanism. They impose a constraint which, in open economies, is more likely to be admitted than a constitutional money supply rule.

Why do even central banks that would be competitive object to international currency competition? It is tempting to adopt a public economics approach: the benefits of currency competition accrue to private money holders and users (lower inflation tax and inflation risk) and to domestic taxpayers (larger external seigniorage), but the cost, the greater difficulty of determining the optimal rate of monetary expansion, has to be borne by the central bankers. After all, bureaucrats tend to be held responsible for the errors they commit rather than for the opportunities they miss.

In the theoretical literature (notably Kareken, Wallace, 1981), we find the objection that competition among central banks (outside monies) renders the equilibrium exchange rate(s) indeterminate because all, and only those, exchange rates which promise to be constant, are compatible with a rational expectations equilibrium. This objection is misleading because it assumes that monies are only stores of value and that they can be perfect substitutes. First of all, different groups of people who consume different baskets of commodities prefer different standards of value: since money serves as a standard of value, they would insofar prefer different monies - i.e., monies that are stable in terms of different commodity baskets. Moreover, if for this reason (or owing to past government intervention) different monies coexist, currency transaction costs will reinforce the tendency toward the formation of (overlapping) payments circuits or currency domains. Thus, if money is also viewed as a standard of value and means of payment, two competing monies will hardly ever be perfect substitutes. The Kareken-Wallace view is not relevant [10].

[10] Haberler (1980, p. 44) writes about the Kareken-Wallace view (in paraphrasing Keynes): "it is an extraordinary example of how remorseless logicians can end up in Bedlam, if they get hold of the wrong assumptions"

3. Currency competition from private suppliers: the case for free entry

If free currency competition between the central banks of different countries has the salutary effect of reducing rates of inflation below the monopolistic rates, it is difficult to see why the case for a competitive supply of money should not also extend to competition from private banks of issue. From a present-day perspective, the suggestion of an unrestricted competitive supply of (distinguishable[11]) private high-powered money must be regarded as truly (counter)revolutionary, and even Hayek needed more than half a year to proceed, in 1976, from the demand for "free choice in currency" to the case for the "denationalisation of money".

Several justifications have been given for the prohibition of currency competition from private suppliers:

1. Profit-maximizing private issuers would increase the supply of their money until its price equals the marginal cost of producing it, namely zero; the result would be hyperinflation[12];
2. Private competitive supply of money renders the price level indeterminate[13];
3. The private banking system is inherently unstable;
4. Monopolistic production of money by the state is an efficient way of raising government revenue;
5. The supply of money is a natural monopoly because of economies of scale in production or use;
6. Money exerts positive external effects; money, or the currency unit, may even be a public good.

The first argument repeats the confusion noted above: it mistakes the price of acquiring money for the price (opportunity cost) of holding money. What private profit maximization reduces to almost zero is not the value of money but the opportunity cost of holding it.

Some authors have objected that private suppliers of money may choose to

---

[11] See Klein (1974).

[12] See Lutz (1936, pp. 4 f.), Friedman (1959 a, p. 7; 1969, p. 39), Pesek, Saving (1967, p. 129), Johnson (1968, p. 976), Meltzer (1969, p. 35) and Gehrig (1978, p. 454). This view has been criticized by Klein (1974, pp. 428-31), Vaubel (1977, pp. 449-52) and Girton, Roper (1981, pp. 21-24).

[13] Gurley, Shaw (1960, pp. 255 ff.), Patinkin (1961, p. 116) and McKinnon (1969, p. 316).

maximize their short run profits rather than their long run profits, thus opting for hyperinflation at the time of their greatest success, when the present value of their confidence capital is at its maximum. Klein (1974, p. 449) and Tullock (1975, pp. 496 f.) have replied that private enterprises tend to have a longer planning horizon than democratically elected governments and their central banks. However, this answer implies that central banks act as profit maximizers as well - in some cases a debatable assumption. The answer is rather that, if there is a danger of "profit snatching", money holders will prefer currencies that offer value guarantees. This point will be further developed in the concluding section. It implies that private money is likely to be inside money. The first objection can only apply to outside money.

The second argument is correct in pointing out that the price level is indeterminate indeed, under any system of money production, for the initial supply of nominal balances is an arbitrarily chosen number. To serve as an objection to private currency competition, the argument would have to show that the rate of change of the price level is indeterminate as well under such a system.

The third argument may justify money production by governments, but it does not justify barriers to entry. Whether claims on the private banking system are excessively risky is a question which each money holder can be left to decide on his own, depending on his individual degree of risk aversion.

Fourthly, even if a system of optimal taxation requires a tax on money balances in addition to the wealth tax, what reason is there to assume that the collection of government seigniorage is more efficient than the taxation of private money creation or of private money holdings?

Fifthly, if money is a natural monopoly good, the central bank does not need a legal monopoly (although it may have to be subsidized[14]). Since we do not even know whether money is a natural monopoly good and what its optimal characteristics are (for instance, whether it should be of stable or increasing purchasing power), barriers to competition from private issuers prevent us from finding out; the mechanism of discovery is blocked. A govern-

---

[14] Subsidies may be justified even if marginal cost pricing is not the aim (because the additional taxation required would create excessive distortions elsewhere in the economy). They may be justified if the natural monopolist has passed the point of minimum average cost; for in this exceptional case, which Sharkey (1982, Ch. 5) has emphasized, an efficient natural monopolist may be unable to produce the optimal quantity of output and to sustain himself against less efficient competitors if the government does not pay him a subsidy (which it should offer to all producers who supply at least as much output). Under Sharkey's assumptions, the subsidy must be sufficient to keep the net-of-subsidy average cost of the most efficient supplier of optimal output at the minimum average cost attainable for any smaller quantity of output.

mental producer of money is not an efficient natural monopolist unless he can prevail in conditions of free entry and without discrimination[15]. Historically, the major central banks have not acquired their national monopoly position in this way[16].

Finally, if money exerts positive external effects or is even a public good, there may be a case for subsidization, or even for governmental production, of money, but not for barriers to entry. The private supply of money would be too small, not too large.

4. Should governments supply money?

The previous section has shown that governmental production of money may be justified, if (i) the private banking system is inherently unstable, or if money is a (ii) natural-monopoly good or (iii) a public good. Whether arguments (i) and (ii) apply is an empirical question which cannot be answered as long as free currency competition from private issuers is not permitted[17]. Monetary history does not provide a clear answer[18]. Whether money is a public good, as has often been claimed, is largely a matter of definition and needs to be clarified[19]. There is no generally accepted definition of a public good. However, most authors seem to consider non-rivalness a necessary and sufficient condition[20]. Others regard non-excludability as an alternative sufficient condition[21]. A few treat the term public good as synonymous with positive consumption externality[22].

---

15 Non-discrimination also implies that the government is willing to accept or pay any currency preferred by its private counterpart. Otherwise, a superior private money may not prevail in the market, merely because the government uses only its own money.

16 The Bank of England, for example, was granted its monopoly not because it was gaining ground in the market but because it was losing out to the other joint-stock issuing banks which had emerged after the Bank's joint-stock monopoly had been abolished in 1826 (for details see Vaubel, 1978 a, p. 389, and White, 1986 b). As Jonung (1985, p. 32) shows, the case of the Swedish Riksbank is analogous (see Section 6).

17 For an econometric test of the natural-monopoly hypothesis and for a list of previous studies on this issue see Vaubel (1984). The results are not conclusive.

18 See Vaubel (1978a, pp. 387-401) and the more recent research surveyed in Section 6.

19 The remainder of section 6 is adapted from Vaubel (1984).

20 The seminal modern contribution is Samuelson (1954).

21 See notably Musgrave (1959, p. 9).

22 Samuelson (1969).

In this analysis we shall retain the benefit of being able to distinguish between the general concept of consumption externality and the polar case of a (pure) public good which, in terms of production units, is equally available to all members of the group in a quantity or quality that is independent of the size of the group (non-rivalness)[23].

We shall call a free good a good for which exclusion is not profitable (non-excludability). The question of whether there are also more limited Pareto-relevant consumption externalities will not be pursued here because they would merely justify subsidies to money holders and users[24].

One group of authors ascribe a public good nature to money because "any one agent, holding cash balances of a given average size, is less likely to incur the costs of temporarily running out of cash, the larger are the average balances of those with whom he trades"[25]. However, money balances do not satisfy the non-rivalness criterion (nor the non-excludability criterion): as long as one person holds a unit of money and benefits from its "liquidity services", nobody else can own it and benefit from it. If he gives it away, he increases his own risk of temporarily running out of cash. Therefore, he will demand a price for it.

For the same reason, it is not true that "the provision of a convertible currency is an international 'public good'" because "a convertible currency can be held and used by foreigners" (McKinnon, 1979, p. 3) or that "the dollar is an 'international public good'" because "the United States provides the world's reserve currency" (Schmidt, 1979, p. 143). Otherwise, any exportable good or asset which happens to be supplied by a government would be an international public good.

Kindleberger refers to "the public good provided by money as a unit of account" (1972, p. 434) and "standard of measurement" (1983, p. 383) and applies the term public good to "money" (1978 a, pp. 9-10), "international money" (1976, p. 61; 1978b, p. 286), "an international unit of account" and "international monetary stability" (1972, p. 435). International monetary stability in the sense of stability of purchasing power or exchange rate stability is not a good but a quality characteristic of the product money. Quality characteristics, it is true, meet the non-rivalness test: enjoyment by one does not

---

23 This is essentially Buchanan's definition (1968, p. 54).

24 For a discussion of confidence externalities, price level externalities and transaction cost externalities see Vaubel (1984, p. 32-45). The analysis shows that there may, but need not, be Pareto-relevant externalities in the demand and supply of money.

25 Laidler (1977, pp. 321 f.). A similar view seems to be taken by Kolm (1972, 1977) and Mundell (Claassen, Salin, 1972, p. 97).

detract from enjoyment by others (nor can they be excluded from them) provided they have bought the good itself. However, this applies to the quality characteristics of all goods. If the publicness of its characteristics made a good a public good, all goods that are sold to more than one person would be public goods.

It might be argued that the benefits of a unit of account (and a price index) can be enjoyed by a person independently of whether he holds and uses the money which it denominates (Yeager, 1983, p. 321). More specifically, a person or organization, by adopting a certain unit of accounta (and by publishing a price index for it), may convey information, a public good, to all others. This would imply that government should suggest a unit of account[26] a and publish a price index for it, but not that it should supply money, let alone the only (base) money or monetary unit.

Brunner and Meltzer (1964, 1971) have emphasized that money itself is a substitute for information because it also reduces transaction costs, and because transaction costs can largely be reduced to the costs of information about possible transaction chains, asset properties and exchange ratios between assets. Since money is a substitute for information and since information is a public good, Hamada (1979, p. 7) and Fratianni (1982, p. 437) conclude, there is a "public good nature of money". However, to show that X is a substitute for a public good is not sufficient to prove that X is a public good. A fence, a dog and an alarm system are all, to some extent, substitutes for police protection but they are not public goods. What has to be shown is not that money is a substitute for information but that it provides the public good of information.

Several authors have argued that "public consensus" or "social agreement" on a common money is a way of creating generally useful knowledge and is thus a public good[27]. The knowledge in question is the predictability of individual behaviour. What becomes predictable is not only the money which each individual accepts but also that each individual in the country accepts the same money.

Public decisions by definition meet the non-rivalness test. However, not all public decisions are public goods - they can be public bads (Tullock, 1971). Since the aim of securing predictability of individual trading behaviour, if

---

26 This conclusion is in fact reached by Engels (1981, pp. 10f.), Hall (1981, p. 21) and Yeager (1983, pp. 324 f.).

27 Hamada (1977, p. 16), Frenkel (1975, p. 217), Tullock (1976, p. 524), Tobin (1980, pp. 86-7) and, with respect to the unit of account, Hall (1983, p. 34) and Stockman (1983, p. 52).

taken to the extreme, may serve to justify the most far-reaching central planning by an omnipotent government (Hirshleifer, 1983, p. 132), the mere fact that a certain act of government generates knowledge is not a sufficient justification. It has to be shown that the knowledge in question is worth its cost and that it is provided more efficiently by the government than by a competitive private sector. Both contentions are controversial.

The only operational proof that a common money is more efficient than currency competition and that the government is the most efficient provider of the common money would be to permit free currency competition[28]. Whether the imposition of a common money or monetary unit is a public good or a public bad depends on whether money is a natural monopoly good or not. Hence, there is no independent public good justification for the government's money monopoly. The public good argument is redundant[29].

5. Forecasting monetary arrangements under free currency competition

If currency competition is to serve as a mechanism of discovery, government must not prescribe the characteristics of the privately issued currencies nor the organization of the private issuing institutions; contrary to some proposals[30], for example, it must not prescribe the monetary unit of account nor the types of assets that may be held by the issuing institutions.

Refusal to prescribe specific arrangements does not prevent us from trying to forecast monetary arrangements under free currency competition; even Hayek (1978a, pp. 70 ff., 122 ff.) has done so. Hayek believes that private money would be stable in terms of "the prices of widely traded products such

---

[28] Friedman and Schwartz (1986, p. 48 f.) explicitly agree with this conclusion; however, they are "highly sceptical that, given the starting point with a government currency firmly established, any private issuers would be likely to compete successfully..." Note that such scepticism - however justified it may be - is not an argument against free entry.

[29] Currency competition might even be desirable if the process were known to converge to the government's money; for the government may not know in advance what type of money to converge to: "The monopoly of government issuing money... has...deprived us of the only process by which we can find out what would be good money" (Hayek, 1978 b, p. 5).

[30] Engels (1981) suggests that the government "has the task of defining the monetary unit...in terms of the market valuation of real assets...and of securing the solvency of issuing banks" (pp. 9 f.). Hall (1983) believes that private money must be denominated in an interest-bearing reserve certificate which is issued by the government and is indexed to the price level. For a critical review of Engels see Vaubel (1982 b).

as raw materials, agricultural food stuffs and certain standardized semi-finished industrial products" (p. 71) and that "competition might lead to the extensive use of the same commodity base by a large number of issue banks" (p. 123). Vaubel (1977) has suggested that "value guarantees...are likely to be a necessary condition for acceptance of a competing money" and that "in the presence of unpredictable fluctuations in the determinants of the demand for money, value guarantees can only be maintained with precision and instantaneously, if they can be validated through exchange rate adjustment vis-a-vis another currency for which a price index is calculated" (p. 451). He believes that this reference currency, which cannot also be indexed (owing to the n-th currency problem), would be the outside money supplied by the government. Hayek, in his most recent article on the subject, takes a similar view; he foresees the emergence of "current accounts in a stable unit - redeemable on demand in such amounts of the currencies generally used as are required to buy a 'basket' of raw materials and foodstuffs..." (1986, p. 9).

Another group of authors argues that the optimal money would appreciate relative to goods. Not all of them claim that the money which they regard as most efficient would also be most attractive to money users and prevail in the market, but this possibility should be considered. One variant is the so-called theory of the optimum quantity of money expounded by Friedman (1969), Johnson (1968), Samuelson (1963, 1969) and others; as Mussa (1977) has emphasized and criticized, it views money only as a store of value and ignores its standard of value function. According to another variant, which is due to Alchian and Klein (1973), the optimal monetary unit is stable in terms of a price index of all assets because the money cost of a given level of lifetime consumption utility ought to be held constant. Engels (1981) has recommended a real asset or pure equity standard because it would stabilize Tobin's q and thereby the business cycle. Engels suggests that such a unit would minimize the monetary risk for borrowers who invest in capital goods. However, the same is not likely to be true for all other debtors nor for all creditors. Bilson (1981) wants to transform money into an equity claim on a portfolio of real and nominal assets in order to render movements in the unanticipated rate of inflation countercyclical. A system of competing private mutual fund monies is also envisioned by Fama (1982) and Greenfield, Yeager (1983). White (1984a) predicts that they would not displace the government's outside money.

Whether privately issued money would appreciate relative to, or be stable in terms of, some composite of goods, cannot be predicted with certainty. However, experience with hyperinflation shows that the value of alternative monies, some of them private monies, tends to be linked to the price of one or more commodities. Whether convergence towards a common standard of value and money is efficient and occurs, depends on how similar the purchase and sale plans of different market agents are and how variable they expect the relative prices among commodities to be (see Vaubel, 1978 a, 1982 b).

What assets are private issuing institutions likely to hold if they are not restricted by government? They would minimize their balance sheet risk by having their assets and their money denominated in the same unit of account. The intermediation risk is zero in the case of equity or mutual fund money. It is also zero in the case of commodity reserve money - however, at the price of a zero real rate of return. The issuer of a money whose value is linked to a commodity price index can earn a positive real rate of return without incurring a monetary intermediation risk, if his assets are indexed as well; but he (and his creditors) cannot avoid a real intermediation risk. Thus, under free currency competition - even more than now - the composition of banks' assets will depend on the risk-yield preference trade-off of money users. Their degree of risk aversion is likely to differ, and it may vary over time. It cannot be reliably predicted - not even by governments.

6. Recent historical research on private competitive note issue: a survey

Examples of free entry for unregulated deposit and note issuing private banks are rare in monetary history. There is a long history of private note issuing banks but they were usually regulated with respect to exchange ratios and reserve ratios, and entry was often restricted. Nevertheless, their monies were frequently more stable than the government's money (Vaubel, 1978, pp. 387 - 401); in hyperinflation private issuers sometimes even adopted stable monetary standards of their own (e.g., in Germany in 1923/24). Chen (1975) reports a case in which a money supplied by private issuers circulated at a fluctuating exchange rate vis-a-vis the government's money for two centuries (China, 1650-1850).

Recent historical research has been less concerned with the evolution of such private parallel standards and their superior stability than with the ability of private note issuing banks to conform to the government's standard in conditions of free entry. The issue has been the stability of the banks rather than the stability of the currency. Whether the value of the money which private banks issue is stable depends on both of these aspects.

The focus of interest has been on Free Banking, i.e., the issue of notes by private banks in conditions of free entry. Free entry distinguishes free banks from chartered banks. But, like the chartered banks, the free banks have been regulated to varying degrees. In the United States (1837-63), the free banks had to back their note issue with state and/or federal bonds (mostly valued at par), redeem their notes in specie at par on demand, meet certain minimum capital requirements and accept double liability[31].

Rockoff, in his pioneering study (1975)[32], emphasized the diversity of experiences with Free Banking in the U.S. While six states suffered from wildcat banking at least initially, other Free Banking states like New York, Ohio and Louisiana benefited from "some of the soundest banking of the era" (1974, p. 163). Thus, wildcat banking cannot have been due to free entry as such. Rockoff attributes it to legal suspensions of specie redemption, legal overvaluation of the bond collateral and the frequent absence of penalties for failure to redeem. He presents some evidence that bank profits were lower in Free Banking states because of free entry. He presents an econometric estimate of the (small) welfare loss due to wildcat banking in the U.S. In his 1985 comment, he also emphasizes that "clearly, if we want to draw a lesson about the wisdom of free entry in modern circumstances, the experience of the developed states rather than the frontier states is what is relevant" (p. 888).

King (1983) analyzes the Free Banking era in New York. He shows that "losses on circulating notes occurred only when...the market value of the securities fell below the value of the notes outstanding" (p. 144) and that "dramatic changes in the prices of state debt occurred as some state governments failed to meet their interest payments...For example, the state debt of Indiana and Illinois sold for less than half its nominal value when auctioned off to pay noteholders" (p. 147). His calculations show that in the twenty year period extending from October 1842 through September 1862, the average annual loss suffered by note holders amounted to about 0.04 percent of the total stock of circulating Free Bank notes and that the notes of failed Free Banks comprised about one-sixth of one percent of the total stock of circulating Free Bank notes; in the case of the chartered banks, this percentage was not much lower (pp. 146-51). King emphasizes that "there appears to be little tendency toward concentration in note issue or the general business of banking during this interval" (p. 154) and that "contemporary discussions...do not

31 Until recently, Free Banking in the United States used to be considered a complete failure. The general image was one of fraudulent and chaotic "wildcat banking" with high bankruptcy rates. Research in the 1970s and 1980s has corrected this impression.

32 Rockoff's book was written as a dissertation at the University of Chicago in 1972. Rockoff (1974) summarizes some of the main themes of the dissertation and adds some further quantitative estimates.

stress circulation of counterfeits as an important feature of the N.Y. banking experience" (p. 155).

In a series of papers, Rolnick and Weber of the Federal Reserve Bank of Minneapolis have analyzed a larger and more representative sample of states. In their 1983 analysis of Free Banking experiences in New York, Wisconsin, Indiana and Minnesota, they estimate that 15 percent of the Free Banks closed with losses to note holders (8 percent of Free Banks in New York) and that the average loss in these cases varied between 11 and 26 percent in New York, Wisconsin and Indiana but reached 70 percent in Minnesota. Over the whole period, the value of a randomly selected Free Bank note was 99.9 percent of its face value in New York, 96.4 percent in Wisconsin and 98.6 percent in Indiana but merely 76.5 percent in Minnesota. Rolnick and Weber estimate that the average life of a Free Bank was 7.9 years in New York, 4.3 years in Wisconsin and 2.0 years in Indiana. Considering all three states together, 86 percent of the Free Banks were in business for more than one year.

Kahn (1985) has re-estimated these figures to allow for truncation bias. He shows that the average life of chartered banks (in Maine, Maryland and New Jersey) was almost three times as long as that of Free Banks (in New Jersey and the four states analysed by Rolnick and Weber)[33]. The expected one-year holding loss of Free Bank note holders was 0.2 percent in New York, 2 percent in Wisconsin and Indiana and 12 percent in Minnesota, if information for the whole sample period is used.

In their 1984 paper, Rolnick and Weber test for two alternative explanations of Free Bank failures. The first, the "wildcat explanation", is that banks were set up to make quick and easy profits by issuing notes when the bonds that were eligible as collateral at par stood below par, and by failing soon after (say, within a year). The alternative explanation is that the bank failures were involuntary and due to the fact that the outstanding note issue could no longer be redeemed when bond prices fell. Rolnick and Weber find that at least 79 percent of the Free Bank failures in New York, Indiana, Wisconsin and Minnesota are consistent with the falling asset price hypothesis, whereas at most 21 percent satisfy the conditions for wildcat banking. 77 percent can only be explained by falling asset prices, 11 percent only by wildcat banking (most of them in Minnesota).Most recently, Rolnick and Weber (1986) have examined the additional hypothesis that the failures of Free Banks were caused by contagious runs. Such runs could either be due to local real shocks ("intrinsic

[33] This is consistent with the expectation that the regulation of entry served to protect the established banks. Thus, as Gorton (1985, p. 273) stresses, the frequency of panics or bankruptcies "is not sufficient evidence for any welfare comparison".

uncertainty") or to random withdrawals of specie ("extrinsic uncertainty"). Rolnick and Weber find that 85 percent of the Free Bank failures in New York, Indiana, Wisconsin and Minnesota may have been due to local real shocks but that "whatever contagion might have existed was limited to specific states" because of the state bond requirement (p. 886). However, in a comment, White (1986a, p. 894) suggests that the state bond requirement itself was a major cause of Free Bank failure, not only because it encouraged wildcatting and unduly exposed the banks to the risk of declining state bond prices, but also because it made the banks susceptible to reserve losses at times when the public desired to hold more currency relative to deposits.

The most ambitious among the recent historical studies of Free Banking is White's book (1984 b) on the highly successful Scottish experience (1716-1844). When in 1716 the legal monopoly of the Bank of Scotland (a private chartered bank) elapsed, entry into the banking industry was no longer restricted. But it was not before 1749 that the first non-chartered banks were established. They also issued notes. In 1756, attempts to form a cartel among the chartered and the free banks failed. While the chartered banks enjoyed limited liability, the free banks were partnerships legally subject to unlimited liability. In 1765 two further regulations were imposed:

-the banks were prohibited to issue small notes (until 1797 and again from 1829 onwards); and

- the banks were obliged to redeem their notes in specie on demand (rather than after six months at 5 percent interest as they could before 1765).

Unlike the American Free Banks, the Scottish free banks could not count on the government suspending redeemability. There was only one general suspension of specie payments in Scotland (1797-1821), and this was not due to a local overissue but part of a governmental suspension that extended to the whole kingdom and was mainly to protect the Bank of England (White 1984 b, pp. 140 f.). Notes circulated at par. A few free banks failed (notably in 1772/73), but creditors were usually paid off in full because the bank owners were fully liable with their personal wealth. The number of free banks issuing notes reached a maximum of about 30 when joint-stock banking spread from 1810 onwards. By 1844, it had declined to 19. In that year, Peel's Bank Act blocked entry into note issuing in all parts of the United Kingdom. Under the Scottish Banking Act (1845), existing Scottish banks had to meet a 100 percent specie reserve requirement for additional note issues.

White (1984 b, pp. 147 f.) draws nine lessons from the Scottish free banking experience.
"1. bad bank notes do not drive out good;
2. counterfeiting does not pose a major problem;
3. banks are not inherently prone to overissue and suspension;
4. banks will not hold chronically insufficient or excessive reserves;
5. bank runs are not an endemic problem[34];
6. there is no clear need for a lender of last resort;
7. no pyramiding of reserves, making credit inherently unstable, takes place;
8. no natural monopoly exists in the production of paper currency[35];
9. proliferation of bank note brands is not a problem".

Finally, Jonung's recent study (1985) of the Swedish experience (1831-1906) ought to be mentioned. Bank notes were not only issued by the Swedish central bank (Riksbank) but also by private banks that were neither subject to specie reserve requirements nor to government inspection. The private issuing banks (enskilda banks) had to apply for a royal charter but many such charters were granted. The applicants had to be partnerships with unlimited liability. Moreover, there were certain disclosure rules and an obligation never to apply for help from the government. In 1846, the following regulations were added:
- a minimum capital was prescribed;
- the part of the private note issue that was not backed by Riksbank notes, coins or deposits was limited to 50 percent of the bank's capital;
- the notes had to be redeemed on demand;
- no small notes were to be issued;
- all offices and branches had to be located in towns.

Later revisions included a minimum for the number of shareholders, a penalty rate of interest (6 percent) for delayed redemption and the requirement that bank directors had to deposit one of their shares with the bank. Unlike the Riksbank notes, the private bank notes were not legal tender, but this did

---

[34] Gorton, in his review essay (1985), emphasizes the theoretical implications of this observation: "It does not appear that the failure of a bank in Scotland ever led to a chain of runs on other banks through some sort of information externality as is often alleged to have happened in the United States" (p. 270)

[35] "No one bank could serve the entire market so cheaply as to exclude others. Scottish experience offers no reason to suppose that there exist 'natural monopoly' characteristics in the production of convertible currency" (White, 1984 b, p. 36). "There was no evidence of natural monopoly in issue, nor even of a natural number of firms that could be called 'small'..." (p. 146).

not prevent them from competing very successfully with the Riksbank notes. From the 1850s onwards the market share of the private bank notes exceeded 50 percent. From the 1870s onwards, the number of note issuing banks was stable at about twenty-six[36]. The notes circulated at par with no failure to redeem (though in two instances private issuing banks did receive financial support from the government). There were no serious problems with counterfeiting in spite of the fact that counterfeiting of private bank notes was not punished as severely as counterfeiting of Riksbank notes. The Riksbank and Parliament (the Riksdag) were generally hostile to the private issuing banks and tried to tax them out of existence; the tax on the private note issue was introduced in 1856 and successively raised from 0.2 percent to one percent (in 1889). In 1897 and 1901, the government made offers to the banks in exchange for their right to issue notes and, in this way, finally managed to establish the legal note issuing monopoly of the Riksbank. Thereafter, the share of notes in the Swedish money stock declined significantly. According to Jonung, "the main reason why the bank of the parliament was turned into a central bank was not that the Riksbank had any dominant competitive advantage on the markets for notes and deposits per se. Rather, the economic inefficiency of this official institution eventually meant that it was empowered through legislation by monopoly powers to protect it from competition from private money producers, thus becoming the central bank of Sweden" (p. 32).

How important are these findings for the debate about currency competition and free entry? From a present day perspective, the important point is certainly not that private banks can be competitive and efficient suppliers of bank notes; of course, they can, just as they can be competitive and efficient suppliers of bank deposits. Nor is it necessary to prove that free entry yields desirable results in the banking industry: we have free entry in deposit banking in most industrialized countries. The important insight, which the recent studies of private competitive money production provide, is that the present degree of banking regulation is not justified. What they cannot show is whether the currency unit is a natural monopoly; for alternative currency units were not permitted in those instances. They falsify the natural monopoly hypothesis for money but not for currencies. A more comprehensive test requires free entry with respect to private and foreign governmental currencies.

---

[36] As Jonung emphasizes, this and the queue of entrants trying to obtain charters "suggests that the production of notes was not a natural monopoly" (p. 33).

References:

Alchian, Armen A., Benjamin Klein (1973), "On a Correct Measure of Inflation", *Journal of Money, Credit and Banking*, 5(1), pp. 173-191.

Bilson, John F.O. (1981), *A Proposal for Monetary Reform*, University of Chicago, unpubl. manuscript, Sept., 30 p.

Brunner, Karl, Allan H. Meltzer (1964), "Some Further Investigations of Demand and Supply Functions for Money", *Journal of Finance*, 19(2), pp. 240-283.

Brunner, Karl, Allan H. Meltzer (1971), "The Uses of Money: Money in the Theory of an Exchange Economy", *American Economic Review*, 61(5), pp. 784-805.

Buchanan, James M. (1968), *The Demand and Supply of Public Goods*, Chicago.

Chen, Chau-Nan (1975), "Flexible Bimetallic Exchange Rates in China, 1650-1850: A Historical Example of Optimum Currency Areas", *Journal of Money, Credit and Banking*, 7(2), pp. 359-376.

Claassen, Emil M., Pascal Salin, Eds. (1972), *Stabilization Policies in Interdependent Economies*, Amsterdam, London.

Engels, Wolfram (1981), *The Optimal Monetary Unit*, Frankfurt.

Fama, Eugene F., *Fiduciary Currency and Commodity Standards*, mimeo, University of Chicago, Jan. 1982.

Fratianni, Michele (1982), "The Dollar and the ECU", *The International Monetary System: A Time of Turbulence*. J.S. Dreyer, G. Haberler, T.D. Willett, Eds., Washington, D.C. pp. 430-453.

Frenkel, Jacob A. (1975), "Reflections on European Monetary Integration", *Weltwirtschaftliches Archiv*, 111(2), pp. 216-221.

Friedman, Milton (1959a), *A Program for Monetary Stability*, New York

Friedman, Milton (1959b), "The Demand for Money: Some Theoretical and Empirical Results", *Journal of Political Economy*, 67(4) pp. 327-351.

Friedman, Milton (1969), *The Optimum Quantity of Money and Other Essays*, Chicago.

Friedman, Milton (1981), *Monetary System for a Free Society*, Hoover Institution, Stanford, unpubl. manuscript, Nov., 14 p.

Friedman, Milton, Anna J. Schwartz (1986), "Has Government Any Role in Money?" *Journal of Monetary Economics*, 17 (1), pp. 37-62.

Gehrig, Bruno (1978), "Brauchen wir monopolistische Zentralbanken?", *Wirtschaft und Recht*, 30(4), pp. 452-464.

Girton, Lance, Don Roper (1981), "Theory and Implications of Currency Substitution", *Journal of Money, Credit and Banking*, 13(1), pp. 12-30.

Gorton, Gary (1985), "Banking Theory and Free Banking History: A Review Essay", *Journal of Monetary Economics*, 16 (2), pp. 267-276.

Grauwe, Paul de (1985), "Should the U.K. join the European Monetary System?", Treasury and Civil Service Committee, Subcommittee *Report on the European Monetary System*, London 1985, Annex, pp. 5-11.

Greenfield, Robert L., Leland B. Yeager (1983), "A Laissez Faire Approach to Monetary Stability", *Journal of Money, Credit and Banking*, 15, pp. 302-15.

Gurley, John G., Edward S. Shaw (1960), *Money in a Theory of Finance*, Washington.

Haberler, Gottfried (1980), "Flexible Exchange-Rate Theories and Controversies Once Again", *Flexible Exchange Rates and the Balance of Payments*. Essays in Memory of Egon Sohmen John S. Chipman, Charles P. Kindleberger, Eds., Amsterdam, New York, Oxford, pp. 29-48.

Hall, Robert E. (1981), *The Role of Government in Stabilizing Prices and Regulating Money*, Stanford University, unpubl. manuscript, Jan., 34 p.

Hall, Robert E. (1983), "Optimal Fiduciary Monetary Systems", *Journal of Monetary Economics*, 12(3), pp. 33-50.

Hall, Robert E. (1984), "A Free-Market Policy to Stabilize the Purchasing Power of the Dollar", *Money in Crisis*, Barry N. Siegel, Ed., San Francisco, pp. 303-321.

Hamada, Koichi (1977), "On the Political Economy of Monetary Integration: A Public Economics Approach", *The Political Economy of Monetary Reform*, Robert Z. Aliber, Ed., London, Basingstoke, pp. 13-31.

Hamada, Koichi (1979), *On the Coordination of Monetary Policies in a Monetary Union*, Paper presented at the Conference on "New Economic Approaches to the Study of International Integration", Florence, May/June, 32 p.

Hayek, Friedrich A. (1976a), *Choice in Currency. A Way to Stop Inflation*. Institute of Economic Affaires, London, Occasional Papers, 48.

Hayek, Friedrich A. (1976b, 1978a), *Denationalisation of Money*, Institute of Economic Affairs, London, Hobart Paper Special, 70.

Hayek, Friedrich A. (1978b), "Towards a Free Market Monetary System", *Journal of Libertarian Studies*, 3, pp. 1-8.

Hayek, Friedrich A. (1984), "The Future Monetary Unit of Value", Money in Crisis. Barry N. Siegel, Ed., San Francisco, pp. 323-335.

Hayek, Friedrich A. (1986), "Market Standards for Money", *Economic Affairs*, London, 6 (4), pp. 8-10.

Hirschman, Albert O. (1970), *Exit, Voice, and Loyalty*, Cambridge, Mass.

Hirshleifer, Jack (1973), "Exchange Theory: The Missing Chapter", *Western Economic Journal* 11(2), pp. 129-146.
Johnson, Harry G. (1968), "Problems of Efficiency in Monetary Management", *Journal of Political Economy*, 76(5), pp. 971-990.
Johnson, Harry G. (1969), "Pesek and Saving's Theory of Money and Wealth", *Journal of Money, Credit and Banking* 1(3), pp. 535-537.
Jonung Lars, (1985), *The Economics of Private Money: The Experience of Private Notes in Sweden 1831-1902*, paper presented at the meeting of the Monetary History Group, London, Sept., 48 p.
Kahn, James A. (1985), "Another Look at Free Banking in the United States", *American Economic Review*, 75 (4), pp. 881-885.
Kareken, John, Neil Wallace (1981), "On the Indeterminacy of Equilibrium Exchange Rates", *Quarterly Journal of Economics*, 96, pp. 202-222.
Kindleberger, Charles P. (1972), "The Benefits of International Money", *Journal of International Economics*, 2 (3), pp. 425-442.
Kindleberger, Charles P. (1976), "Lessons from Floating Exchange Rates", *Institutional Arrangements and the Inflation Problem*. Karl Brunner, Allan H. Meltzer, Eds., Amsterdam, New York, Oxford, pp. 51-77.
Kindleberger, Charles P. (1978a), *Manias, Panics and Crashes* London, Basingstoke.
Kindleberger, Charles P. (1978b), "Dominance and Leadership in the International Economy: Exploitation, Public Goods, and Free Rides", *Hommage a Francois Perroux,* Grenoble, pp. 283-291.
Kindleberger, Charles P. (1983), "Standards as Public, Collective and Private Goods", *Kyklos* 36(3), pp. 377-396.
King, Robert G. (1983), "On the Economics of Private Money", *Journal of Monetary Economics*, 12 (1), pp. 127-158.
Klein, Benjamin (1974), "The Competitive Supply of Money", *Journal of Money,Credit and Banking*, 6(4), pp. 423-453.
Kolm, Serge-Christophe (1972), "External Liquidity : A Study in Monetary Welfare Economics", *Mathematical Methods in Investment and Finance,*. Giorgio P. Szegö, Karl Shell, Eds., Amsterdam, London, New York, pp. 190-206.
Kolm, Serge-Christophe (1977), "Fondements de l'économie monétaire normative: seignieurage, liquidité externe, impossibilité de remunérer les espèces", *Revue Economique*, 28(1), pp. 1-35.
Laidler, David E.W. (1977), "The Welfare Costs of Inflation in Neoclassical Theory - Some Unsettled Problems", *Inflation Theory and Anti-Inflation Policy,* Erik Lundberg, Ed., Boulder, Col., pp. 314-328.
Lutz, Friedrich A. (1936), *Das Grundproblem der Geldverfassung*, Berlin.

McKean, Roland N. (1958), *Efficiency in Government through Systems Analysis*, New York.

McKinnon, Ronald I. (1969), *Private and Official International Money: The Case for the Dollar*, Essays in International Finance, Princeton, 74.

McKinnon, Ronald I. (1979), *Money in International Exchange*, New York, Oxford.

Meltzer, Allan H. (1969), "Money, Intermediation and Growth", *Journal of Economic Literature*, 7(1), pp. 27-56.

Mussa, Michael (1977), "The Welfare Cost of Inflation and the Role of Money as a Unit of Account", *Journal of Money, Credit and Banking*, 9(2), pp. 276-286.

Musgrave, Richard A. (1959), *The Theory of Public Finance*, New York, Toronto, London.

Patinkin, Don (1961), "Financial Intermediaries and the Logical Structure of Monetary Theory", *American Economic Review*, 51(1), pp. 95-116.

Pesek, Boris P., Thomas R. Saving (1967), *Money, Wealth and Economic Theory*, London.

Rockoff, Hugh (1974), "The Free Banking Era: A Reexamination", *Journal of Money, Credit and Banking*, 6 (2), pp. 140-167.

Rockoff, Hugh (1975), *The Free Banking Era: A Reexamination*, New York.

Rockoff, Hugh (1985), "New Evidence on Free Banking in the United States", *American Economic Review*, 75 (4), pp. 886-889.

Rolnick, Arthur J., Warren E. Weber (1983), "New Evidence on the Free Banking Era", *American Economic Review*, 73 (5), pp. 1080-1091.

Rolnick, Arthur J., Warren E. Weber (1984), "The Causes of Free Bank Failures", *Journal of Monetary Economics*, 14 (2), pp. 267-291.

Rolnick, Arthur J., Warren E. Weber (1986), "Inherent Instability in Banking: The Free Banking Experience", *Cato Journal*, 5 (3), pp. 877-890.

Samuelson, Paul A. (1954), "The Pure Theory of Public Expenditure", *Review of Economics and Statistics*, 35(4), pp. 387-389.

Samuelson, Paul A. (1963), "D.H. Robertson (1890-1963)", *Quarterly Journal of Economics*, 77(4), pp. 517-536.

Samuelson, Paul A. (1969), "Pure Theory of Public Expenditures and Taxation", *Public Economics*, Julius Margolis, Henri Guitton, Eds., London, pp. 98-123.

Schmidt, Wilson E. (1979), *The U.S. Balance of Payments and the Sinking Dollar*, New York.

Scitovsky, Tibor (1954), "Two Concepts of External Economies", *Journal of Political Economy*, 62(1), pp. 143-151.

Sharkey, William W. (1982), *The Theory of Natural Monopoly*, Cambridge.

Stockman, Alan C. (1983), "Comments on R.E. Hall's Paper", *Journal of Monetary Economics*, 12(1), pp. 51-54.
Tobin, James (1980), "Discussion", *Models of Monetary Economies*, J.H. Kareken, N. Wallace, Eds., Federal Reserve Bank of Minneapolis, pp. 83-90.
Tullock, Gordon (1971), "Public Decisions as Public Goods", *Journal of Political Economy*, 79(4), pp. 913-918.
Tullock, Gordon (1975), "Competing Monies", *Journal of Money, Credit and Banking*, 7(4), pp. 491-497.
Tullock, Gordon (1976), "Competing Monies: A Reply", *Journal of Money, Credit and Banking*, 8(4), pp. 521-525.
Vaubel, Roland (1976), "Freier Wettbewerb zwischen Währungen?" *Wirtschaftdienst* (Hamburg), 56(8), pp. 422-428.
Vaubel, Roland (1977), "Free Currency Competition", *Weltwirtschaftliches Archiv*, 113(3), pp. 435-461.
Vaubel, Roland (1980), *Strategies for Currency Unification: The Economics of Currency Competition and the Case for a European Parallel Currency*, Tuebingen.
Vaubel, Roland (1978b), "The Money Supply in Europe: Why EMS may make inflation worse", *Euromoney*, Dec., pp. 139-142.
Vaubel, Roland (1978b), "International Shifts in the Demand for Money, their Effects on Exchange Rates and Price Levels, and their Implications for the Preannouncement of Monetary Expansion", *Weltwirtschaftliches Archiv*, 116(1), pp. 1-44.
Vaubel, Roland (1982a), "West Germany's and Switzerland's Experience with Exchange-Rate Flexibility", *The International Monetary System: A Time of Turbulence*, J.S. Dreyer, G. Haberler, T.D. Willett, Eds., Washington, D.C., pp. 180-222.
Vaubel, Roland (1982b), "Private Geldproduktion und Optimale Währungseinheit" (Review of 'The Optimal Monetary Unit' by Wolfram Engels), *Weltwirtschaftliches Archiv*, pp. 581-585.
Vaubel, Roland (1984), "The Government's Money Monopoly: Externalities or Natural Monopoly?", *Kyklos*, 37(1), pp. 27-58.
Vaubel, Roland (1985), "International Collusion or Competition for Macroeconomic Policy Coordination? A Restatement", *Recherches Economiques de Louvain*, 51 (3-4), pp. 223-240.
White, Lawrence H. (1984a), "Competitive Payments Systems and the Unit of Account", *American Economic Review*, 74 (4), pp. 699-712.
White, Lawrence H. (1984b), *Free Banking in Britain: Theory, Evidence and Debate, 1800-1845*, Cambridge.

White, Lawrence H. (1984c), "Free Banking as an Alternative Monetary System", *Money in Crises*. Barry N. Siegel, Ed., San Francisco, pp. 269-302.

White, Lawrence H. (1986a), "Regulatory Sources of Instability in Banking", *Cato Journal*, 5 (3), pp. 891-897.

White, Lawrence H. (1986b), "Depoliticizing the Supply of Money", *Political Business Cycles and the Political Economy of Stagflation*, Thomas D. Willett, Ed., Pacific Institute.

Yeager, Leland B. (1983), "Stable Money and Free Market Currencies", *Cato Journal*, 3 (1), pp. 305-326.

Comment by Eduard J. Bomhoff (Erasmus University)

Why do governments wish to monopolize the supply of money? The historical answer is without doubt the possession of a flexible means of taxation: issuing money provides seigniorage to the issuer. Compared to other forms of taxation, collection of seigniorage has two advantages: it does not require legislative approval and the citizens may not be able to identify the true identity of the tax collector. Inflation can be blamed on unions, other monopolists or foreigners, making people overlook that the issuers of money collect seignorage at the expense of the current holders of money.

In his authoritative survey Roland Vaubel points to some real costs of this government monopoly and makes the case for competition in the supply of money. I find his warnings against an international cartel of Central Banks quite convincing. The debate in the U.K. about the introduction of an anti-inflation policy in the late 1970's, for instance, was positively influenced by the visible example of more virtuous monetary policies abroad.

Vaubel's exposition of the arguments for domestic competition in the supply of currency is stimulating. His discussion casts more light, however, on the stability or instability of various banking arrangements than on the case for private supply of currency. For, he limits his inquiry to whether private suppliers would be able to provide stable money. The answer then depends on two points: is it in their interest to do so, and are they able to do it? Vaubel marshals the historical evidence to argue for a positive answer to both questions. He does not consider the possibility, however, that monetary policy should amount to something more than providing stable money[1] For example, do we want the suppliers of money to react immediately to incipient potential financial panics? Or, do we want the money supply to be accommodative in the face of a sudden surge in (some) import prices? How should the money supply react to an exceptional increase in the national wage level, as for example in France in june 1968? To me it is not obvious that the interests of competitive privatized suppliers of money automatically coincide with the national interest.

---

[1] See his list of possible justifications for prohibiting private issue of currency. It does not include potential conflicts between the interest of profit-maximizing banks and the national interest under circumstances when a quick reaction to some unforeseen problem may be asked from the suppliers of currency.

In many ways the supply of money can be analyzed like the supply of drinking water and Vaubel rightly points out that monopolies are dangerous and that private suppliers might do a superior job of providing stable, non-inflationary money. But what if we want the suppliers of money to be not only stable (almost always) but also flexible when required? The full case for private money requires either the assertion that stability of supply is all that is required or an analysis that profit-maximizing private suppliers would react to emergencies in a way that reflected the social interest, or at least was not inferior to the observed record of our official Central Banks.

Assume, for example, that we have an equilibrium with both private and government supply of currency and that all private monies circulate at par with respect to the government currency. Now a national strike results in a 25 percent wage increase for all workers. The unions are careful to stipulate that the wage rise applies to wages measured in all circulating monies. Obviously, an inflexible monetary policy now endangers the private sector. Thus, the government puts pressure on its Central Bank to increase its circulation of currency by some 25 percent. However, it is powerless over the private suppliers, who may feel that they can gain reputation and market share by keeping their supply of currency fixed. To me, it is not clear whether such a hypothetical state of affairs is preferable to a single supplier of currency under ultimate political control, although one could argue that privatized money reduces the temptation to go for monopolistic pricing in goods and labour markets in the first place.

Comment by G.A. Kessler (De Nederlandsche Bank)

I am both impressed and amazed by the essay contributed by Professor Vaubel. Impressed by the tremendous amount of thought that has gone into it. It is, as Professor Vaubel indicates, a synthesis of his writings on the subject of free currency competition from the past ten years. I am also impressed by the tremendous amount of thought that has been devoted to the same subject by many other writers, witness the lengthy reference list annexed to Professor Vaubel's contribution. I am also amazed however. For me, a central banker, it is like hearing a story form another world, one completely different to our own and very far from reality. As an economist I also wonder how it is possible for a dichotomy to persist for so long in economic thinking and in the perception of reality. I am almost tempted to apply Professor Vaubel's quotation of Haberler to the whole line of thinking on free currency competition: "an extraordinary example of how remorseless logicians can end up in Bedlam if they get hold of the wrong assumptions". But please do not think that I am conceited enough to pass judgement, I shall limit myself to briefly indicating those aspects of his essay that strike me as being particularly doubtful.

The proponents of free currency competition seem to claim that such competition would contribute to the general economic welfare by reducing inflation and instability, by promoting the emergence of optimal currency areas and an optimal differentation between different types of money, and possibly also by leading to an optimal unification of currencies. In comparison to Professor Vaubel's earlier writings, however, in his latest paper the prospect of currency unification seems to have receded into the background. Whether, and if so why, his opinion on this matter has changed may be an interesting discussion question. To arrive at free currency competition governments would have to abolish all restrictions on the use of all foreign currencies as a means of payment, a store of value or a standard of value. In addition, and this is far more revolutionary, they would have to grant similar freedoms to the use *and the creation* of currencies by any number of domestic private banks of issue. This denationalisation of the creation of base money would imply a complete abstinence from any governmental attempt at monetary control, and with regard to other countries it would also imply the free flotation of all currencies and the nondesirability or even the nonpossibility of international governmental monetary coordination.

The mechanism that could produce the salutory outcome of less inflation, more stability and optimal product differentiation would depend on the healthy effects of free competition and consumer choice, which are well-known in the good markets. Agents and holders of money would express their preference for the currencies that suited them best by demanding payment in and market conversion into those currencies. They would naturally prefer currencies with the lowest opportunity costs, i.e. those whose purchasing power is expected to perform the best, to depreciate the least, to be the most stable, or even to appreciate in value. The producers of money, the banks of issue, would therefore be challenged and would need to be disciplined to meet these requirements in order to survive and maximize their profits and seigniorage. Contrary to the so-called law of Gresham, good money would in due course drive out bad money.

So much for the gist of the argument. I have many doubts and criticisms though. It would be completely misleading to characterize a modern central bank as an institution that seeks to maximize its profits by choosing an optimally high monopolistic rate of inflation. Modern central banks are very aware of their public function and of their co-responsibility for keeping the purchasing power of their currency as stable as possible. To this end they use monetary instruments to influence the amount of money, creating assets in the banking system for which they act as lender of last resort. If free currency competition were indeed to lead in due course to the survival of the strongest and most stable currencies, the central banks responsible for those currencies would be in exactly the same position as modern central banks today. Why should we therefore have to undergo the chaos of an intermediate period of manifold currency competition when we could embark with renewed vigour on the task of achieving and maintaining monetary stability right away?

It is true that governments, overruling central banks, may impair monetary stability by having excessive recourse to monetary financing. The proponents of free currency competition could perhaps claim that under their system the inflationary creation of outside money would be ruled out de facto. The competing central banks would have to be completely independent of governments. This however does not seem to be a very realistic proposition. Although the prime responsibility for monetary policy should certainly rest with the central banks, governments, partly for democratic reasons, are unlikely to surrender all power. In the real world the basic for an enlightened and harmonious monetary policy is for central banks and governments to work together.

The immediate effects of free currency competition however are even more doubtful. Competition between national currencies implies a domestic competition between units of account and competing means of payment and therefore competing systems of pricing and competing circuits of settlement. It is difficult not to see this as an extremely chaotic and harmful development. It would complicate if not disrupt the national goods, factor and asset markets and therefore run counter to what I understand to be one of the main objectives of the Austrian approach. The costs of uncertainty and of information would rise considerably, depriving the national economy of the very benefits inherent in the use of money as generally accepted means of exchange. The consideration that strongly depreciating currencies are bound to disappear is of little comfort if it is far form certain how quick and permanent the disappearance would be, and in the meantime considerable damage would be done. In my opinion it is a mistake to think that indexation clauses could intrinsically improve the pricing and payments situation. These clauses may be a device to cope with some aspects of the problem of unstable currencies, but they do not get to the root of the problem.

With respect to the derived functions of money, money as a store and a standard of value, the desirability of optimal product differentiation provides no valid argument in favour of free currency competition. In most countries there is already ample scope for the differentiation of and competition between these derived functions within a single domestic currency system, see for example the commercial banks' many different types of monetary liabilities and the wide range of denominations and valuations of non-monetary financial instruments. There may be sound reasons for removing any remaining restrictions in these fields, but such deregulation should be approached pragmatically rather than dogmatically. It is very important for the sake of general welfare that the monetary authorities should retain enough leeway and power to be able to influence at least the rate of monetary expansion and to ensure that financial institutions pay adequate attention to prudential safeguards. An approach that is directed at maximizing the consumer surplus of the holders of money without taking these general welfare considerations into account is dangerously one-sided and therefore misleading.

Much the same is true for further deregulations of the use of foreign currencies as a unit of account, a means of payment, a standard of value or a store of value. Central bank cooperation has made an active contribution to the extension and harmonization of the prudential supervision of the commercial banks' foreign lending activities. The issue of whether and if so how special instruments should be made available in order to control, if necessary, the amount of liquidity creation via the so-called Euromarkets is still unresolved but in my opinion this issue cannot be dismissed as being irrelevant to the attainment and maintenance of monetary stability.

As to the issue of free floating, there is again no justification for dogmatism. Dr. M.W. Holtrop, a former president of "De Nederlandsche Bank"

(Dutch Central Bank) was one of the first to stress the important and welcome disciplining effect of a balance of payments deficit under a system of fixed exchange rates. It seems to me that such a quantitative contracting and disciplining effect may well be much stronger and more beneficial than currency depreciation, to which Professor Vaubel alludes under the heading "Exit" in his essay. On the other hand is has to be acknowledged that fixed exchange rates may give rise to the "import of inflation" due to liquidity inflows into strong currency countries. In my opinion the problem of exchange rate flexibility has to be analyzed in terms of the distinction between different types of international disturbances, viz. cyclical disturbances, financial disturbances and fundamental disturbances.

In view of the unmeasurable cost and welfare advantages resulting from currency unification and taking into account that governments will always want to retain final responsibility and power for their national currency, it seems to me that is is utterly unrealistic to assume that any government would ever be willing to experiment with the device of allowing different banks of issue to manage competing domestic currency systems. Irrespective of whether the concept of "natural monopoly" is or is not applicable, countries are well-advised to stick to the practice of granting a legal monopoly to their central banks. Given the justified existence of a national differentiation of currencies, the international coordination of monetary policy is of great importance. In this respect the possible desirability of the establishment of an area of closely connected or even unified currencies no doubt deserves full attention. However, even here free currency competition cannot be relied upon to arrive at optimal currency regions. The choice and character of currency blocs will depend partly on the economic structure of the countries concerned, but more importantly on the available leeway for an effective harmonization of monetary and other macroeconomic policies. In addition the willingness of governments to surrender part of their authority for the sake of currency unification is highly significant.

My conclusion therefore is that the idea of free currency competition certainly provides a provocative and thought-stimulating impulse for economists, and this idea has been admirably presented by Professor Vaubel, but to my mind it has to be considered as a non-starter in almost all respects.

Author index

Subject index